REVOLUTION AND GENOCIDE IN ETHIOPIA AND CAMBODIA

REVOLUTION AND GENOCIDE IN ETHIOPIA AND CAMBODIA

Edward Kissi

LEXINGTON BOOKS

A Division of
ROWMAN & LITTLEFIELD PUBLISHERS, INC.
Lanham • Boulder • New York • Toronto • Oxford

LEXINGTON BOOKS

A division of Rowman & Littlefield Publishers, Inc.
A wholly owned subsidiary of The Rowman & Littlefield Publishing Group, Inc.
4501 Forbes Boulevard, Suite 200
Lanham, MD 20706

PO Box 317
Oxford
OX2 9RU, UK

British Library Cataloguing in Publication Information Available

Library of Congress Cataloging-in-Publication Data

Kissi, Edward, 1961–
    Revolution and genocide in Ethiopia and Cambodia / Edward Kissi.
        p. cm.
    Includes bibliographical references and index.
    ISBN-13: 978-0-7391-0691-4 (cloth : alk. paper)
    ISBN-10: 0-7391-0691-0 (cloth : alk. paper)
    ISBN-13: 978-0-7391-1263-2 (pbk. : alk. paper)
    ISBN-10: 0-7391-1263-5 (pbk. : alk. paper)
    1. Ethiopia—History—Revolution, 1974. 2. Cambodia—History—
Civil War, 1970–1975. 3. Genocide—Case studies. 4. Genocide—
History—20th century. I. Title.
    DT387.95.K47 2006
    963.07—dc22   2005011853

Printed in the United States of America

♾^{TM} The paper used in this publication meets the minimum requirements of
American National Standard for Information Sciences—Permanence of Paper
for Printed Library Materials, ANSI/NISO Z39.48-1992.
Manufactured in the United States of America.

For Afua Tenkorama, the memories of Kofi Ntiri, Alex Effah, and the love of Daphne, Frank and Akosua

CONTENTS

ACKNOWLEDGEMENTS

This book is the product of a two-year post-doctoral research fellowship (January 1998–December 1999), supported by the Andrew W. Mellon Foundation, Inc., in the Genocide Studies Program (GSP) at the Yale Center for International and Area Studies. I am especially grateful to the Mellon Foundation for its support and to the fellowship committee at Yale University for giving me the opportunity to undertake the research that led to this book. I am also immensely grateful to Professor Ben Kiernan for his commitment to my work in the GSP and for his friendship and eagerness to share with me his vast knowledge of the Khmer Rouge revolution and the Pol Pot regime. Professor Frank Chalk of the Department of History at Concordia University, Montreal, Canada, from whom I learned my first lessons in the history and theory of genocide, deserves special mention for offering me the guidance of a mentor in the completion of this work. The Southeast Asian Studies program at Yale University generously offered me the stipend that allowed me to continue my study of Cambodia and the Khmer language at the Southeast Asia Summer Studies Institute held at the University of Oregon in the Summer of 1998. GSP research associates Thavro Phim gave me my first rudimentary lessons in the Khmer language for my research and Dr. Toni Shapiro-Phim offered me illuminating insights into the anthropology of Cambodia. Yale alumnus Alex Boateng offered the moral support that was required to complete this book and, above all, taught me how to drive an automobile essential for immersing oneself in the brisk environment that is New Haven. I also found comfort and pleasure in my friendship with Charles Mironko and Susan Cook, then students at Yale University. Not only did they make my stay in New Haven and association with Yale a memorable experience, but they also offered me the needed space for research, writing and rest at their residence in Addis Ababa, during my field-work on the book, in 1999, while they worked for the erstwhile Organization of African Unity, in Ethiopia. Tekalign Wolde-Mariam of the History department at Addis Ababa University, Ebenezer First-Quao of the United Nations Economic Commission office in Addis Ababa and Sophie Abraham First-Quao shared their memories of the Ethiopian revolution with me and arranged for me to interview key surviving participants in the revolution.

Robert Melson, whose pioneering work in comparative genocide studies inspired the title of this book, read earlier drafts of the manuscript and provided helpful comments on content, structure and analysis. Yehuda Bauer, then visiting scholar at the Strassler Family Center for Holocaust and Genocide Studies at Clark University, Worcester, Massachusetts, also read a revised draft of the manuscript and suggested intriguing lines of inquiry. My colleagues Deborah Dwork, Paul Ropp, Shelley Tenenbaum, Tatyana Macaulay, Margaret Hillard and Simon Payaslian offered friendship and support that kept me sane and serene as I ploughed through the thickets of this book as a visiting assistant professor at Clark. At the University of South Florida, the book benefitted from the assistance of graduate student Sherri Anderson who traced and copied articles I had misplaced with a smile. Trevor Purcell took pleasure in discussing the fine points of revolutionary theory with me while Cheryl Rodriguez and Deborah Plant shared with me their experiences of academic and collegial life in the Department of Africana Studies. Emmanuel Akyeampong of the Department of History at Harvard University, Thomas Owusu of the Department of Environmental Science and Geography at William Paterson University of New Jersey, Ismail Rashid of the Department of History at Vassar College, Edmund Abaka of the Department of History at University of Miami, Mr. E. K. T. Osam, my favorite teacher at Swedro Secondary School, and Jeripher Yaw Oppong and Charles Amoakohene of Montreal, Canada, have been great sources of inspiration. To the Institute on Black Life at the University of South Florida, especially its able director Geoffrey Okogbaa and Office Manager Cheriese Edwards, I owe an immense debt of gratitude for the financial help offered for the typesetting and indexing of this book. I thank the anonymous reviewers, and the editorial staff of Lexington Books for their perceptive comments and gentle prodding that moved the tedious, but delightful work on this book forward. I am, however, solely responsible for the imperfections of this work which highlight the complexities of the creative process.

INTRODUCTION

Ethiopia, in northeast Africa, and Cambodia, in southeast Asia, are far apart in geographical location and territorial extent. But some scholars and writers would argue that they may be quite close to each other in history. Prior to 1975, Ethiopia and Cambodia shared many of the characteristics of traditional agrarian monarchies. Their predominantly peasant societies were changing into full-fledged modern nation-states. From 1975 to 1979, these two agrarian societies in transition also experienced violent revolutions including mass murder. Indeed some scholars and writers have suggested that one or the other or both societies experienced genocide in the course of those revolutions. Others go as far as to suggest that the Cambodian and the Ethiopian revolutions, and the "genocide" purported to have occurred in their wake, actually resembled each other. That comparison has generated some controversy.

Journalist Jean-Claude Guillebaud aptly captures that controversy in his article published in the French newspaper *Le Monde* and reprinted in the British *Guardian Weekly* of February 26, 1978. Guillebaud asks whether the terror and murder that characterized the revolution in Ethiopia was "Lunacy?" or "A red madness already become Cambodian?"[1] The comparison is very striking. Eleven years after Guillebaud wrote (in 1989), Dawit Wolde Giorgis, a former member of Ethiopia's revolutionary government who defected to the United States, appears to have answered Guillebaud's question in the affirmative. Dawit has argued that the Ethiopian revolution and the murders committed in its wake mirrored the Cambodian experience.

He explains that:

> From 1975 to 1979 . . . Pol Pot presided over a reign of terror in Kampuchea, . . . that left one and half million people dead. . . . [L]ike Pol Pot, Mengistu . . . massacred thousands . . . , and brought death, suffering, and displacement to millions.[2]

Undoubtedly, Mengistu and Pol Pot led two of the most ruthless revolutionary regimes in Africa and Asia in the late twentieth century. But did revolutions in Ethiopia and Cambodia lead to genocide in both cases, and how similar or different were they?

No detailed comparative study of the Ethiopian and Cambodian experiences exist, so far, beyond the superficial parallels that some scholars and writers occasionally draw between the two. In many cases, these parallels are limited to the death toll and the terror of the two revolutionary regimes. Dawit and Ethiopian political scientist Paulos Milkias estimate that the Ethiopian revolution claimed the lives of 1.2 to 2 million Ethiopians out of a pre-revolutionary population of 45 million—an estimated 2.7 to 4.4 percent of the population.[3] That death toll, some argue, is comparable to the annihilation of 1.7 to 3 million Khmer and other groups—between 21 and 38 percent of the pre-revolution population—by the Khmer Rouge during the Cambodian revolution, according to estimates by demographer Patrick Heuveline.[4] The population of Cambodia before that country's revolution in 1975 was 8 million.

The controversy over the nature of the Ethiopian and Cambodian revolutions is part of a broader debate, among scholars and other writers, about the bloody history of Communism in the twentieth century, the prevalence of terror in countries claiming to adhere to Marxist-Leninist ideologies and the relationship between revolutions and genocide. While political scientist Barbara Harff considers the Cambodian revolution led by the Khmer Rouge as "the one extreme case that defies comparison to other modern revolutions," John Dunn, the political scientist, concludes that it is, indeed, comparable to other revolutions.[5] In his study of modern revolutions, Dunn identifies "at least three revolu-

tions since 1971" whose common characteristics mark them as the most
extreme revolutions of the twentieth century. According to Dunn, the
Cambodian revolution joins those of Iran and Ethiopia in a class of revolutions whose "brutal domestic repression" not only defied prior expectations, but also defiled the ideals of revolution. As Dunn argues, a
"belligerently . . . reconstituted Amhara military domination [under]
Colonel Mengistu," replaced the "archaic and ancien regime" of Emperor Haile Selassie in Ethiopia while, in Cambodia, Pol Pot "carried
the political reconstruction of post-colonial Indochina through the
ghastly killing fields."[6]

Dunn's characterization of the Mengistu regime as dominated by the
hegemonic Amhara ethnic group in Ethiopia is inaccurate. In fact the
Mengistu regime was multi-ethnic in its composition. Although it upheld traditional Amhara notions of nationhood (the unity of Ethiopia),
the regime did not identify itself with the Amhara ethnic group or other
elements of Amhara identity: Christianity and monarchy. According to
Dawit, Mengistu's peers preferred him as leader of the Ethiopian revolution precisely because of his non-Amhara ethnicity and his well-known
resentment of centuries of domination of Ethiopia by the Amhara.
Mengistu's humble social origins and his affable demeanor (which
masked a lust for power) endeared him to the junior military officers
who wanted to end Amhara "class arrogance and racism" in Ethiopia.[7]
While one cannot discount ethnic factors in any theoretical analysis of
the origins of revolution as a mechanism of social change in Ethiopia,
one cannot at the same time overlook the empirical evidence that the
Mengistu regime promoted religious and ethnic equality for the precise
purpose of weakening centuries of "Amhara domination" of Ethiopia.

Sociologist Heinz Kaufeler has made an impressive comparative
study of the revolutions which took place in Ethiopia and Iran—two
ancient agrarian monarchies—in the 1970s. To Kaufeler, the urban
origins and secular character of the Ethiopian revolution distinguish it
from the Iranian experience which was "a social millenarian movement with religious messianic leadership."[8] Unlike other scholars and
writers who reach for a Cambodian equivalent of the Ethiopian experience, Kaufeler concludes that the Ethiopian case mirrors the classic
European revolutions: an anachronistic monarchy removed by an ascending elite and replaced by a regime subscribing to radical social

transformation but actually practicing ruthless power politics and terror. Kaufeler is partially correct.

Since 1990, social scientists who study genocide from a comparative perspective or examine situations and contexts favorable to genocide have focused their research on the connections between revolution and genocide. In his pioneering work in this field of genocide studies, political scientist Robert Melson argued that revolutions accompanied by war have often provided the contexts as well as pretexts for states, governments, liberation movements and other armed non-state groups to annihilate specific groups of people in their quest to redefine the essence and identity of their nations. Melson cites the genocide against the Christian Armenians by the Muslim Young Turks revolutionary regime in the tottering Ottoman empire in old Turkey, during World War I, and the Holocaust perpetrated by Nazi Germany against European Jews, Gypsies and other ethnic and religious groups, in the course of World War II, as examples of genocidal revolutions of the twentieth century.[9] He has added the destruction of the kulaks in the former Soviet Union [1930–37], the mass murder of Cambodia's upper and middle classes by the Khmer Rouge [1975–79], and the organized and systematic killing of the Tutsis in Rwanda by armed Hutu militias [April–July 1994] to his list of twentieth century genocides that occurred in the context of revolution and war.[10] But Melson is careful to emphasize that although some revolutions lead to genocide as the examples above indicate, it is not true that all revolutions lead to genocide or every genocide is the consequence of revolution. What happened in Ethiopia proves Melson's caveat. Certainly, the Ethiopian revolution was as bloody as the French and Cambodian revolutions, but it did not lead to genocide as the crime and concept have been strictly defined in international laws.

Unlike the Ethiopian revolution led by Mengistu Haile Mariam, the horrors of the Cambodian revolution led by Pol Pot have been well-documented.[11] Historian Ben Kiernan's comprehensive work on the Pol Pot regime based on internal Khmer Rouge documents sums up the basic features of the Cambodian experience. Kiernan argues that in "the first few days" after taking power, the Khmer Rouge evacuated all cities, emptied hospitals of their patients, closed schools and factories, scattered or burned libraries, abolished money and markets, closed monasteries and defrocked Cambodia's Buddhist Monks. For nearly four years, the Khmer Rouge suppressed all fundamental freedoms. It curtailed the freedom of the press, restricted free movement of people, suppressed religious worship and destroyed freedom of organization, association and discussion. As Kiernan notes, by 1977 the Khmer Rouge had destroyed traditional social institutions such as the bonds of loyalty between parents and children. It restructured traditional family life to the extent that parents and children could eat only in controlled communal mess halls and not in the comfort of their homes.

Kiernan describes revolutionary Cambodia as "a prison camp state" where eight million people lived as prisoners in solitary confinement. Worse still, the Khmer Rouge sealed Cambodia off from the rest of the world. By expelling foreign dignitaries and journalists, shutting down newspapers and television stations, confiscating radios and suppressing the use of mails and telephones, the Khmer Rouge stifled all forms of domestic communication and contact with the outside world. The Pol Pot regime did not reward skills or harness intellectual accomplishments for social change. Rather, it viewed possession of knowledge, and ability to speak foreign languages, as evidence of debilitating foreign contamination to be purged by extermination.[12] Above all, the Khmer Rouge was a racist regime that sought to revive and purify the Khmer race as the Nazi party attempted to do in Germany. To pursue that supremacist ideology, the Khmer Rouge decreed, in 1975, that "[i]n Kampuchea there is one nation, and one language, the Khmer [l]anguage. From now on the various nationalities . . . do not exist any longer. . . ."[13]

From a casual perspective, the conduct of the Khmer Rouge looked like the *Dergue* (the Ethiopian revolutionary government). Seven months after taking power, the revolutionary regime in Ethiopia nationalized all lands including those of the Ethiopian Orthodox Church, closed down the schools of some Protestant churches and killed and intimidated some religious figures. It pursued an ideology of absolute national unity, ethnic-pluralism and obedience to the state by suppressing ethnic-based armed secessionist movements and killing people who opposed the military's leadership of the revolution. The Mengistu regime controlled the movement of peasants and their political loyalties by urging them to join agricultural cooperatives and also by resettling those in dissident and insurgent areas in state-controlled regions. In its search for total power, the Dergue ruthlessly suppressed political opponents. This is where the similarities end, in my view.

Much has been written about the Cambodian revolution and the internal history of the Pol Pot regime as compared to the scant and often speculative literature on the Ethiopian revolution and the Mengistu regime. Dawit Wolde Giorgis, a member of Ethiopia's revolutionary regime who defected in 1985, has written perhaps the only comprehensive book on the Ethiopian revolution dealing with the internal history of the Dergue and the motivations of its leadership. But Dawit's judgments appear to be colored by his post-defection metamorphosis in the United States. He claims, contrary to the historical evidence, that the revolutionary Ethiopian government was similar to the Pol Pot regime.[14] That orthodox view was first floated by the *Wall Street Journal* in January 1986, three years before Dawit wrote his book, *Red Tears*. In its editorial of January 27, 1986 captioned "Today's Holocaust," the journal characterized the deaths which resulted from the forced resettlement program undertaken by the Mengistu regime in the mid-1980s as "government-organized group murder" and "mass extermination" comparable to "the Khmer Rouge killing fields" and the "deportation of Armenians [by the Young Turks revolutionary regime] in 1915."[15] Certainly, the atrocities of the Mengistu regime conjure up visions of the crimes of the Khmer Rouge. As Robert Kaplan, the journalist, has stated, "the manner in which Ethiopians died [under the Mengistu regime] evoked the well-known slaughter of millions of Cambodians by the Khmer Rouge in the mid-1970s."[16] But the extent to which the Ethiopian revolution mirrored or differed from the Cambodian experience should be demonstrated rather than assumed. The problem seems to lie in the approach to comparison as a social science methodology.

Political Scientist Arend Lijphart has argued that comparative studies should discover common relationships and avoid "the danger of being overwhelmed by large numbers of variables."[17] This book concurs and goes beyond that approach. It draws on the views of historians Charles Maier, about the comparative method, and Robert Gellately, Ben Kiernan and Robert Cribb about the urgent need to integrate mass murder in the non-Western world, especially Africa and Asia, into the comparative study of genocide.[18] As Maier notes, "comparison is a dual process that scrutinizes two or more systems to learn what elements they have in common and what elements distinguish them." While comparison, according to Maier, should help "to discern a common causal mechanism" between the events compared, "any comparison that fails to emphasise the persisting differences is . . . undertaken in bad faith." Every comparative study of events or systems should add to our knowledge. For it to be worth the effort, in the opinion of Maier, comparison "should go beyond mere taxonomy" to "reveal a wider historical process at work."[19]

Today, the Ethiopian and Cambodian revolutions of the 1970s raise new and important questions not only about the nature of some of the revolutions that took place in Africa and Asia in the late twentieth century, but also the relationship between revolutions and genocide. They also raise questions about the orthodox conception of the state, in genocide studies, as the main perpetrator of genocide. The two cases highlight some of the problems in the definition of genocide itself; the comparative study of genocide, the challenges of prosecuting perpetrators of genocide and the relationship between historical memory, national identity and genocide. By comparing the Cambodian and Ethiopian experiences, this book seeks to offer some perspectives on these issues. It is, therefore, the task of this book to identify and explain what the Ethiopian and Cambodian revolutions of the early 1970s had in common; what set them apart and the lessons to be drawn from a comparison of them. It pays particular attention to four issues. First, the causes and objectives of the two revolutions. Second, the cultural and historical circumstances that gave them their common and distinctive characteristics. Third, the conduct of the revolutions, especially the choices the leaders, opponents and followers made. Fourth, the specific nature of the genocide or other crimes against humanity that occurred in the course of the two revolutions.

The Ethiopian revolution began on September 12, 1974 and came to an end on May 28, 1991 when a domestic coalition of armed opponents overthrew the revolutionary regime. On the other hand, the Cambodian revolution started on April 17, 1975 and was terminated on January 7, 1979 by an external invasion from Vietnam, Cambodia's neighbor to the east. Arguably, 1975 to 1979 was the most crucial period of the two revolutions. It was during this period that the revolutionary regimes struggled to consolidate their power and impose their respective visions of change and social order. Therefore, a detailed study of these critical years is intended in this book. The book argues that although genocide did occur in Cambodia, it did not in Ethiopia. And far from what has been asserted in some of the literature, the Dergue was not Ethiopia's Khmer Rouge.

Mass death in Ethiopia in the course of that country's revolution, was a product of state terrorism, civil war and famine. The Dergue (Ethiopia's revolutionary government) alone was not responsible for the 2 million estimated deaths. Other non-state actors also practiced terrorism and political killings. These were violent and brutal measures, but they do not constitute an attempt to destroy, totally or partially, a national, ethnic, racial or religious group as such. Unlike in Cambodia where there was extensive genocide against ethnic and religious groups as well as urban-based middle and upper classes, such destruction was limited in Ethiopia to organized and armed political opponents in a protracted domestic war for political power and secession. Differences in social structure in Ethiopia and Cambodia and the ideology of the Dergue and the Khmer Rouge, among other "wider historical processes, " explain why two revolutions which began almost at the same time, and had some elements in common, produced different results and ended at different periods though under similar circumstances.

In its composition, revolutionary ideology, target groups and scope and scale of killing, the Ethiopian revolutionary regime (*Dergue*) was qualitatively different from the Khmer Rouge (*Angkar*). The Dergue was a military junta that had come to power by exploiting insurrection in the capital city initiated by civilian groups. The junior military officers who formed the Dergue took the calls of the civilians for "revolution" to improve living conditions in Ethiopia as an opportunity for the military to seize power and impose its own vision of change and national identity. The Dergue was multi-ethnic in composition. Throughout its seventeen-year rule, it exercised only tenuous control over a pluralist society of about eighty ethnic groups previously divided along ethnic, religious and occupational lines. By contrast, the Khmer Rouge was a civilian organization which had established its own guerrilla army. This civilian armed movement composed predominantly of members of the Khmer ethnic group seized power in Cambodia after a five-year civil war. Unlike the Dergue, the Khmer Rouge exercised absolute control over a population which was 80 percent Khmer. Here is a significant difference between the two revolutions.

Whereas, ideologically, the Ethiopian regime demonstrated that it was pragmatic, populist, opportunist and egalitarian, the Khmer Rouge proved that it was ambitious, fanatical, utopian and racist. In fact, Ethiopia's soldier-revolutionaries had no clearly-defined revolutionary ideology beyond imposing national unity and religious and ethnic equality in an ethnically-diverse society. The Ethiopian regime adopted the Marxist vocabulary of its armed civilian competitors even as it fought them for control over the revolution. As a person, Mengistu Haile Mariam, the eventual leader of the Ethiopian revolution, had sentiments against aristocratic privileges and ambitions for unchallenged power that were similar to Pol Pot's. But as a leader of a revolutionary regime, Mengistu was more pragmatic and nationalistic and not as utopian as Pol Pot. The Khmer Rouge ideology of racial purity and Khmer ethnic dominance was the direct opposite of the Dergue's pursuit of inter-racial unity through suppression of ethnic chauvinism. The revolutionary military regime in Ethiopia also resisted pressure from left-wing civilian allies and competitors to seal Ethiopia off from the rest of the world as the Khmer Rouge did Cambodia.

The Khmer Rouge had messianic and communist views of social transformation which motivated it to conduct the world's "first pure revolution" or, as it put it, to do what had "never been done before in history."[20] The revolutionary regime in Cambodia targeted national and religious groups such as the Vietnamese, Chinese, Buddhists, Christians and Muslims for annihilation. The Pol Pot regime viewed the Vietnamese and Chinese in particular as the embodiment of foreignness and debilitating contamination in Cambodia to be eradicated from the "pure" and "new" revolutionary society. Besides transforming the ethnic demography of Cambodia, the Khmer Rouge invaded the territory of its neighbors. To the extent that the Dergue had territorial aims, it showed a preference for the preservation of existing frontiers and not their expansion. The Mengistu regime made the defense of Ethiopia's national borders from domestic ethnic secessionism and neighboring Somali irredentism the keystone of its revolution. That was a significant difference between the two revolutionary regimes.

Furthermore, the Mengistu regime had no messianic and utopian views of social transformation such as the Khmer Rouge had. The Dergue did undertake a radical land reform program in March 1975. But that land reform program was not aimed at changing Ethiopia's rural society along ethnic lines. The Dergue's rural transformation measures were limited to the organization of peasants into associations for collective cultivation of nationalized agricultural lands. That was a strategy aimed at courting the support of peasants in the regime's battle against ethnic insurgencies and in Mengistu's quest for enhanced personal power. Here, the Ethiopian revolution was unlike other twentieth century revolutions in Africa, Asia or Latin America. It was not a "peasant revolution" in the sense of being organized and led by peasants, but rather a revolution that went in search of peasants in order to legitimize itself and survive in a peasant society.

The Dergue's assaults on the clergy, as similar as they appear to the conduct of the Khmer Rouge, actually had a different intent. They were aimed at enhancing the power of the military regime and its leader by weakening the economic strength and social influence of the Ethiopian Orthodox Church, and other Christian denominations. These measures did not signify an ideological commitment to abolishing religion in Ethiopia as Khmer Rouge assaults on religion in revolutionary Cambodia clearly demonstrated. It is true that the Dergue, as well as the Khmer Rouge, failed to prevent famine in the course of their revolutions though they made agricultural development a key objective. But the Khmer Rouge bears more responsibility for famine in Cambodia given the fact that unlike Ethiopia, Cambodia had no history of famine. And the responses of the Khmer Rouge and the Dergue to famine differed too. The Khmer Rouge rejected foreign assistance in the name of "self-reliance." The Dergue accepted international famine aid and made Ethiopia a symbol of international relief operations in the 1970s and 1980s.

The scope of killing in Pol Pot's Cambodia was much broader than in Ethiopia. The mono-ethnic Khmer Rouge regime, with its ideology of ethnic purity, had no scruples about destroying other minority ethnic groups. In Ethiopia, it was impossible for the multi-ethnic Mengistu regime, with an ideology of ethnic plurality and national unity, to successfully target a specific ethnic or religious group for destruction. However, given the domestic political climate under which the Dergue operated, it attempted to consider all the Tigrinya-speaking people of Tigray and neighboring Eritrea as potential supporters of the rebel

Tigrayan Peoples Liberation Front (TPLF), which sought to overthrow the Dergue, and the Eritrean Peoples Liberation Front (EPLF) which fought for the secession of Eritrea from Ethiopia. Here, it was the revolutionary regime's ideology of absolute national unity that tempted the Dergue to convert particular ethnic groups into political enemies to be destroyed.

The leaders of the Dergue and the Khmer Rouge had the same feeling of insecurity. Because of the proliferation of ethnic insurgencies against the Dergue, Mengistu faced the greater political challenge. But whereas Pol Pot responded to insecurity and sometimes created it by moving rapidly with communist transformation of Cambodia, and forging ahead with purges of racial, ethnic, national and religious groups as well as urban middle and upper classes, Mengistu moved cautiously to solidify ethnic-unity-in-diversity and sacrificed communist transformation of Ethiopia to enforced national unity, but at the cost of the lives of his political opponents, particularly revolutionaries. Here, the extent of the Dergue's atrocities against political groups are clear, but an overall intent of the military regime to completely or partially annihilate the ethnic groups from which its opponents came is difficult to detect. What is certain is the overtly political nature of the Dergue's killing in the sense that political beliefs, affiliation and opposition was important in the Dergue's targeting of its victims. As Robert Cribb has accurately argued, the quasi-ethnic nature of Khmer Rouge crimes is clear because class, racial and religious background played important roles in the selection of groups for destruction in revolutionary Cambodia.[21]

The Ethiopian case also highlights the problems that plague the relationship between genocide and law. The absence of protection of political groups (the Dergue's principal targets), in the UN Genocide Convention, would make prosecution of the leaders and followers of Ethiopia's revolutionary government for genocide, under existing international law, very difficult. In domestic Ethiopian law, however, the killing of political opponents or people on grounds of their political beliefs constitutes genocide. Many implications and complications arise from this clash of legal conceptions of genocide. Robert Cribb has boldly identified some in his observation that "two . . . unpleasant consequences [could] arise if we accept that mass political killings can be [considered as] genocide." As Cribb argues from his assessments of genocide in the non-Western world, if genocide is only a product of "racism," then it can be appropriately regarded as morally and intellectually wrong to annihilate a group on grounds of its ethnic or racial origin. But, if genocide is viewed as a consequence of "politics," then for the study of genocide to have any analytical and predictive value to policymakers, the behavior of both victims and perpetrators in that political conflict warrants attention. This method of analysis would have serious ethical implications for the study of genocide in the Western world such as the Holocaust and the Armenian genocide. Certainly, to suppose that the victims of the Holocaust or the Armenian genocide may have provoked their fate, or bear some responsibility for what happened to them, is to step beyond what is morally, politically and intellectually acceptable. Thus, in the view of Cribb, "in admitting political killing as genocide, the world of genocide studies sets up for itself an enormous conflict."[22]

But, one might also surmise that in not admitting political killing as genocide, perpetrators of genocide could convert real ethnic and racial groups into political enemies to be murdered with impunity. Perhaps, one resolution of the "conflict" that Cribb has identified would be to redefine the concept of "political groups" and draw a careful distinction between armed insurgent or militia groups that pursue certain political agendas with violence and defenseless groups who hold particular political opinions. That redefinition of "political groups" should also be accompanied by the development of a new regime of international law outlining the legal obligations of non-state armed political groups or militias and dealing with their conduct and atrocities. The conflicts over definitions and comparisons of genocide, the connections between revolution, war and genocide, genocide and law, genocide and the state and non-state groups make the on-going efforts by social scientists to study genocide and resolve its many conundrums through comparative studies informed by empirical data worthwhile. This book contributes to this new trend in genocide studies.

NOTES

1. Jean-Claude Guillebaud, "Dergue's red terror," *The Guardian Weekly* 118, no. 9 February 26, 1978): 11.

2. Dawit Wolde Giorgis, *Red Tears: War, Famine and Revolution in Ethiopia* (Trenton, N.J.: The Red Sea Press, 1989), 57.

3. Dawit, *Red Tears*, 57; Paulos Milkias, "Mengistu Haile Mariam: Profile of a Dictator," *Ethiopian Review* (February 1994): 51.

4. Patrick Heuveline, "Between One and Three Million: Toward the Demographic Reconstruction of a Decade of Cambodian History (1970–1979)," *Population Studies* 52 (1998): 59.

5. Barbara Harff, "Cambodia: Revolution, Genocide, Intervention," in *Revolutions of the Late Twentieth Century*, ed. Jack A. Goldstone, Ted Robert Gurr and Farrokh Moshiri (Boulder, CO: Westview Press, 1991), 218, 233; John Dunn, *Modern Revolutions: An Introduction to the Analysis of a Political Phenomenon*, 2nd ed. (Cambridge: Cambridge University Press, 1989).

6. Dunn, *Modern Revolutions*, xxiii–xxiv.

7. Dawit, *Red Tears*, 17.

8. Heinz Kaufeler, *Modernization, Legitimacy and Social Movement: A Study of Socio-Cultural Dynamics and Revolution in Iran and Ethiopia* (Zurich: Ethnologische Schriften, 1988), 12–13.

9. Robert Melson, *Revolution and Genocide: On the Origins of the Armenian Genocide and the Holocaust* (Chicago: University of Chicago Press, 1992), xvi, 1. See also Levon Chorbajian and George Shirinian, ed., *Studies in Comparative Genocide* (New York: St. Martin's Press, 1999).

10. Robert Melson, "My Journey in the Study of Genocide," (Paper presented at the Sawyer seminar of the Genocide Studies Program, Yale University, September 2000), 12.

11. For books on the internal history of the Pol Pot regime, see Ben Kiernan, *The Pol Pot Regime: Race, Power, and Genocide in Cambodia under the Khmer Rouge, 1975–79* (New Haven: Yale University Press, 1996); Michael Vickery, *Cambodia, 1975–1982* (Boston: South End Press, 1985); David Chandler, *Brother Number One: A Political Biography of Pol Pot*, revised edition (Boulder: Westview Press, 1999); Elizabeth Becker, *When the War Was Over: Cambodia and the Khmer Rouge Revolution* (New York: Public Affairs, 1998).

12. Kiernan, *The Pol Pot Regime*, 8–9.

13. Elizabeth Becker, *When the War Was Over: The Voices of Cambodia's Revolution and its People* (New York: Simon and Schuster, 1986), 253.

14. Dawit, *Red Tears*, 57.

15. The *Wall Street Journal*, "Today's Holocaust," January 27, 1986, 24.

16. Robert Kaplan, "The African Killing Fields," *The Washington Monthly* 28, no. 8 (1988): 32.

17. Arend Lijphart, "Comparative Politics and the Comparative Method," *American Political Science Review* 65, no. 3 (1971): 690.

18. Charles S. Maier, *The Unmasterable Past: History, Holocaust and German National Identity* (Cambridge, Mass.: Harvard University Press, 1997), 69; Robert Gellately and Ben Kiernan, eds. *The Specter of Genocide: Mass Murder in Historical Perspective* (Cambridge: Cambridge University Press, 2003), 9; Robert Cribb, "Genocide in the non-Western World," *International Institute for Asian Studies Newsletter* 25 (July 2001): 6.

19. Maier, *The Unmasterable Past*, 69.

20. David P. Chandler, "Seeing Red: Perceptions of Cambodian History in Democratic Kampuchea," in *Revolution and Its Aftermath in Kampuchea: Eight Essays*, ed. David P. Chandler and Ben Kiernan, Monograph Series no. 25 (New Haven: Yale University Southeast Asia Studies, 1983), 34.

21. Cribb, "Genocide in the non-Western World."

22. Cribb, "Genocide in the non-Western World." See also Robert Cribb, "Genocide in the Non-Western World: Implications for Holocaust Studies," in *Genocide: Cases, Comparisons and Contemporary Debates*, ed. Stephen L.B. Jensen (Copenhagen: The Danish Center for Holocaust and Genocide Studies, 2003), 127, 139.

1

SOCIETY AND STATE IN PRE-REVOLUTIONARY ETHIOPIA AND CAMBODIA

Pre-revolutionary Cambodia and Ethiopia did not differ significantly from each other in their political and economic institutions. But they stood far apart in aspects of their history. Before the 1970s, Ethiopia and Cambodia were two of the best examples of ancient monarchies with a predominantly agrarian economy. About 90 percent of the 45 million pre-revolutionary Ethiopian population as well as the 8 million pre-revolutionary Cambodian population resided in rural areas where they pursued their ancient craft: agriculture. Cambodia's peasants produced rice as a national food crop, and the kingdom exported rubber as its cash crop. On the other hand, Ethiopia's peasants produced *teff*, the national food crop, and provided much of the labor for the production of coffee, the empire's main export crop.

What distinguished the two societies was the different nature of their ecology and ethnic demography. Ecologically, Ethiopia's location in northeast Africa gave it a more temperate weather condition than the tropical climate that enveloped Cambodia in southeast Asia. As the tenth largest country on a continent of fifty-four countries, Ethiopia is an enormous land mass.[1] The country's 431,000 square miles of land embraces an area equal in size to the combined U.S. states of California, Oregon, Missouri and Idaho. But only parts of the central and southwestern provinces of Shoa, Arsi and Keffa, have relatively good soil and favorable weather conditions to permit adequate food production. Hence famine has been a persistent problem in northern Ethiopia. Much of the land in southern Ethiopia is dry and only useful for pastoral activities.[2]

The enormous size of Ethiopia contrasts sharply with Cambodia's 69,000 square miles—about the size of the state of Missouri. Cambodia is the third smallest nation in southeast Asia.[3] Nevertheless, nature endowed Cambodia with resources that it deprived Ethiopia. Heavy and adequate rainfall provided the peasants of pre-revolutionary Cambodia with wet weather conditions for the production of adequate food. Cambodia's irrigated and mechanized rice fields of the northwest contrast with the poor soil and rugged topography of northern Ethiopia which put teff, Ethiopia's most widely grown and preferred national food crop, at the mercy of nature. With favorable weather conditions and vast arable lands, Cambodian peasants rarely experienced famine and mass death from starvation as their counterparts in Ethiopia did.[4] However, the geographical locations of the two monarchies made conflict over territory a central element in their relations with neighboring states. David Chandler has described Cambodia as a "walnut caught in the open jaws of its three large neighbors [Thailand, Laos and Vietnam]."[5] In the same vein, Ethiopia could be described as a Christian walnut lodged in the suspicious gullet of its Muslim neighbors: Egypt, to the north, Sudan, to the west and Somalia, to the east.

Pre-revolutionary Cambodia and Ethiopia had a similar political institution—monarchy—but they had a different political history. As we shall observe in the next chapter, the distinctive political histories played significant roles in the uneven development of revolutionary ideas in the two monarchies. Whereas Cambodia was the victim of European colonial politics, Ethiopia was its chief beneficiary. During World War II, Vichy France ceded to Thailand about one-third of Cambodia's territory which contained crucial economic assets. After World War II, Ethiopia gained parts of Somalia's land which Britain had once possessed as a colony. British Somaliland (Ethiopia's present Ogaden region) contained pastoral areas; crucial economic assets for ethnic Somali nomadic groups who live there. The Ogaden, in southeastern Ethiopia, became a bone of contention between Ethiopia and

Somalia, after 1961, in a manner similar to the antagonism over the same issue of territory between Cambodia and its eastern neighbor, Vietnam, and western neighbor, Thailand.

ETHNICITY, RACE AND CLASS

Ethnically, Ethiopia is the most culturally diverse nation in Africa accommodating over eighty different ethnic and linguistic groups. The largest ethnic group, the Oromo, constituted about 40 percent of Ethiopia's 45 million population at the beginning of the revolution in 1974. The Amhara and Tigre, the hegemonic ethnic groups and political class, together made up another 40 percent. Minority ethnic groups such as the Konso (1 percent), Afar (4 percent), Somali (6 percent), Gumuz (6 percent) took up the remaining 20 percent.[6] *Amharinya*, the language of the Amhara ethnic group, was the official language of pre-revolutionary Ethiopia. By contrast, 80 percent of the 8 million-pre-revolutionary Cambodian population was Khmer and spoke the Khmer language.

Inter-ethnic relations in Ethiopia's plural society were as cordial as the relatively non-violent social relations which existed in Cambodia's homogeneous society. But social harmony in Ethiopia and Cambodia was achieved at the cost of the suppression of the identities of other groups. The difference was in degree and method. Pre-revolutionary Ethiopia was, arguably, a Christian monarchy. About 50 percent of the population professed Christianity, another 45 percent Islam and the remaining 10 percent other religious beliefs. Despite fighting to maintain its sovereignty during the European colonization of the African continent, Ethiopia had an imperial creed. In their state-building processes, Amhara monarchs from the central Ethiopian province of Shoa integrated Ethiopia's minority groups into a dominant Amhara Christian culture. By the turn of the twentieth century, citizenship or national identity in Ethiopia was defined by acceptance of *Amharinya*, the language of the Amhara ethnic group, as the national language, Christianity, the religion of Amhara emperors, as the national religion and the Emperor himself as the symbol of nationhood, the source of state authority and the theoretical owner of all cultivable land in the empire.[7] The *Amharicization* of Ethiopian society made many ethnic minorities less distinct. In fact to be Ethiopian—that is to have access to economic and political privileges in the period before the revolution—Oromos, Gurages, Konso and all ethnic minorities had to take Amhara names and assume other Amhara identities.

This method of ethnic assimilation as well as centuries of intermarriage created a complex social structure in Ethiopia. That diminished individual and group appeals to some primordial ethnic or racial purity as a framework of identity and social relations. In fact, no one ever claimed to be the "original" or "pure Amhara" as Pol Pot, according to Kiernan, claimed to be "the Original Khmer."[8] As John Young has argued about Ethiopia, "there are few Amhara who do not have Oromo [or some other non-Amhara] blood in them."[9] Emperor Haile Selassie himself was part Oromo and part Gurage, but assumed Amhara identity to legitimize his leadership. Being an Amhara, as political scientist Christopher Clapham notes, was "more a matter of how one behaved rather than who one's parents were."[10] In fact land ownership, religion and occupation, rather than ethnicity or race defined class and power in Ethiopia. Class and power were buttressed by myth and well-cultivated personality cults. Clapham has aptly called Ethiopian society the "tough man system."[11] People acquired power by demonstrating a capacity for strong leadership and not nobility of birth. They preserved leadership through charisma and personal success. Without the capacity of strong state leaders to assimilate other ethnic groups into a core Amhara-Tigre culture which, until the Ethiopian revolution, was accepted as the national culture, Ethiopia would not have been able to survive as an empire and preserve its independence from European colonialism. This is a fundamental difference between pre-revolutionary Ethiopia and Cambodia.

Cambodia's experience of French colonialism, more than any indigenous state-building processes, accounted for its ethnic demography. As a result of French colonial policy in Indochina, a substantial, but unintegrated number of Vietnamese, Chinese, Lao, Thai, Cham and sixteen other small ethnic groups, made Cambodia their home. Cambodia's ethnic minorities, who constituted 15 percent of the pre-revolutionary Cambodian population, were much more distinct than those in Ethiopia.[12] The largest minority ethnic group in Cambodia, before 1970, were the Vietnamese—about 450,000. They were followed by the Chinese

(425,000), the Muslim Cham (250,000), Thai (20,000), Lao (1,800) and the Kola (2,000). The Chinese and Vietnamese ethnic groups were more visible in the cities. The 80 percent Khmer population of pre-revolutionary Cambodia was predominantly Buddhist in religious faith.

Walter P. Zenner has studied the relationship between economics and group identities. He has observed that people who occupy strategic positions in the economic life of societies have often been "the objects of some of the most violent attempts at 'final solutions' of intergroup conflicts in the twentieth century." He mentions the Jews in Europe, Indians and other East Asians in East and South Africa, Lebanese in West Africa and Chinese in Southeast Asia as examples of what he calls "middleman minorities" who have borne the brunt of "subtler racism" often perpetrated against "stigmatized groups of middle economic positions."[13] Between 1970 and 1975, the Lon Nol regime expelled about half of the Vietnamese ethnic group from Cambodia and killed several thousand. Beside that obvious state repression, the dominant Khmer population did not persecute the Cham ethnic and religious minorities or the Vietnamese and Chinese middle class.[14]

Before the Ethiopian revolution, the Amhara and Tigre lived in amity with their assimilated minority ethnic groups. But Ethiopia's seemingly integrated national identity obscured the stigmatization of certain ethnic groups on the bases of their occupation and religion. Ethiopians, especially the Amhara, used their orthodox Christian religion to rationalize what Ethiopian historian Teshale Tibebu calls the "segregative division of labor." Ethiopia's stigmatized ethnic groups were the non-Christians such as the Oromo, who were predominantly Muslim, and the Beta Israel (Ethiopian Jews), who practiced an archaic form of Judaism.

Ethiopia's "middleman minorities" or "stigmatized groups of middle economic position" included hunters, weavers, carpenters, tanners, blacksmiths and fishermen. They were forbidden to own land or engage in agriculture regarded as the noble occupation in the monarchy. Ethiopian mythology inspired contempt for these economic groups.[15] According to Teshale Tibebu, Ethiopian mythology taught that woodcarvers and carpenters made the cross upon which Jesus was crucified. Many Ethiopians regarded these socioeconomic groups as either "unclean" or possessing "evil eyes."[16] A different situation existed in Cambodia. There, the Khmer

Loeu, a semi-nomadic highland people, hunted with dignity, in their sparse settlements in northeastern Cambodia. Until 1975 when the Khmer Rouge used their revolution to redefine citizenship and national identity in Cambodia, the Cham, a Muslim ethnic community, wove silk and raised their cattle in relative peace.

The kingdom's and empire's "middleman minorities" also included immigrants. In Cambodia, Chinese and Vietnamese immigrants provided the backbone of the market economy of the kingdom. In Ethiopia, Arabs, Greeks and Armenians constituted the mercantile class and dominated the retail economy of the empire. Yet in a society which put a premium more on land than the market, the social value of agriculture in Ethiopia made trade and money-lending unenviable professions. Merchants and immigrant communities such as Greek, Arab and Armenian traders operated without hindrance in Ethiopia. An essential point to be made here in relationship to Zenner's middleman minority theory is that although Ethiopians stigmatized or demonized non-agrarian occupational groups, they never entertained the idea of exterminating them.

RELIGION AND POLITICS

Prior to 1974, the political legitimacy of Emperor Haile Selassie of Ethiopia was firmly anchored in Orthodox Christian teachings just as the power and authority of King Norodom Sihanouk of Cambodia were rooted in the Buddhist religion. Buddhist and Christian doctrines also rationalized the patrimonial political structures and social and economic inequalities in the Empire of Ethiopia and the Kingdom of Cambodia. From Christian doctrines, peasants in pre-revolutionary Ethiopia came to regard periodic famines as acts of God, and state famine relief aid as the gracious gifts of a benevolent emperor. Similarly, Khmer Buddhism interpreted poverty as the consequence of bad *karma* in previous existence.

Cambodian and Ethiopian peasants believed that only by doing good deeds could they alter their social status or obtain a better life in the next world. In Ethiopia, the requirements for status alteration included obedience to authority, payment of taxes and tithes to the state and the Church and such good works as giving alms to the poor. Similarly, by giving food to monks or by becoming a monk, individuals in pre-revolutionary Cambodia hoped to obtain a better life in a future reincarnation. But the Cambodian monk's life of asceticism stood in stark contrast to the ostentatious lifestyles of the priests of the Orthodox church in Ethiopia.[17] As John Young has argued about Ethiopia, despite the Church's religious interpretation of power, poverty and social inequalities, Christianity was the institution which the majority of Ethiopians, especially the peasants, held in high esteem.[18] But as Michael Vickery argues about religion and peasants in Cambodia before the revolution, the teachings of Khmer Buddhism turned off younger Cambodians. Vickery put it controversially that Cambodian Buddhism had already been "desecrated" and discredited before the Khmer Rouge seized power in April 1975.[19]

LAND TENURE AND PEASANT LIFE

Unlike Ethiopia, land tenure was not a major problem in Cambodia. Abundance of land and equitable distribution of it to peasants made land tenure and landlordism issues less important in the formation of political views. Thirty-one percent of farming families in Cambodia owned less than one hectare of land in 1962 which made them poor given the low rice yields of one ton per hectare of land. But the poor peasants were in the minority. As Ben Kiernan argues, a majority of Cambodia's peasants owned about one to four hectares of land which guaranteed them a modicum of subsistence. Moneylenders, rather than landlords, constituted Cambodia's social overlords. More than half of Cambodia's rural peasants suffered from indebtedness thus making rural living standards low despite the richness of the Cambodian countryside which was generally well-watered and with low population density. Cambodia's moneylenders were mainly Chinese immigrants. It was their influence which preoccupied the Cambodian revolutionary elite.[20]

On the other hand, unequal distribution of land in pre-revolutionary Ethiopia reduced a substantial number of peasants in the empire to the status of tenants in a feudal empire.[21] Before March 1975, Ethiopia had two main types of land-tenureship known in *Amharinya*, the official language of Ethiopia, as *rist* and *gult*. *Rist* was the dominant system of land-holding in the northern highlands where the Christian Amhara and Tigre lived. Unlike their Cambodian counterparts, many of the peasants in the *rist* regions of northern Ethiopia held not more than ten hectares of land. As heritable lineage property, claimants subjected *rist* lands to division as frequently as descendants of those lineage groups asserted rights to the land. Frequent litigation over the size and location of land robbed *rist* landholders of absolute title to land. Moreover, peasants who cultivated small plots of such insecure land had neither the desire to increase output beyond subsistence nor the incentive to improve their holdings. Centuries of cultivating small plots of marginal fertility, within the institutional constraints of *rist* land-tenure, exposed the northern Ethiopian peasants of Wollo, Eritrea and Tigray to cyclical famine and starvation.

Gult was land granted by the Emperor as reward to people whose military services and religious devotion to the monarchy earned them "special grace." Since Haile Selassie could not afford to diminish the reward for loyal services to him by giving infertile land to the politically important, he offered large tracts of the most fertile land in the empire, mostly in the central and southern provinces, to members of the privileged group of patriots and Imperial loyalists. To the Ethiopian Orthodox Church, from which he obtained his sanctity and political legitimacy, he offered *semon* land, a type of *gult*, which the church held in perpetuity. Although very little data exists to clarify the popular perception in pre-revolutionary Ethiopia that the Church owned one-third of the land in the empire, it is probable that as the fount of religious doctrine and overseer of imperial coronations, the Ethiopian Orthodox Church owned a considerable quantity of some of the best lands.[22]

Land grants to patriots, soldiers, civil servants and the clergy formed part of Haile Selassie's strategy of building and consolidating domestic alliances to buttress the security of his reign. The absence of reliable external military allies in the midst of fear of external invasion from neighboring Muslim countries made the use of land for the creation of political balance imperative. About 28 percent to 45 percent of land in the fertile south was owned by absentee landlords. Tenancy and landlessness were widespread in Ethiopia. About 75 percent of peasants in Hararghe, in southeastern Ethiopia, 67 percent in Shoa, in central Ethiopia, and 62 percent in Keffa, in southern Ethiopia, had no land. They survived on rent, labor and sharecropping. This astounding statistic compares with 15 percent landless peasants in the northern provinces of Beggemdir (Gondar), 20 percent in Gojjam and 25 percent in Tigre. *Gult* landowners in southern Ethiopia operated sharecropping arrangements which often took one-third or one-half of the annual produce of their tenants rendering them poor and destitute.

Ethiopia's poor peasants faced arbitrary evictions by their landlords as the value of land rose with commercial farming and mechanization in the late 1960s. The looming fear of eviction compelled many tenant peasants to exceed their tenancy obligations by offering gifts and free labor services to their landlords in order to retain their favor. In many cases, tenant-peasants transported food, at their own expense, from the rural areas to their landlords who lived in the capital city.[23] These inherent flaws in Ethiopia's land tenure system penalized hard work instead of rewarding it.

The Emperor and officials of the Imperial Ethiopian Government came from the privileged class of landlords. The Imperial Ethiopian Government (IEG) controlled the scope, pace and direction of change in Ethiopia's agrarian economy. The substantial food stocks which landlords obtained from their tenants made radical land reform measures seem unattractive to them. This became more evident when landowners who dominated the Imperial Parliament made the legislature a barren field for the discussion of land reform issues. In the end, the plight of Ethiopia's peasants mobilized the empire's revolutionary elite many of whom were children of peasants. Land reform and the destruction of the landlord class became their persistent quest. That quest found extreme expression in the revolution of 1974.

HISTORICAL MEMORY AND NATIONAL IDENTITY

The Khmer of Cambodia and Amhara and Tigre of Ethiopia claim to have great traditions of nation-building. Archaeologists and anthropologists affirm these claims. French archaeologists considered pre-revolutionary Cambodia as the successor of the ancient northwestern Cambodian kingdom of Angkor. Similarly, British archeologists regarded Ethiopia as the successor of the ancient northwestern Ethiopian kingdom of Aksum. Angkor and Aksum reached the zenith of their glory between the first and the sixteenth centuries AD.

The ancient Khmer kingdom of Angkor dominated the Southeast Asian mainland. Its cultural influence extended over much of present day Thailand, Vietnam and Laos. Similarly, Aksum embraced the whole of the northern highland of present day Ethiopia and stretched beyond it to incorporate parts of southern Arabia. Legend has it that Aksum developed intricate commercial and cultural ties with the Greeks, Romans and the ancient Egyptians. Through these interactions, the fourth century Aksumite king, Ezana, was converted to Christianity by Egyptian monks.[24] Consequently, Christianity, the religion of the court, became the established religion of the empire, and the only faith which Ethiopian emperors were expected to profess. The kingdoms of Aksum and Angkor distinguished themselves in their material culture. Angkor produced the magnificent Angkor Wat temple at the same period (in the twelfth century) that Aksum built obelisks and rock-hewn churches to celebrate the might and opulence of its priest-kings. While Angkor Wat served as a monument to the worship of Buddhist deities, Aksumite temples received the devotees of Christ.

European archaeologists and anthropologists who popularized the history and memory of Angkor and Aksum gave Cambodians and Ethiopians a powerful ideological tool. Khmer and Amhara and Tigre educated elites extracted from their historical memory exaggerated ideas of the grandeur of their ancestors. From that social identity emerged a sense of political entitlement. The inscriptions, art, architecture and agriculture of Angkor gave the Khmer elites the impression that "their ancestors had been . . . the most powerful and gifted people of mainland Southeast Asia."[25] A group of the Khmer elite of the 1970s led by Pol Pot sought to recreate the civilization of ancient Angkor. For Ethiopians, Aksum invoked memory of the might and glory of highland Christian Amhara and Tigrean kings as well as memory of descent from the royal house of King Solomon of Israel. The Amhara and Tigre claim of semitic descent is tenuously based on a legendary liaison between a Queen Sheba, believed to have come from Aksum, and King Solomon of Israel in the tenth century BC.[26] The most grandiose appeal to this royal genealogy occurs in the 1955 revised constitution of Ethiopia which Emperor Haile Selassie (1930–1974) "graciously" offered to his subjects. The fourth article of that constitution proclaimed that "By virtue of His Imperial Blood, as well as by the anointing which he has received, the person of the Emperor is sacred, His dignity is inviolable and His power indisputable."[27] It was not belief in semitic origins of royalty alone that shaped the identity of the Aksumites and their Amhara and Tigre descendants. A culture of writing reinforced that. Aksum's Geez script matched ancient Egypt's famous *hieroglyphics* on a continent which Europeans such as Friedrich Hegel had dismissed, in the 1830s, as "uncivilized" and, therefore, "lying beyond the day of self-conscious history" because of its presumed lack of an alphabet or written texts.[28] The presence of indigenous scripts in Ethiopia and Cambodia set these monarchies apart from many of the ancient kingdoms in Africa and Asia. It assured the Amhara and Tigre of Ethiopia and the Khmer of Cambodia of the uniqueness of their civilization and history.

In 1863 when Cambodia succumbed to French colonial "protection" in Southeast Asia, Ethiopia withstood similar encroachments from the Portuguese and Italians. Nineteenth century Ethiopian emperors successfully contained the attempts of Portugal and Italy to colonize Ethiopia and convert its Coptic Christian court to Catholicism. In the end, Ethiopia stood alone as the only African empire to remain sovereign during the European scramble for colonies on the African continent. Ethiopia's famous defeat of Italian troops sent to conquer the northeast African empire in March 1896 continues to be a central theme in Ethiopian nationalism. Discoveries of early human skulls and bones in Ethiopia by European archaeologists, in the 1950s and 1970s added to Ethiopia's fame and prestige. Many scholars now take it as axiomatic that Ethiopia is "the birthplace of humankind."[29]

Myth and memory created in both monarchies individual illusions of grandeur and group delusions of superiority. No Cambodian found memory of ancient Angkor and Cambodia's national decline, in the late twentieth century, more incompatible than Pol Pot who led the Khmer Rouge revolution. He declared in 1977 that "If we [Cambodians] can build Angkor, we can do anything."[30] From a political and comparative perspective, Pol Pot's perception of Khmer ability and the superiority of Cambodia in Southeast Asia resembled Amhara and Tigre notions of their superiority in Ethiopia, and Ethiopia's conception of its uniqueness in Africa.

Tragically, memories of Angkor and of Aksum became the barometer by which the post–World War II Ethiopian and Cambodian educated elites measured the progress of their societies. Ethiopian students interpreted the inability of their society to feed itself and their dependence on international food aid in the 1970s as a blemish on national dignity.[31] Cambodian elites did not have to think about the implications of famine for national honor. Favorable weather conditions and equitable distribution of land had provided the kingdom with higher levels of food production for four centuries. But they viewed Cambodia's inability to respond to threats from Thailand and Vietnam, in the 1960s, and defend Cambodia against American economic and military attacks in the 1970s, as painful evidence of national decline.[32] Thus, the contrast that Ethiopian and Cambodian elites drew between their glorious past and their decadent present produced in them a crisis of identity which acted as a catalyst for the development of revolutionary ideas.

Angkor and Aksum may have provided the historical bases of Cambodian and Ethiopian nationalism. But the two ancient kingdoms left myth, militarism and personality cults as their enduring political legacies. Reverence for leaders, ability to project military force and annihilate political opponents were at the core of state-building in Cambodia and Ethiopia. Seizing power by killing political rivals, either in battle or by intrigue, would shock twenty-first century human rights activists as an immoral act. But that was not an unusual political practice in the history of Ethiopia and Cambodia. Neither was manipulating the economic life of peasants to bolster political loyalties seen as a bad social practice. Ethiopian and Cambodians had a political culture which allowed an individual thought to be affable, charismatic and meritorious, to exercise enormous power. King Norodom Sihanouk and Emperor Haile Selassie epitomized that culture.

ABSOLUTE MONARCHY AND MODERNIZING ELITES

Cambodia was identified with Sihanouk in the same way as Ethiopia was identified with Haile Selassie. Both monarchs remained popular among the peasants. Sihanouk had been chosen by the French to become king in Cambodia in 1941. In that same year, British soldiers and colonial troops and Ethiopian patriots restored Haile Selassie to his throne after defeating the Italians who had re-invaded and occupied Ethiopia since 1936. That re-invasion had caused the Emperor to seek refuge in London.

Emperor Haile Selassie and King Norodom Sihanouk were obsessed with power and self-glorification. A well-cultivated cult of personality stripped both monarchs of all human attributes. School children chanted songs praising the Emperor and the King and wishing them longer life.[33] This theater of imperial canonization made acquiescence to political authority the political norm in Ethiopia and Cambodia. As David Chandler has argued, obsession with power made it difficult for Norodom Sihanouk to distinguish between political dissent and treason.[34] King Sihanouk shared this political flaw with Emperor Haile Selassie.

Haile Selassie's own sense of insecurity fostered unquestioned obedience to the Emperor. While victory over Italian forces at Adwa in 1896 became a major part of the Ethiopian national epic, the memory of the Emperor's flight to England, when the Italians re-invaded Ethiopia in 1936, echoed with dissonance. Sections of the Ethiopian aristocracy never forgave him for seeking exile rather than accepting martyrdom in battle against Italian forces.[35]

Khmer communists such as Pol Pot, Ieng Sary and Hou Yuon disliked Sihanouk's personal rule from early in their careers. Nowhere was the distaste for monarchy more clearly articulated than in an article attributed to Pol Pot in a Khmer student magazine. In it, Pol Pot described monarchy as "a doctrine which bestows power on a small group of men who do nothing to earn their living," but "exploit the majority of the people at every level." To him, monarchy as a political institution constituted "a malodorous running sore" in human society that "just people" had the moral obligation to "eliminate."[36] Ethiopia's educated elites were not that forthright in their condemnation of that political system. Even those who resented Haile Selassie's claim to a divine right of rule, and wished to see an eventual demise of the social institutions that nurtured royal absolutism, actually admired the Emperor and regarded his intentions as noble. They blamed his officials for failing to carry out the Emperor's "gracious edicts."[37]

As leaders, Sihanouk and Haile Selassie had different political inclinations in moments of change. While Haile Selassie barred the formation of political parties in his empire, Sihanouk encouraged party political activities in his kingdom and even founded a political party—the Popular Socialist Party. What distinguished Sihanouk from Haile Selassie was that he abdicated his throne for direct participation in party politics in the 1955 atmosphere of decolonization and nationalism in much of Africa and Asia. Haile Selassie held on to power till he was deposed and killed at the age of 82 having ruled Ethiopia for more than fifty years against all appeals from Monks and other close advisors to yield power.[38]

DIPLOMACY

Ethiopia and Cambodia benefited from American aid. In the 1950s, Cambodia received U.S. economic assistance. It also accepted American military aid and advice in the early 1960s. But while Norodom Sihanouk avoided total dependence on the United States, and even broke diplomatic relations with Washington in 1965, Haile Selassie centered his diplomacy on relations with the United States.[39] American influence was conspicuous in two key areas of Ethiopian national life: defense and education. In both equipment and training, the Ethiopian Airforce remained, in the pre-revolutionary period, as the "most prestigious show-piece of American military aid to Ethiopia."[40] Over 2,500 Ethiopians including the future leader of the Ethiopian revolution, Mengistu Haile Mariam, studied in either American military academies or universities between 1953 and 1968. By 1970, Ethiopia was the largest recipient of U.S. military aid to Africa (about 60 percent).

To secure full American diplomatic and military protection, Haile Selassie granted the United States the right to operate a military communications installation at Kagnew in Asmara, Eritrea, for a period of twenty-five years starting in 1953. However, the United States did not always extend reciprocal diplomatic and military support to Ethiopia. The Emperor did not hide his displeasure at the failure of the United States to provide Ethiopia with the military assistance it needed to meet "the burden of national defence."[41] The visit of Haile Selassie to Moscow, in 1959, and his acceptance of a Soviet loan of 400 million roubles clearly demonstrated that while Christian Ethiopia found communism unattractive, it viewed the ancestral home of the communist ideology as a compelling source of military assistance. This view of Moscow did not change during the revolution. Despite the American reluctance to fully meet Haile Selassie's military needs, Ethiopia's educated elites of the 1950s and 1960s viewed the United States as "providing the infrastructural . . . support for the consolidation of [royal] absolutism" in Ethiopia.[42] They resented American influence in Ethiopia and regarded it as the clearest evidence of American global imperialism. For the Cambodian elite, U.S. bombardment of Cambodia in the early 1970s demonstrated even more pointedly that Cambodia had fallen prey to external forces despite Sihanouk's non-aligned foreign policy. That palpable sense of loss of national identity and prestige became a moving force in the revolutionary thinking of the Cambodian elite.

CONCLUSION

Power and land were the two key factors that defined life and status in pre-revolutionary Ethiopia. They also served as catalysts for social and political change. The degree to which land tenure and the exercise of power by monarchs alienated the political elite from the ascending educated class determined the nature of the ideas of change that the educated class nurtured. Peasants in Cambodia and Ethiopia took their low status in society for granted despite their experiences of social inequalities and economic oppression. They thought that their leaders had earned their status in society. Therefore, ideas of a just society, to be created through radical transformation of the existing social order were not widespread among peasants. They concentrated on what they considered to be their business: harvesting their crops and organizing religious festivals.

It was the salience of land and the resolute opposition to its equitable distribution by landlords—a section of the Ethiopian political elite—that would make land reform the focus of the revolutionary thoughts of the Ethiopian educated class. That was not at all the case in the kingdom of Cambodia. Cambodia's peasants did not have an oppressive land-owning class as their social overlords. The peasants in the kingdom would become revolutionary agitators after the educated elites, who blamed many of the things that went wrong in Cambodia on foreign influence, made peasants the vanguard of elite grievances against the monarchy.

NOTES

1. Relief and Rehabilitation Commission, *Ethiopia: An Overview* (Addis Ababa: RRC Public Relations and Information Service, 1995), 13.

2. Provisional Military Government of Socialist Ethiopia, Ministry of Agriculture, Planning and Programming Department, "Food Crop Development Information," July 1978, *Ministry of Agriculture Archives*, Addis Ababa, Ethiopia, 1.

3. David P. Chandler, *The Land and People of Cambodia* (New York: Harper Collins Publishers, 1991), 9.

4. Chandler, *The Land and People of Cambodia*, 22; Ben Kiernan, *How Pol Pot Came to Power: A History of Communism in Kampuchea, 1930–1975* (London: Verso, 1985), xv.

5. Chandler, *The Land and People of Cambodia*, 22.

6. Relief and Rehabilitation Commission, *Ethiopia: An Overview*, 13.

7. Patrick Gilkes, *The Dying Lion: Feudalism and Modernization in Ethiopia* (New York: St Martin's Press, 1975), 13–15. See also Addis Hiwet, *Ethiopia: From Autocracy to Revolution* (London: The Review of African Political Economy, 1975), 1–3.

8. Ben Kiernan, "The Cambodian genocide—1975–1979," in *Century of Genocide: Eyewitness Accounts and Critical Essays*, ed. Samuel Totten, W.S. Parsons and Israel W. Charny (New York: Garland, 1997), 336. See also Kiernan, *How Pol Pot Came to Power: Colonialism, Nationalism, and Communism in Cambodia, 1930–1975*, second edition (New Haven: Yale University Press, 2004), xxi.

9. John Young, *Peasant Revolution in Ethiopia: The Tigray People's Liberation Front, 1975–1991* (Cambridge: Cambridge University Press, 1997), 46–47.

10. Christopher Clapham, *Transformation and Continuity in Revolutionary Ethiopia* (Cambridge: Cambridge University Press, 1988), 24.

11. Clapham, *Transformation and Continuity*, 22–23.

12. Ben Kiernan, *The Pol Pot Regime*, 5. In 1975, the Khmer Rouge statistically wrote off Cambodia's ethnic minorities by claiming that they constituted only 1 percent of the Cambodian population. See Ben Kiernan, "The Cambodian Genocide—1975–1979," 340–42, and Elizabeth Becker, *When the War Was Over: The Voices of Cambodia's Revolution and its People*, 253.

13. Walter P. Zenner, "Middleman Minority Theories: a Critical Review," in *The Persisting Question: Sociological Perspectives and Social Contexts of Modern Antisemitism*, ed. Helen Fein (Berlin: de Gruyter, 1987), 255–59.

14. Chandler, *The Land and People of Cambodia*, 29; Kiernan, "The Cambodian Genocide—1975–1979," 340–42.

15. Teshale Tibebu, *The Making of Modern Ethiopia, 1896–1974* (Lawrenceville, NJ: The Red Sea Press, 1995), 67.

16. Teshale, *The Making of Modern Ethiopia*, 69.

17. Teshale, *The Making of Modern Ethiopia*, 82, 85.

18. John Young, *Peasant Revolution in Ethiopia*, 76–77.

19. Vickery, *Cambodia, 1975–1982*, 11.

20. Ben Kiernan and Chanthou Boua, *Peasants and Politics in Kampuchea, 1942–1981* (London: Zed Books, 1982), 4; Charles H. Twinning, "The Economy," in *Cambodia 1975–1978: Rendezvous with Death*, ed. Karl D. Jackson (Princeton, NJ: Princeton University Press, 1989), 113–114; Pierre Rousset, "Cambodia: Background to the Revolution," *Journal of Contemporary Asia 7*, 4 (1977): 521; Vickery, *Cambodia 1975–1982*, 16.

21. Bahru Zewde, *A History of Modern Ethiopia: 1855–1974* (London: James Currey, 1996), 178; Author's taped interview with Tesfaye Mekasha Amare, former vice-Minister of Foreign Affairs in the Imperial Ethiopian Government, Addis Ababa, July 31, 1995.

22. Michael Stahl, *Political Contradiction in Agricultural Development* (New York: Africana Publishing Company, 1974), 66–67; Patrick Gilkes, *The Dying Lion*, 3–4, 16–20, 55–57; Randi R. Balsvik, *Haile Selassie's Students: The Intellectual and Social Background to Revolution, 1952–1977* (East Lansing, MI: Michigan University Press, 1985), 149.

23. Tekalign Wolde-Mariam, "A City and Its Hinterlands: The Political Economy of Land Tenure, Agriculture and Food Supply for Addis Ababa, Ethiopia, 1887–1974," (diss., Boston University, 1995), 299, 320, 350–51.

24. Tefera Haile-Selassie, *The Ethiopian Revolution: From a Monarchical Autocracy to a Military Oligarchy* (London: Kegan Paul, 1997), 1–2.

25. Chandler, *The Land and People of Cambodia*, 6; *Brother Number One*, 12–13.

26. Bahru, *A History of Modern Ethiopia*, 1, 7.

27. Quoted in Bahru, *A History of Modern Ethiopia*, 206. See also Teshale, *The Making of Modern Ethiopia*, 105.

28. Georg Wilhelm Friedrich Hegel, *The Philosophy of History*, translated by J. Sibree (New York: Dover Publications, Inc., 1956), 91.

29. Teshale, *The Making of Modern Ethiopia*, xii.

30. David P. Chandler, *The Tragedy of Cambodian History: Politics, War, and Revolution Since 1945* (New Haven: Yale University Press, 1991), 6.

31. Author's taped interview with Professor Mesfin Wolde-Mariam, Chairman, Ethiopian Human Rights Council, Addis Ababa, March 8, 1995.

32. Chandler, *The Tragedy of Cambodian History*, 6.

33. Bahru, *A History of Modern Ethiopia*, 202; Chandler, *The Tragedy of Cambodian History*, 4.

34. Chandler, *The Tragedy of Cambodian History*, 4.

35. Edward Kissi, "Famine and the Politics of Food Relief in United States's Relations with Ethiopia: 1950–1991," (diss., Concordia University, Montreal, Canada, 1997), 44; Bahru Zewde, "Hayla Sellassie: From Progressive to Reactionary," in *Ethiopia in Change: Peasantry, Nationalism and Democracy*, ed. Abebe Zegeye and Siegfried Pausewang (London: British Academic Press, 1994), 41.

36. Chandler, *Brother Number One*, 37.

37. Mesfin Wolde-Mariam, *Rural Vulnerability to Famine, 1958–1977* (London: Intermediate Technology Publications, 1986), 37, 42–43; Dawit, *Red Tears*, 259; Balsvik, *Haile Sellassie's Students*, 245–46.

38. Bahru, *A History of Modern Ethiopia*, 206.

39. Kenton J. Clymer, "The Perils of Neutrality: The Break in U.S.-Cambodian Relations, 1965," *Diplomatic History* 23, no. 4 (Fall 1999): 613; Bahru, *A History of Modern Ethiopia*, 184–186.

40. Bahru, *A History of Modern Ethiopia*, 184–86.

41. See Imperial Ethiopian Government, Ministry of Foreign Affairs, "Summary of Remarks Made by His Imperial Majesty At Audience Granted on 12 March 1957 to the Vice President of the United States," and also Embassy of the United States of America "Aide Memoire for James P. Richards, Special Assistant to the President of the United States," April 17, 1957, *United States National Archives* (USNA), Record Group (RG) 59, Lot File No. 57, D616, Box 13.

42. Bahru, *A History of Modern Ethiopia*, 178.

2

GROWTH AND DISSEMINATION OF REVOLUTIONARY IDEAS

In the 1950s, those who championed revolution as a process of change in Cambodia were "relatively moderate," largely rural and very religious Buddhist Monks. Their revolutionary mentors were Vietnamese Communists who had helped to establish a Communist Party in Cambodia in 1951.[1] Ethiopia's revolutionaries of the 1950s were a secular and urban group of students at home and the few who were studying in France, The Netherlands, United States and the former Soviet Union. They admired the Chinese cultural revolution and felt inspired by it. But there is no evidence that the Ethiopian student-revolutionaries of the 1950s sought or obtained any form of assistance from China until after the 1970s when the revolution was actually launched.

As in all revolutionary movements, changes occurred in the leadership, ideology and objectives before the revolution began. The leadership of the revolutionary movement in Cambodia shifted, in the 1960s, from its moderate, rural and religious veterans to a group of younger and urban Cambodians who had studied in France. And their ideological mentors changed too. These extremist revolutionaries sought ideological support from China rather than Vietnam as the older veteran leaders had done. However, these changes in leadership and ideological orientation did not alter the key objective. Many Cambodian revolutionaries wanted a strong and self-reliant Cambodia. In hindsight, this noble objective appears to have obscured other morbid aspirations that the younger and more radical revolutionaries had. That became apparent after the revolution broke out in the 1970s. Ethiopia had similar transitions. In the 1960s, the student-revolutionaries at home tried to entice members of Ethiopia's armed forces to lead the revolutionary movement. The initial attempt, on December 13, 1960, by a section of the Ethiopian military to launch a revolution failed. However, their objective of overthrowing the emperor and eradicating social inequalities in the kingdom lived on to inspire fresh efforts in the 1970s.

Ethiopia's student and soldier-revolutionaries of the 1950s and 1960s did not seek a self-reliant and strong state as their counterparts in Cambodia did. Rather, they wanted to reform the existing land tenure system which had created a rigid class society of rich landlords and impoverished tenant peasants. But some agents of revolution in Ethiopia wanted more than land reform. They viewed the prevailing land tenure system as intricately connected with the plight of ethnic minorities as it had been with the poor conditions of the peasants. For them, self-determination for some of Ethiopia's ethnic minorities remained as the key objective of revolution. But ethnic self-determination did not become a stronger revolutionary objective in Ethiopia until after the revolution broke out. These different characteristics of Ethiopia's and Cambodia's revolutionary movements should not obscure one salient commonality about their social context. The society the revolutionaries in both monarchies sought to change was predominately rural and agrarian.

WHICH IDEOLOGY FOR WHAT REVOLUTION?

Saloth Sar (alias Pol Pot), who led the revolution in Cambodia in the 1970s, came from a privileged landowning family. He was, reportedly, "a mediocre student," who later became a successful teacher with "a reputation for fairness."[2] In the 1950s, while Pol Pot studied radio electricity in France, he met and struck up a deep friendship with Ieng Sary. Like Pol Pot, Ieng Sary was born into a land-owning family, but in Vietnam. In France, both men joined a Marxist study group affiliated with the

French Communist Party and closely followed political developments at home. As school teachers in Cambodia, in the 1960s, Pol Pot and Ieng Sary joined the Cambodian Communist Party. They even married sisters. Their colleague, Khieu Samphan, was the son of a judge. Like Pol Pot and Ieng Sary, Khieu Samphan became a communist during his studies in France. As David Chandler argues, there was much beyond France that shaped the ideas of Cambodia's agents of change. They developed their communist ideas in the era of Stalinism, the first Indochina war (1946–54), the Korean war (1950) and the first non-aligned conference in Bandung in 1955. Their exposure to world events broadened their worldview and "set them apart from Cambodian students at home."[3]

The more revolutionary-minded Ethiopians of the 1960s came from privileged social backgrounds as well. They too had studied in France and the United States. Notable among them was Haile Fida, a student in France often regarded as the "ideological leader" of the Ethiopian Students Union in Europe. Fikre Merid, another key revolutionary, was the son of a prominent Amhara soldier in a society in which military service granted access to land ownership and lucrative political careers. Fikre's father, General Merid Mengesha, was a close relative of Emperor Haile Selassie. Similarly, Tilahun Gizaw, the student leader who was assassinated in Ethiopia in 1965, possibly by government agents, was the son of a Tigrayan nobleman whose sister had married the Emperor's son. Berhane Meskal, the founder of the Ethiopian People's Revolutionary Party, in 1975, came from "a poor Tigrean peasant family."[4] But like Khieu Samphan, Berhane Meskal was raised in the comfortable home of a high court judge, his uncle. Ethiopian students abroad had opportunities which their colleagues at home did not have. Their access to uncensored revolutionary literature, and familiarity with the American civil rights struggle and social revolutions in Latin America, gave them a broader perspective on international affairs and a theoretical understanding of revolutions than their colleagues at home.

A key contrast in the social and intellectual history of revolution in the two monarchies is that teachers rather than students led the movement for revolution in Cambodia. In 1953, Cambodian radical students in France such as Pol Pot, Son Sen, Khieu Ponnary and her sister Khieu Thirith returned home and embarked on teaching careers. By late 1960, when only Ethiopian students at home bore the burdens of protest against the Haile Selassie government, former Cambodian teachers, and their loyal students, organized and led rebellions against the Sihanouk government from their rural sanctuaries.

Despite their common quest for change, Khmer communists of the 1960s were seriously divided over revolutionary "ideology and tactics." A chauvinist, anti-Vietnam and anti-Sihanouk group led by Pol Pot, and including Ieng Sary, Son Sen, Nuon Chea and Khieu Samphan, considered "true revolutions" and "rational" ideologies as those that ultimately produced an economically viable and a militarily strong Cambodia capable of regaining territories lost to Thailand and Vietnam. To the Pol Pot group of communists, a revolutionary Cambodia could only draw its domestic strength from the peasantry and external support from China. The second group of Khmer Communists led by Tiv Ol, Phouk Chhay and Hu Nim, was moderately anti-Sihanouk, in its domestic politics. But, ideologically, the group looked to the "mass democracy" idea of China's cultural revolution for lessons about revolutions. This pro-China group nevertheless saw the Cambodian Communist Party as a part of an international socialist movement. It, however, shared the Pol Pot group's commitment to rapid social transformation. The third group comprising Khmer communists trained in Vietnam supported the Vietnamese model of revolution and socialism and sought cooperation with Vietnamese communists. This pro-Vietnam group was not as committed to radical and rapid social change as the Pol Pot group.[5] As we shall later observe, the Pol Pot faction of the Cambodian Communist Party imposed ideological uniformity within the party by killing their ideological opponents.

The absence of a communist party in Ethiopia, as a result of the ban on political parties, did not deprive the empire of political factions and revolutionary views. Pre-revolutionary Ethiopia had "liberals," "conservatives," "monarchists," "theocrats," "socialists" and "communists."[6] With no Communist Party, and without sufficient data on other political groups, the study of the intellectual and social background to revolution in Ethiopia has narrowly focussed on the students as the main agents of revolution. It is the students who have left traces in the archival record about their revolutionary thoughts and intentions. That archival record reveals ideological rifts among Ethiopian student socialists and communists as serious as those that divided the Cambodian Communist Party into three opposing camps. Not all Ethiopians who wanted revolution viewed the overthrow of the Emperor's government as the only means of effecting change. There was a group of students who participated in the fashionable class analysis of Ethiopian society, in the 1960s, but sought the status rewards that came with fealty to the emperor. This group wanted change to be gradual rather than sudden.[7]

The gradualists perceived "Socialism" and "Marxism" as no better substitutes for Ethiopian "feudalism." For them, the problems affecting Ethiopia needed to be solved in an "Ethiopian way" rather than through foreign ideologies that bred division and hatred. With that perspective, the gradualists called their evolutionary ideology "Ethiopianism." The political thinking of this group reflected the traditional Ethiopian contempt for foreign influence and ideas. But Ethiopians who had studied abroad, especially in France and the United States, had a different opinion. They held tenaciously to the view that socialism was a universal concept that has no local versions.[8] The difficulty of resolving the tension between the gradualist advocates of Ethiopianism and the radical proponents of socialism can be discerned from the initial ideological compromises that the revolutionary government made when the Ethiopian revolution began in the early 1970s.

Kiflu Tadesse has argued that Ethiopian soldiers shared the idea of revolution that the students had.[9] That is not accurate. Ethiopian soldiers were just as conscious of the terrible conditions of Ethiopia's peasants as the intelligentsia. But that consciousness did not turn the soldiers into radical revolutionaries or marxists. As Major Dawit Wolde Giorgis, a member of the military government which led the Ethiopian revolution in the 1970s has noted, Ethiopian soldiers, unlike the students, were "educated in a nationalist tradition." If the soldiers had anything resembling an ideology, it was nationalism. And their nationalism emphasized "love of country and loyalty to the Emperor."[10] Thus, conflict in the Ethiopian army was not over Marxist or Communist ideology or even revolutionary strategy as was the case among the Ethiopian students and within the Cambodian Communist Party. Rather, it was over the prestige attached to the places of military training and Haile Selassie's strategic cultivation of the senior officers of the military with gifts of land, houses and money.

Ethiopian soldiers who graduated from the Haile Selassie Military Academy at Harar, which trained the sons of noble families and the best college students, regarded themselves as the elite corps. They received three years of military training and a university-level education. Their training differed from that of the cadets with elementary and high school backgrounds at the Genet Military School at Holeta. Soldiers at the Holeta Academy trained for a shorter period of six months to a year. It is noteworthy that the majority of the members of the military junta that seized power and launched revolution in Ethiopia in the early 1970s came from the less prestigious academy at Holeta. Ethiopian soldiers wanted improvement in conditions of service, fair allocation of military ranks, respect for junior officers and modernization of the means with which they defended a multi-ethnic empire.[11]

Without a Communist Party and a cohesive student movement, the only well-organized sector of pre-revolutionary Ethiopian society capable of seizing power to effect change was the military. But contrary to Kiflu Tadesse's assertion, the political necessity for the generals to preserve state power and enjoy the privileges that military service brought made the Ethiopian military potentially the strongest defenders of the Ethiopian monarchy and the most unreliable revolutionaries. Officers of the military benefited from the existing land tenure system which Ethiopian radical civilians made the focus of their revolutionary agitation. Moreover, the unity of Ethiopia that some student agitators questioned, and sought to change through revolution, was the basis of nationhood that members of the military had pledged to defend in their profession. The different views that Ethiopian soldiers had on land and national identity put the military into an antagonistic relationship with the civilian revolutionaries.

Whatever the differences between the Cambodian and the Ethiopian revolutionary movements, revolution as an idea of change was an urban and elite preoccupation. It was nurtured from despair. In Ethiopia, the preconditions for revolution were mainly economic and rural. They were the poverty, landlessness and famine that characterized rural life and impaired the international image of an uncolonized African empire. These economic and rural conditions did not plague Cambodia. As we have already noted, the kingdom of Cambodia did not have as rigid a class structure as the empire of Ethiopia. Land was not inequitably distributed and famine was not endemic as in the Ethiopian empire. As David Chandler correctly argues, "the customary spurs for revolutionary mobilization" (an exploitative class of landlords and shortage of land) were absent in Cambodia.[12] Thus, from a comparative perspective, pre-revolutionary Cambodia may have been a happier place than Ethiopia. The relative economic contentment made Cambodian peasants unlikely revolutionary agitators.

Even during the worst economic conditions, Ethiopian peasants did not become revolutionary agitators. They did, however, express their economic discontent and desires for change through occasional revolts. But Ethiopia's "peasant revolts" differed from the student agitations in their nature, duration and motivation. Peasant revolts in Ethiopia were nothing more than localized protests against taxation, land tenure, usury and social and economic conditions which affected this rural group directly. In duration, peasant rebellions lasted for a few days to several months. Ideologically, they lacked a motivation to alter the social character of society. Their impact was also minimal. None of the peasant revolts in Bale, in southeastern Ethiopia, in the 1940s and 1960s, for instance, developed into a nation-wide movement seeking radical social transformation. Nor did they attract the attention which student protests captured. The situation was not different in Cambodia.[13] Therefore, the usefulness of peasant protests for understanding the social background to revolution in Ethiopia and Cambodia lies in invocation of them by the intellectual elite to project popular support for their own political causes or to give their quest for revolution an idealistic interpretation.

FOCUS OF REVOLUTIONARY IDEAS

Ideas of rebellion for the purpose of establishing an egalitarian social order, changing the political leadership and the bases of power, and transforming modes of thought grew faster in Cambodia than they did in Ethiopia. Cambodian communists who wanted revolution as a vehicle for social transformation had a clearly-defined ideology and revolutionary program as well as a communist political party to propagate their competing ideas. The Khmer Peoples Revolutionary Party (KPRP), formed in 1951, served as a legal vehicle for revolutionary politics in Cambodia. In the 1960s, Pol Pot and other French-educated Khmers took control of the KPRP and transformed it into the Communist Party of Cambodia, with a clear revolutionary program. At this period of time, the Ethiopian students movement existed only as a pressure group. It was not until twenty-five years after the foundation of the KPRP that the most marxist and radical of Ethiopia's revolutionary movements, the Ethiopian Peoples Revolutionary Party (EPRP), was formed.[14]

It was the radical few among the Ethiopian students at home who laid the foundations of revolution in Ethiopia. But Christianity and the absence of a colonial experience must have inhibited the development of a clear revolutionary program in the Ethiopian empire. Ethiopian revolutionaries could not organize a political party to articulate a well-defined revolutionary program or compete for political power as their Cambodian counterparts did. Yet, as determined advocates of change, they constituted a significant political group bound together by their common belief that a "complete social transformation" of Ethiopia in the "framework of socialism," constituted the only means to change.[15]

It is important to note that despite their common professions of socialism as their ultimate revolutionary goal, Ethiopian and Cambodian revolutionaries differed considerably in their knowledge of socialism as a political ideology and a theory of social organization. The different levels of knowledge of the political and economic theories of Karl Marx in Ethiopia and Cambodia were partly the consequence of unequal levels of literacy and the political contexts of operations. Higher literacy rates in Cambodia had produced "a mass of politically aware teachers and students."[16] By 1967, when a majority of Cambodians had acquired basic education, only a small proportion of the Ethiopian population had received basic elementary education. In Ethiopia, 70 percent of students who had entered the less than 200 primary schools had not even reached twelfth grade by 1967. And the drop-out rate was extremely high.[17] In 1968, Cambodia had nine universities compared to the one university which Ethiopia established in 1961, and which remained the empire's sole institution of higher learning until the outbreak of revolution in 1974. Moreover, the imbalance in the spread of educational opportunities in the Ethiopian empire meant that the capital city, Addis Ababa, at the center, and the province of Eritrea, in the north, had the highest number of schools and students. By 1970, only a small number of Ethiopians had even made it to university. To reach that level of education, one had to "negotiate a narrow passage which eliminated all but the most able and socially privileged."[18]

It is not surprising that the low level of literacy in pre-revolutionary Ethiopia bred attitudes of deference and obedience to authority. Whereas Khmer communists disliked Sihanouk's personal rule from early in their careers as students and later teachers, not all of Ethiopia's socialists and communists resented Haile Selassie's personal rule or wanted to overthrow the monarchical system. Many Ethiopians, including some revolutionaries, admired the Emperor as the symbol of nationhood. They even considered absolutism as an inevitable characteristic of a monarchy. Cambodian revolutionaries, on the other hand, had different attitudes toward monarchy as a political institution.[19]

Despite the different levels of literacy, at home, and the cultural and political atmosphere in which they operated, Ethiopian and Cambodian agents of change abroad had better exposure to radical ideas. From the late 1950s, hundreds of Ethiopian and Cambodian students left their homes every year to pursue further studies abroad under state sponsorship. France served as the intellectual sanctuary of Cambodian students. By 1970, the United States had the largest number (700) of Ethiopian students, followed by France, the Netherlands and the Soviet Union.[20] Ability to interpret the domestic and global conditions affecting their societies imbued Ethiopian and Cambodian students abroad with an abiding belief in change and progress under their leadership.

As Kiernan and Chandler argue, rising unemployment in urban areas made a great majority of Cambodia's educated elite passionate advocates of radical social change.[21] The situation was not different in Ethiopia. What Kiflu Tadesse has called "the painful reality" in Ethiopia, and historian Bahru Zewde considers "the objective basis" for radicalism, transcended what the students considered as "the greed of the [Ethiopian] ruling elites" and the "worsening condition of the peasants [famine]." That painful reality included the worsening condition of the "urban masses [unemployment]."[22] In short, the revolutionaries framed their own despair over unfulfilled expectations in broader and more idealistic terms. Cambodian and Ethiopian revolutionaries of the 1960s epitomized what Kiflu Tadesse has called "a generation . . . at odds" with

the fealty and submission which their feudal culture and other indigenous traditions demanded of them in a changing world suffused with
ideas of progress and development.[23] However, the common elite discontent did not produce similar revolutionary visions. Ethiopians who
sought revolutionary transformation of their society wanted to abolish
landlordism, Amhara ethnic hegemony and deal with mass death of
peasants from famine.[24] By contrast, Khmer revolutionary consciousness
had some of its roots in Cambodia's colonial experience. The French
had prevented Cambodia from being annexed by Thailand from the
West and Vietnam from the East in the nineteenth century. But foreign
patronage made Cambodia neither stronger, militarily, nor bigger, terri-
torially. Cambodian intellectuals such as Pol Pot put the preservation of
the territorial integrity of Cambodia from Thai and Vietnamese encroachments at the center of their revolutionary visions. Kiernan has argued that for the Pol Pot group of Khmer communists, preserving the
territorial integrity of Cambodia also meant rejecting all foreign cultures
and influences, particularly those of Vietnam.[25] Chandler has clarified
that cultural isolationism—the idea that Cambodia should be cut off
from other cultures—persisted in many Cambodian regimes before the
Pol Pot group violently enforced it in 1975.[26]

The leadership and direction of revolutionary politics changed in
Ethiopia, in the 1960s. From this period onwards, the more radical intellectuals enticed sections of the military to carry out what the civilians
could not accomplish alone. Thus, Ethiopia attempted to carry out its
revolution fifteen years before Cambodian communists launched theirs.
Girmame Newaye, an Ethiopian educated at Columbia University, in
the United States, convinced his brother General Mangestu Newaye, an
officer of the Imperial Bodyguard, a detachment of the Ethiopian army
which protected the Emperor and the palace, to lead a coup to overthrow the Imperial Ethiopian Government on December 13, 1960. In
their first radio announcement, the coup plotters compared what they
viewed as the underdevelopment of Ethiopia to what they claimed as
the "fantastic progress achieved by the new independent African states."
Their declared intention was to launch a "revolution" to achieve six main
objectives. First, to restore Ethiopia to her "ancestral place in the
world." Second, to give peasants "every assistance . . . to raise agricultural production." Third, to offer traders "assistance to improve [their]

business." Fourth, to establish schools so that "many young Ethiopians ... seen loitering in the streets ... [could] find employment." Fifth, to give the "armed forces more clearly-defined ... personal freedom." Sixth, to unify the Ethiopian army by abolishing the "two separate titles" of the armed forces: Imperial Bodyguard and the Imperial Ethiopian Army.[27]

Ethiopia's first revolutionary proclamation gave a foretaste of the reformist and moderate objectives of the monarchy's soldier-revolutionaries. The coup plotters demonstrated in their first policy statement that their country's "malodorous running sore" was not the monarchy as an institution as Pol Pot's group of Khmer communists felt about their society, but rather the inability of their monarch's officials to prevent famine from developing into mass starvation and thereby tarnishing the image of a proud nation. Thus, it was mass death of Ethiopian peasants from recurrent famine that delegitimized the Ethiopian monarchy and encouraged a section of the army to promote revolution in the name of liberating the peasants. When recurrent famine delegitimized the Ethiopian monarchy, radical Ethiopian students became even more strident in their mockery of official references to Ethiopia's "richness" and "3000 years" of independence.[28] They now fearlessly questioned Ethiopia's achievements in the midst of mass death of the empire's predominant population, the peasants, from famine. For the Imperial Government, not acknowledging that famine was a problem in Ethiopia, and persistently explaining the worsening conditions of peasants as temporary aberrations in a wealthy empire, had some political benefits. It enabled the Emperor and his officials to downplay the need for land reform.[29] Obviously, one of the requirements for improving the conditions of peasants was land reform. Ethiopian advocates of revolution made that their key objective. Land reform meant the breaking up of large land estates and redistributing them to landless peasants. That had the potential of reducing peasant tax and food supply obligations to the state and landlords. But land reform threatened the landlord class: the clergy and senior officers of the Ethiopian army whose wealth, power and status depended on the prevailing land tenure system.[30]

It is worth noting that the December 1960 coup d'etat failed as a result of the anti-revolutionary attitude of the landlords, the top brass of the army and the Ethiopian Orthodox Church.[31] Though the coup plotters were

quickly apprehended and hanged, their action and proclamation left an enduring legacy. The willingness of some Ethiopian soldiers to lead a revolution to change the social, economic and political system of which they were
a crucial part and had sworn to defend demonstrated that by the end of
1960 key sections of the Ethiopian military, instigated by civilian socialists,
were eager to identify with the more radical civilians in spite of their divergent visions of revolution. The coup also alerted the Imperial Government to the fact that military fealty—already taken for granted—could no
longer be guaranteed in the face of student agitation in the capital city.

RELIGION, ETHNICITY AND REVOLUTION

Ethiopian radical students and Cambodian communists blamed many of
the social problems of their day on religion. But whereas Ethiopian revolutionaries had no intention of abolishing religion except dispossessing
the Church of its material wealth and social influence, their Cambodian
comrades contemplated the abolition of Buddhism altogether. Radical
Ethiopian students questioned the morality of the Ethiopian Orthodox
Church in a society where millions starved to death while the clergy promoted a view of famine as the unfolding of a divine plan. As Randi
Balsvik and Shiferaw Bekele note, if radical Ethiopian students of the
1960s had their wish, all church lands in Ethiopia would be nationalized,
the state separated from the church, all religions accorded equal privileges, and above all, "rich people in authority" dispossessed of their
wealth and power.[32]
     Ethiopian revolutionaries of the 1960s were not alone in viewing reli-
gion as a fatalist institution. For many Cambodians, the hypnotic power
of Buddhism lay in its explanation of life as a consequence of conduct. As
Michael Vickery argues, by entering the monastery, doing good deeds, or
"giving up . . . part of one's own economic surplus" to Monks, Cambodians hoped to accumulate merits for a better future life. Drawing upon
May Ebihara's research, Vickery concludes that by 1959 many poor and
wealthy Cambodians had come to resent Buddhism's fatalistic explanations of life.[33] Vickery and David Chandler have attributed the loss of interest in religion in Cambodia manifested in the "decline of Buddhist
practices among the urban middle class," in the 1950s and 1960s, to "the

expansion of literacy and mass education" in the kingdom. According to Vickery, many Cambodian teachers and "middle class youth", in the 1960s, "openly ridiculed religious traditions" and viewed the Monks as "social parasites." The teachers and youth expressed their disaffection with religion and monastic life in "destruction of religious paraphernalia."[34] Thus, in the opinion of Vickery, anti-religious feeling in Cambodia preceded the Cambodian revolution of 1975. Ethiopians had different attitudes toward religion as an institution. Even in their disaffection with the Orthodox Church, Ethiopian revolutionaries held religious symbols and images in awe. The issue that they considered important in their revolutionary thought was land tenure and not religious belief.

. Undoubtedly, land tenure issues inflamed Ethiopia's second most important revolutionary spur: ethnicity. Whereas the break-up of Ethiopia into ethnic polities appealed to some Ethiopian revolutionaries, especially students from the northern province of Eritrea, as the inevitable result of revolution, the indivisibility of Cambodia remained the keystone of the Cambodian Communist Party's idea of revolution. It needs to be emphasized that the kingdom of Cambodia did not have anything resembling the "nationalities problem" that became a contentious source of revolutionary agitation in the Ethiopian empire. By 1962, ethnic nationalism had inspired a stern resolve by Tigrinya-speaking nationalists in Eritrea to seek independent statehood for the northern province through armed liberation struggle. Ethiopians who opposed ethnic self-determination acknowledged the inherent problems in the prevailing definition of Ethiopian nationhood that elevated Amhara identity and language over all other ethnicities and languages and privileged Christianity over all other religions. Yet most Ethiopian student-revolutionaries, both at home and abroad, chose to focus on what they considered as the important issue: land-based class distinctions. Secessionists within the student revolutionary movement saw class and ethnicity as inseparable.[35] Here, the future battle lines were drawn.

COMMON IDEOLOGIES, DIFFERENT OBJECTIVES

Certainly, Ethiopian students and Cambodian communists considered socialism, Marxism and communism as ideological paths to a brighter future. Khmer communists and Ethiopian marxists or "radical students" found Marxism as a useful analytical tool. The social liberation of the poor and the improvement of the lives of the common people which Marxism and Socialism promised had a stronger appeal to them. In 1964, a group of students in Ethiopia led by Berhane Meskal, Zeru Kehishen and Gebru Gebre-Wold formed a marxist group known as the *Crocodile Society*. Fourteen years earlier (in 1950), a small group of Cambodian students in France led by Pol Pot, Khieu Samphan and Ieng Sary had also formed a *Marxist Circle* or study group affiliated with the French Communist Party. The Ethiopians in the *Crocodile Society* and the Cambodians in the *Marxist Circle* promoted a view of their two societies as a class-based society of peasants and aristocrats in a world divided between the forces of socialism and imperialism. They had similar class enemies. Ethiopian Marxists counted big landlords, members of the imperial family, the nobility and the clergy among their class enemies.[36] Khmer communists included the royal family, Vietnamese and the Chinese middlemen minorities in Phnom Penh, moneylenders, corrupt government officials and pro-American Khmers among theirs.[37]

Formation of Marxist study-clubs in Ethiopia should not mislead one into concluding that Ethiopian Marxists had more than rudimentary knowledge of Marxism or that socialism was a big factor in Ethiopia before the revolution. Former Ethiopian student leader, Gebru Mersha, has admitted that even the most "socialist-minded" political science students at Haile Selassie I University had only a "limited acquaintance with Marxism." For many Ethiopian student radicals of the 1960s, the appeal of Marxism resided in its "captivating slogans."[38] Dawit Wolde Giorgis, another former student Marxist who joined the revolutionary military regime, has noted that it was fashionable to be considered a "radical" in Ethiopia in the 1960s, and intellectually respectable to be able to quote Mao, Che, Lenin or Marx.[39] The toxic effects of this form of cosmetic Marxism in Ethiopia became more apparent in student debates about whether Ethiopia was an "empire-state," "imperial power," "kingdom state," "feudal," "capitalist," or "feudo-bourgeo-capitalist."[40] Marxist students interpreted every national problem exclusively in marxist terminologies and sought uncompromising solutions. Lack of tolerance for opposing views in revolutionary discourse can be attributed to the absence of a serious democratic tradition in Ethiopia under Haile Selassie.

Not only did Cambodian and Ethiopian revolutionaries differ in their knowledge of Marxism, but also the symbolism and interpretation that they attached to socialism and communism in their agrarian, religious and feudal societies. Cambodian revolutionaries saw communism as a mechanism for liberating Cambodia from French colonialism and Cambodian feudalism. The socialism of the Pol Pot group of Khmer communists emphasized "self-reliance and independence" from Vietnamese influence, a strong state and a national army capable of having "mastery" over the destiny of the Khmer race and the national borders of Cambodia.[41] In Cambodia where Buddhism and communism were not considered as incompatible, "communist," as an ideological label, had an inspiring ring to it. Prince Sihanouk once quipped that "Buddha was red, or pink anyway."[42] To be a communist in Cambodia meant having simple tastes, a good education, aversion to corruption and a sense of justice and sympathy for the poor.

In Christian Ethiopia, socialism and communism were associated with atheism. Not even the most ardent radical happily sought the label "socialist" or "communist." When Ethiopian socialists talked about socialism, they meant "a complete restructuring of property relations in land" and not ethnic purity and territorial expansion. They wanted land reform to bring social justice to rural Ethiopia. Social justice meant the ability of all peasants to own land and those dispossessed of their land to have it restored to them. Socialism also meant the narrowing of social gaps. In Ethiopia that meant abolishing social hierarchies and noble titles with their land-based privileges. The Marxist or Socialist slogan of the 1960s was "Land to the Tiller."[43]

Cambodian and Ethiopian revolutionaries of the 1960s looked more to China than the Soviet Union for pathways to revolution. As Chandler argues, Pol Pot and his comrades found "China's triumphant revolution" more appealing and worthy of emulation than "Vietnam's arduous, unfinished struggle." The "Red Khmers" or *Khmer Rouge*, as King Sihanouk derisively called Cambodian Communists, drew from Maoism and Chinese communism ideas of self-reliance, mobilization of peasants and elimination of class enemies. But according to Ben Kiernan, Cambodia's Marxists learned their "organizational tactics and control techniques" from the Soviet Union under Stalin. Elizabeth Becker contends that the Khmer Rouge may have borrowed their revolutionary ideology and organizational strategies from elsewhere, but their practice of communism was indigenous. It was deeply influenced by the "Buddhist background of members of the Khmer Rouge."[44] Ethiopian revolutionaries drew inspiration from the Chinese cultural revolution as a result of the parallels they saw between the historical experiences of Ethiopia and China. Personality cults and the deification of national leaders had deep resonances in the Chinese past and the Ethiopian present. Ethiopian marxists, especially those who studied in the United States in the 1960s, drew some of their revolutionary lessons from the civil rights movement in the United States, the Cuban revolution and the Marxist ideas of Che Guevara.[45]

ANTI-AMERICANISM AS REVOLUTIONARY IDEOLOGY

Despite their different conceptions of socialism, Ethiopian and Cambodian revolutionaries wanted to live in a society freed from American influence. Their anti-American proclivities had deeper roots in aspects of their political histories. In the 1950s and 1960s, the Imperial Ethiopian Government had relied heavily on American economic and military aid for the stability of the Ethiopian monarchy. American military presence in Ethiopia had been the price that the Haile Selassie government had paid for Ethiopia's receipt of the largest American aid grants in Africa at that time. About 6,000 Americans lived in Ethiopia. Half of this large number were soldiers and technicians who maintained the American military installation in northern Ethiopia which facilitated U.S. telecommunications between Europe and the Far East.[46]

The kingdom of Cambodia was not as dependent on U.S. aid, or as ideologically pro-American, as the Empire of Ethiopia. In the Cold War period of the 1960s, Sihanouk pursued a neutral foreign policy and even permitted Cambodian Communists to criticize U.S. foreign policy in a manner that reflected Sihanouk's own antipathy towards the United States. But as Kiernan has also noted, Sihanouk's foreign policy was aimed at "keeping Cambodia out of the escalating conflict in neighboring Vietnam." We now know that that strategy did not keep Cambodia safe from American bombs during the Vietnam War. But in 1963, Sihanouk did what Haile Selassie could not even contemplate. He suspended the limited U.S. military and economic aid to Cambodia—which had accounted for 14 percent of state revenue—and broke off diplomatic relations with Washington two years later.[47]

Anti-American feeling in Cambodia intensified over the American bombardment of Cambodia from 1969 to 1973 and accelerated the outbreak of revolution there. In 1969, the United States dropped 100,000 tons of bombs on Cambodian soil in a bid to destroy Vietnamese Communist forces using Cambodian territory as a hideout and to move supplies. By 1973, U.S. aerial bombardments of the Cambodian countryside had wiped out entire villages and killed up to 150,000 civilians. Kiernan and Chandler argue that the Cambodian Communist Party (the Khmer Rouge) would not have gained power in 1975 had the U.S. military action not destabilized Cambodia economically. Khmer Rouge cadres succeeded in convincing many young peasants that the Lon Nol regime had requested the air strikes and the only means to stop them was to overthrow the regime. The bombing also increased the anti-urban sentiment in the revolutionary ideology of the Pol Pot faction which dominated the Communist Party. Peasants who had endured the American bombing had practical reasons to join the Khmer Rouge in their thousands, and the Khmer Rouge used the national outrage against the bombing and the Cambodian political leadership as an excuse to purge the moderates and monarchists within its ranks.[48]

Anti-American feelings in Ethiopia initially grew from American aid and cultural influence in the empire itself. The student-revolutionaries at home viewed American military assistance to the Haile Selassie regime as providing the Emperor's government with the means to suppress student protests. They also opposed "the American way of life" which their colleagues returning from their studies in the United States tried to promote. Above all, Ethiopian students at home and abroad found their clearest example of American global imperialism in the Vietnam war. U.S. military actions in Vietnam and Cambodia caused Ethiopian revolutionaries to draw critical comparisons between the bombardment of Cambodia and what the United States could do in Ethiopia if it felt its interests in the empire were threatened. In the late 1960s, rumors that the United States intended to build new military bases in Ethiopia heightened student resentment of American influence in the empire.[49]

TERRITORIAL EXPANSIONISM
AND RACIST ULTRANATIONALISM

A key nationalist aspiration of the Pol Pot group of Khmer Communists was to regain all territories once lost to Thailand and Vietnam and to re-unite into one nation all Khmers who lived in Cambodia, Thailand and Vietnam.[50] Here, the viability of the Khmer race and the Cambodian nation was a prominent feature of Khmer Rouge revolutionary national-ism. To the extent that Ethiopian student radicals were concerned about "race" or ethnicity, it was about the right of ethnic minorities to secede from the Ethiopian empire and not the preservation of the "purity" of a particular race or ethnic group or the expansion of historical territories.

The majority of Ethiopia's student-revolutionaries saw the prospect of an independent Eritrea as an ominous signal for ethnic groups in the multi-ethnic empire to invoke real or imagined oppression as a basis for declaring independence or taking up arms to achieve it. The lack of pop-ular support for secessionism had historical reasons. According to Ethiopian historian Bahru Zewde, before the Italians gained control over the northern territory making up Eritrea, in 1890 and 1935, that territory had served as a strategic corridor to mainland Ethiopia. The Italians had used the now independent Eritrea as a base to invade Ethiopia in 1896 and again in 1935. In September 1952, the former Ital-ian colony of Eritrea was federated with Ethiopia by the United Na-tions. But security concerns strengthened the interest of the Imperial Ethiopian Government (IEG) to prevent Eritrea, situated along the Red Sea coast, from becoming a base for future external attacks on the heart-land of Ethiopia.

The IEG saw the restoration of Eritrea to the "Motherland" as the "only means of disposing of the (colonial status) of Eritrea."[51] Conse-quently, Ethiopia annexed Eritrea in November 1962 in violation of the September 1952 U.N. agreement which had granted Eritrea au-tonomous status within Ethiopia. Far from assuaging the security dilem-mas of the IEG, the annexation of Eritrea actually fuelled the flames of secessionism in the province and accentuated the fears of the Ethiopian monarchy about the disintegration of the empire. Eritrean revolutionary nationalists, however, viewed independent statehood for Eritrea as the only way of disposing of "Ethiopian colonialism" in Eritrea.[52] They made

Eritrean independence the central objective of their conception of revolution. The lack of national support for ethnic-separatism in Ethiopia (including independence for Eritrea), in the 1960s, meant that Eritrean nationalists could achieve their idea of revolution only through armed struggle against the Ethiopian state. That meant fighting their revolutionary colleagues who did not share their idea of revolution.

Fear of a break-up of the Ethiopian empire intensified after July 1960 when the U.N. Trust Territory of Somaliland and part of British Somaliland were merged into the Republic of Somalia to the east of Ethiopia. The Somali government sought to "reunite" under the new republic all ethnic Somalis who lived outside of Somalia, especially in the Ogaden region of southeastern Ethiopia—a portion of the former British Somaliland. With support from the government of Somalia, the more nationalistic Ogaden Somalis demanded the conversion of the Ogaden region into an independent state of Western Somalia. They founded the Western Somalia Liberation Front (WSLF), in 1961, to wage a war of secession against the central government in Ethiopia to achieve that objective.[53] A year after the formation of the WSLF (1962), Eritrean nationalists also established an armed liberation movement, the Eritrean Liberation Front (ELF), to seek independent statehood for Eritrea. In their armed struggle for independence, Eritrean nationalists interpreted "Eritrea" as a lost territory and "Eritreans" (who are actually speakers of the Tigrinya language spoken mainly in northern Ethiopia) as a distinct and oppressed ethnic group. Having politicized ethnicity in this manner, the ELF proceeded to view ethnic solidarity among all "Eritreans" as more important than their membership in a particular social or economic class in the Ethiopian empire.[54]

Ethiopia's fear of Somali irredentism had a striking parallel in Cambodia's fear of Thai and Vietnamese expansionism. But that fear of Somali irredentism as well as Eritrean and Ogaden Somali ethno-nationalism did not have the same strong racial overtones as the anti-Vietnamese sentiments of the Pol Pot group of Khmer Communists. While Eritrean and Ogaden-Somali revolutionaries made independence for oppressed ethnic groups, the focus of their revolutionary nationalism, Ethiopian soldiers who had since December 1960 accepted revolution as a mechanism of change made the preservation and unity of the Ethiopian empire their revolutionary ideology. Here, again, the future battle lines were rigidly drawn. The pan-Ethiopianist orientation of the soldiers had some of its roots in the casualties they suffered during the brief Ethiopia-Somali border war of 1967 and their unceasing defense of the Ethiopian state against Eritrean and Ogaden-Somali armed nationalists. It is accurate to state that the revolutionary nationalism of Ethiopia's soldier-revolutionaries mirrored the predominant Amhara nationalist ideology which elevated the unity of Ethiopia within the empire's traditional borders over ethnic self-determination, secessionism and the redrawing of national boundaries. It was this well-organized and disciplined, but non-Marxist group (the Ethiopian army), that seized state power in Ethiopia in the early 1970s and took leadership of the revolution away from the civilians.

MARKETING REVOLUTION BEYOND THE CITY

Cambodian communists had more success than their Ethiopian compatriots in propagating their revolutionary ideas. That happened despite Sihanouk's determination to suppress communism in Cambodia through gruesome measures such as decapitation and disembowelment of known Communists. When gruesome persecution in the city forced Cambodian Communists to flee to the countryside, they slowly built and deepened peasant hatred for the cities.[55] While the Khmer Rouge may not have enjoyed majority peasant support, they undoubtedly commanded the loyalty of a larger number of peasants than the student-revolutionaries and soldiers did in Ethiopia. U.S. bombardment of Cambodian villages in the 1960s and the freedom that Sihanouk allowed the communists, amid the persecutions, to propagate their revolutionary ideas in the previous decade helped to radicalize the Cambodian peasantry.

Ethiopian student revolutionaries did not succeed in capturing the peasants and turning them against the state and the capital city as the Khmer Rouge did. Between 1964 and the outbreak of the revolution in 1974, Ethiopian students at home used a national service program in which university students spent a year in the rural areas teaching secondary schools to spread their revolutionary ideas. But they failed to politicize Ethiopian peasants to join a campaign to overthrow the Emperor. Haile Selassie treated Ethiopian revolutionaries as Sihanouk did

Cambodia's. His security forces incarcerated, tortured and assassinated student activists.[56] But whereas persecuted Cambodian Communists fled to the countryside, repressed Ethiopian radicals left the empire altogether. Many of them ended up in Canada and the United States. Ethiopia's exiled revolutionaries returned home only after junior military officers seized power in 1974. Their long exile abroad had alienated them from the peasantry. It even put them in conflict with their comrades who had stayed at home. The struggle between the exiles and the comrades at home to control the leadership and direction of the revolution after 1974 was bloody.

Although Ethiopia was the first to attempt a revolution through a coup d'état that failed, it was in Cambodia that a more successful coup took place. The coup of March 18, 1970 that toppled the Sihanouk monarchy was led by General Lon Nol. In October 1970, the Cambodian coup-makers renamed the kingdom, the Khmer Republic. That was a revolutionary event that ended two thousand years of monarchical rule in Cambodia. The overthrow of Prince Norodom Sihanouk led to a strange political alliance between Sihanouk and his former political enemies, the Khmer communists. That alliance to oust the Lon Nol regime marked the significant beginning of the transformation of the Cambodian Communist Party into a popular political group. Through the alliance, the Khmer Rouge exploited Sihanouk's popularity to rally forces against the U.S.-backed Lon Nol military regime in a bloody domestic war which began anew in 1970 and ended in a victory for the Pol Pot faction of Khmer Communists in 1975.[57]

Two different domestic developments brought the agents of revolution to power. In Cambodia, it was civil war which catapulted Cambodia's civilian Communists—the most vocal advocates of revolution—into power. In Ethiopia, it was famine which brought Ethiopia's military reformers and ardent nationalists to power. Mass death of peasants from famine between 1972 and 1974 created, in Ethiopia, the Cambodian version of unusual political alliances. The Ethiopian famine of the 1970s which killed an estimated 2 million people united soldiers, radical students and other civilians in the capital city who wanted change behind the banner of revolution. Although the alliance between the soldiers and the students did not last, it enabled the soldiers to appropriate the students' revolutionary slogans and their objective of land reform to promote their own vision of revolution. That happened in September 1974.

CONCLUSION

Cambodia and Ethiopia had some things in common as agrarian monarchies in transition. But different conditions facilitated the growth and acceptance of revolution as the answer to change. Unlike Ethiopia, much of the land in Cambodia was in the hands of its tillers. Therefore, redistribution of land did not become as crucial a factor in revolutionary thought in Cambodia as building a strong state and recapturing lost historical land. Socially, Cambodian and Ethiopian revolutionaries came from the same group of educated elites in two predominantly peasant societies. They drew inspiration from the Chinese and other worldwide struggles for social justice. But if that were all, there would be little to distinguish Cambodia's agents of change, and their idea of revolution, from their Ethiopian counterparts and their vision of social transformation.

There were other notable differences. What distinguished Khmer Communists and Ethiopian radical students was more important than what they had in common. Cambodian revolutionaries had a Communist Party to propagate their ideas and mobilize national support. The Pol Pot group which ultimately dominated the revolutionary movement in Cambodia saw revolution as an instrument for preserving the dominant Khmer race and expanding the borders of Cambodia. It was the beneficiary of economic and military aid from Vietnam and China. And civil war provided the group an opportunity to amass considerable rural support which helped it to plan the seizure of power. Ethiopian revolutionaries had only a pressure group of students and not a well-organized political party. They depended on an organized, but unreliable institution— the military—to bring the change they desired. They operated in a political culture which inhibited the propagation of political ideas. Thus, Ethiopia's revolutionaries could not even plan their seizure of power before revolution dawned upon them through an accidental convergence of events.

NOTES

1. Kiernan, *How Pol Pot Came to Power*, 2nd ed., xxi.

2. For detailed biographies of Cambodia's leading communists, see Kiernan, *How Pol Pot Came to Power* [first issue], 25–29 and Chandler, *Brother Number One*, 18–22, 37.

3. Chandler, *The Tragedy of Cambodian History*, 52.

4. For detailed biographies of Ethiopia's leading revolutionaries, see Kiflu Tadesse, *The Generation: The History of the Ethiopian People's Revolutionary Party, Part I, From the Early Beginnings to 1975* (Trenton, NJ: The Red Sea Press, 1993), 37, 41–42, 73; and Randi R. Balsvik, *Haile Selassie's Students: The Intellectual and Social Background to Revolution, 1952–1977* (East Lansing, MI: Michigan State University, 1985), 237.

5. Ben Kiernan, "Conflict in the Kampuchean Communist Movement," *Journal of Contemporary Asia* 10, 1 (1980): 8, 24, 38; Dmitry Mosyakov, "The Khmer Rouge and the Vietnamese Communists: A history of their relations as told in the Soviet archives," *Yale Center for International and Area Studies, Genocide Studies Program Working Paper* No. 15, n.d.

6. Joseph Simonson, U.S. Ambassador to Ethiopia, to Secretary of State, "Comments on a New Generation of Ethiopians," April 21, 1955, *United States National Archives* (USNA), Washington, D.C., Record Group (RG) 59: British Africa: 1955–1959, Box 4881.

7. Balsvik, *Haile Selassie's Students*, 67, 166, 189. See also Kiflu, *The Generation: Part 1*, 44, and Bahru, *A History of Modern Ethiopia*, 225–226.

8. Balsvik, *Haile Selassie's Students*, 174.

9. Kiflu, *The Generation*, Part I, 28–29.

10. Dawit, *Red Tears*, 7, 18.

11. Author's interview with Col. Tadesse Chernet, Army Ordnance Officer, Ground Forces, Addis Ababa, Ethiopia, May 12, 1999.

12. Chandler, *Tragedy of Cambodian History*, 48, 89, 108.

13. For detailed surveys of peasant politics in Ethiopia, see Gebru Tareke, *Ethiopia: Power and Protest, Peasant Revolts in the Twentieth Century* (Cambridge: Cambridge University Press, 1991), 50–51; Dessalegn Rahmato, *Famine and Survival Strategies: A Case Study from Northeast Ethiopia* (Uppsala: Nordiska Afrikainstitutet, 1991), 33; Bahru, *A History of Modern Ethiopia*, 215–220. In Cambodia, see Ben Kiernan and Chanthou Boua, *Peasants and Politics in Kampuchea*, 5, 13, 37; Vickery, *Cambodia, 1975–1982*, 16.

14. Kiernan, *How Pol Pot Came to Power*, 155; Balsvik, *Haile Selassie's Students*, xiii.

15. Balsvik, *Haile Selassie's Students*, 251.

16. Kiernan, *The Pol Pot Regime*, 6.

17. For detailed statistical analysis of education in Cambodia, see Kiernan, *How Pol Pot Came to Power*, xiii; Vickery, *Cambodia, 1975–1982*, 18, and in Ethiopia, see Balsvik, *Haile Selassie's Students*, 6–7.

18. Bahru, *A History of Modern Ethiopia*, 221–22. See also Kiflu, *The Generation*, Part I, 15.

19. Balsvik, *Haile Selassie's Students*, 245–46; Chandler, *Brother Number One*, 37.

20. Kiflu, *The Generation*, Part I, 40.

21. Kiernan, *How Pol Pot Came to Power*, 2nd ed., xxii; Chandler, *Brother Number One*, 67.

22. Kiflu, *The Generation*, Part I, 1; Bahru, *A History of Modern Ethiopia*, 222.

23. Kiflu, *The Generation*, Part I, 1.

24. The Ethiopian Students Union in North America, *Repression in Africa* (Cambridge, MA: Africa Research Group, 1971), 8; Richard Greenfield, *Ethiopia: A New Political History* (London: Pall Mall Press, 1965), 339–41, 398–402; Tekalign, "A City and Its Hinterlands," 389.

25. Kiernan, "Conflict in the Kampuchean Communist Movement," 7, 9.

26. Chandler, *Tragedy of Cambodian History*, 53.

27. Greenfield, *Ethiopia: A New Political History*, 402–3.

28. Balsvik, *Haile Selassie's Students*, 240.

29. Kissi, "Famine and the Politics of Food Relief," 131, 146.

30. John Cohen and Dov Weintraub, *Land and Peasants in Imperial Ethiopia: The Social Background to a Revolution* (Assen, The Netherlands: Van Gorcum & Co., 1975), 20.

31. Interview with Tesfaye Mekasha Amare.

32. Balsvik, *Haile Selassie's Students*, 241, 245, 251; Shiferaw Bekele, "The Evolution of Land Tenure in the Imperial Era," in *An Economic History of Ethiopia, Volume 1: The Imperial Era, 1941–74*, ed. Shiferaw Bekele (Senegal: CODESRIA, 1995), 122–123.

33. Vickery, *Cambodia, 1975–82*, 9.

34. Chandler, *Tragedy of Cambodian History*, 7; Vickery, *Cambodia, 1975–82*, 10.

35. Kiflu, *The Generation*, Part I, 52.

36. Balsvik, *Haile Selassie's Students*, 118, 251; Bahru, *A History of Modern Ethiopia*, 223; Kiflu, *The Generation*, Part I, 44; author's interview with Gebru Mersha, former student leader, ex-member of the EPRP and professor of Political Science at Addis Ababa University, Addis Ababa, Ethiopia, 4 May 1999.

37. Chandler, *Tragedy of Cambodian History*, 108.

38. Interview with Gebru Mersha. See also Bahru, *A History of Modern Ethiopia*, 226. Bahru is professor of History at Addis Ababa University.

39. Dawit, *Red Tears*, 10.

40. Kifle Wodajo, "Remarks by Kifle Wodajo at a Conference on the Horn of Africa Sponsored by the New School of Social Research," New York City, May 17, 1986, 5. See also Bahru, *A History of Modern Ethiopia*, 226.

41. Kiernan, *How Pol Pot Came to Power*, 49, 123.

42. Conversation with historian Ben Kiernan, New Haven, May 23, 1999.

43. Balsvik, *Haile Selassie's Students*, 175, 250–51.

44. For the debate on the origins of Khmer Rouge revolutionary ideology and practice, see Kiernan, "Conflict in the Kampuchean Communist Movement," 22; "The Cambodian Genocide—1975–1979," in *Century of Genocide*, 350–351; Chandler, *Brother Number One*, 72; Elizabeth Becker, *When the War Was Over: Cambodia and the Khmer Rouge Revolution* (New York: Public Affairs, 1998), 185–189. See also Serge Thion, "The Idea of Revolution," in *Revolution and Its Aftermath*, 28.

45. Kiflu, *The Generation*, Part I, 37, 44–45.

46. For detailed analysis of U.S. economic and military aid to Ethiopia from 1950 to 1974, and the growth of anti-American feeling in Ethiopia, see Bahru, *A History of Modern Ethiopia*, 223, and also Kissi, "Famine and the Politics of Food Relief," chapter 2.

47. Kiernan, *How Pol Pot Came to Power*. Second edition, xxi.

48. For a detailed assessment of the impact of the U.S. bombing of Cambodia on the Khmer Rouge revolution, see Ben Kiernan, *The Pol Pot Regime*, 19–22, 23–25, and David P. Chandler, *Brother Number One*, 96–97.

49. Balsvik, *Haile Selassie's Students*, 175, 201; Bahru, *A History of Modern Ethiopia*, 189; Kiflu, *The Generation*, Part I, 39.

50. Kiernan, *How Pol Pot Came to Power*. Second edition, x–xi.

51. Bahru, *A History of Modern Ethiopia*, 181.

52. See Basil Davidson, Lionel Cliffe and Bereket Habte Selassie, *Behind the War in Eritrea* (Nottingham: Spokesman, 1980), 34, and James Firebrace, with Stuart Holland, *Never Kneel Down: Drought, Development and Liberation* (Trenton, NJ: The Red Sea Press, 1986), 167–68.

53. For a discussion of the origins and political aims of the WSLF, see Fred Halliday and Maxime Molyneux, *The Ethiopian Revolution* (London: Unwin Brothers, 1981), 76, and Jason Clay and Bonnie Holcomb, *Politics and the Ethiopian Famine, 1984–1985* (Cambridge, MA: Cultural Survival, Inc., 1986), 24.

54. Firebrace with Holland, *Never Kneel Down*, 167–68.

55. Chandler, *Tragedy of Cambodian History*, 91; Kiernan, *The Pol Pot Regime*, 13–14; Jean-Louis Margolin, "Cambodia: The Country of Disconcerting Crimes," in *The Black Book of Communism: Crimes, Terror, Repression*," ed. Stephane Courtois et al. (Cambridge, MA: Harvard University Press, 1999), 618.

56. Balsvik, *Haile Selassie's Students*, 245; Bahru, *A History of Modern Ethiopia*, 221–22, 225–26.

57. Jean-Louis Margolin, "Cambodia: The Country of Disconcerting Crimes," in *Black Book of Communism*, 581; Timothy Carney, "The Unexpected Victory," in *Rendezvous with Death*, 13.

3

EMPIRE AND KINGDOM
IN REVOLUTION

Ethiopia and Cambodia experienced "revolution," in the late twentieth century, in the sense in which Samuel P. Huntington has defined the phenomenon: "a rapid, fundamental and violent . . . change in the dominant values . . . , myths . . . , political institutions, social structure, leadership, . . . government activities and policies" of a society.[1] But the different durations of the revolutions—seventeen years in Ethiopia, and three years, eight months and twenty days in Cambodia—and the different transformations that occurred in the two societies, raise some puzzling questions about the nature of the two revolutions. Tep Vung, a Buddhist survivor of the violence of the Cambodian revolution captures one of the puzzling questions when he asks whether history has any examples of countries and revolutions in which the leaders "eradicated religion, massacred . . . monks and . . . fellow countrymen, plundered sacred articles of worship, destroyed pagodas, temples, and Buddhist tombs."[2] One can easily point to Cambodia and Pol Pot in the history of revolutions of the late twentieth century. But how about Ethiopia?

Some of the scholars who have attempted to address the questions that the Ethiopian and Cambodian revolutions raise have often argued that revolutions, like trees, must be judged by the fruits they bear. Judging the nature of a revolution by its ultimate result has led these scholars to conclude that only marxist and communist revolutions lead to murder, genocide or terror of the kind that the Cambodian and Ethiopian revolutions of the 1970s produced. Thus, the two revolutions, often described as Marxist and communist, become two more examples of the normality of terror and murder in communist and marxist theory and practice. Jean-Louis Margolin asserts this thesis even more bluntly in *The Black Book of Communism*. He argues that "[t]he crimes of the Khmer Rouge should be judged rigorously and objectively so that the Cambodian experience can be compared to the other great horrors of the [twentieth] century, and its proper weight assigned in the history of Communism."[3] While these scholars seem certain about the ideological spur of the Cambodian revolution, thanks to the voluminous literature on the Pol Pot regime, they seem uncertain about the Ethiopian case given the limited literature on that country's revolutionary experience. In Yves Santamaria's article on "Afrocommunism" or African versions of communist practice in Ethiopia, Angola and Mozambique, in the same book, the author argues that communism appealed to leaders in the Third World because of the ideology's "illusory remedy for underdevelopment." But Yves is somewhat uncertain about the practice of Marxism and commitment to Communism in revolutionary Ethiopia. The author laments that "[p]eople have often denied Mengistu Haile Mariam [the leader of the Ethiopian revolution] the label "Communist" in the same way it was denied to Stalin himself by the extreme Marxist left and by the Trotskyites in particular." Yves' certainty about the communist nature of revolutionary Ethiopia and its leaders seems to be based on the controversial assertion that "these African movements made serious references to Marx, Bolshevism, and the USSR throughout the period 1974–91, and these references were taken seriously by the protagonists and their supporters in the Soviet Union and the Communist International."[4]

The failure to note and draw a distinction between rhetoric and reality or ideological conviction and opportunistic self-labelling is, perhaps, the most glaring weakness in Yves's argument about Ethiopia. Afterall, the communist nature of the Mengistu regime, as well as Pol Pot's, their comparable features, the specific nature and the overall context of the crimes they committed, ought to be demonstrated, empirically, rather than assumed, theoretically. A major contribution that this comparative study of Ethiopia and Cambodia makes to the larger debate on marxist revolutions and genocide lies in its penetration of the radical Marxist rhetoric of the leaders of the Ethiopian revolution. This book would reveal that contrary to the arguments made by Yves Santamaria and other scholars and writers, the Mengistu regime, from the available historical record, was not the radical and "communist" revolutionary regime that it was made out to be by the extreme non-Marxist right. That, indeed, the Ethiopian regime's Marxism was nothing more than an opportunistic self-labelling that was strategic in purpose and shallow in content as compared to the Khmer Rouge's. This chapter in particular argues that the form that revolution took in Cambodia and Ethiopia depended largely on how the two revolutionary regimes acquired power. And the scope and pace of the changes the leaders of the revolution made in the dominant values of their society, and how they treated their fellow citizens, also depended on the degree of control they exercised.

Ben Kiernan, arguably, the leading scholar of the Pol Pot regime, has identified eight characteristics of the Cambodian revolution. First, the emphasis the Khmer Rouge put on peasants as the vanguard of their revolution. Second, the reliance of the revolutionaries on agriculture as the backbone of the national economy. Third, their pursuit of absolute self-reliance as a revolutionary ideology. Fourth, their affirmation of the supremacy of the Khmer ethnic group in Cambodia. Fifth, their violent repression of particular social groups, middlemen minorities, and political dissenters. Sixth, their atomization of Cambodian society through the dissolution of pre-existing institutions such as religion, family structures, schools and leisure. Seventh, the absolute control that a half-dozen leaders of the communist party exercised in revolutionary Cambodia. Eighth, the uncompromising demand of the Khmer Rouge that all goals be achieved at all cost.[5]

Kiernan has argued that the leaders of the Khmer Rouge intended their revolution to "wipe the [Cambodia] slate clean." That meant ensuring a rapid and fundamental break from the old Cambodian society to the reconstruction of a completely new one. That mentality caused the Khmer Rouge leadership to order the evacuation of the capital city, Phnom Penh, abolition of money and markets, defrocking of the monks and turning these religious icons into peasants, execution of the leaders of the Lon Nol regime, establishment of cooperatives with communal eating, and the expulsion of the Vietnamese minority population.[6] From a comparative perspective, the Ethiopian revolutionary government had a very modest and practical outlook. The Ethiopian revolution had only three characteristics: land reform with the intention of combatting persistent famine, ethnic pluralism with the intention of ridding Ethiopia of Amhara ethnic domination, and national unity. The brutal war which the soldiers who led the revolution waged against ethnic nationalism and secessionism in Ethiopia highlights the determination of the Mengistu regime to impose national unity and ethnic pluralism in the multi-ethnic revolutionary society. National unity and ethnic pluralism were not new revolutionary priorities. They had been the dominant political and social values of the pre-revolution Ethiopian society. The desire of Ethiopia's revolutionary regime to maintain an indivisible multi-ethnic nation while the Khmer Rouge sought to create an ethnically-homogenous Khmer nation would suggest that Ethiopia's revolutionary regime was different from Cambodia's in its nature. Indeed, to the extent that it was "revolutionary" at all, the Ethiopian regime merits that characterization only in its successful land reform program which fundamentally altered the pre-existing land tenure system and the political and economic privileges that were associated with it.

Kiernan has also demonstrated that racism dominated the worldview of the top leaders of the Khmer Rouge. For them, "conceptions of race overshadowed those of class" in their idea of revolutionary struggle.[7] The opposite was the case for Ethiopia's revolutionary leaders. By contrast, in revolutionary Ethiopia, class overshadowed race in the revolutionary thinking of the Dergue not out of genuine interest in Marxism, but for its usefulness as a conceptual tool for maintaining political power and enforcing national unity.[8] These sharp differences in the thinking of the Ethiopian and Cambodian revolutionary regimes stemmed from how the leaders of the revolution acquired power.

ACQUISITION OF POWER

Scholars who study genocide or link revolutionary ideologies, communist regimes, military-led revolutionary governments, and authoritarian states to mass murder often look for the "preceding conditions" or circumstances that bring these murderous regimes to power. Helen Fein, a leading exponent of this approach, has argued, in her comparative study of murderous revolutionary regimes in Cambodia and Indonesia, that "political discrimination of a suppressed ethnoclass" in a society is the common cause of rebellions that ultimately lead to acquisition of power by murderous elites.[9] Empirical evidence on the Ethiopian case challenges this theory. In fact, the Ethiopian revolution happened by default. It was, indeed, an accidental product of urban and barrack protests over high fuel prices, the cavalier response of the Haile Selassie government to famine in 1974 and poor conditions of military service. The protesting soldiers and their student supporters were the most privileged ethnoclass in Ethiopia. The soldiers in particular had supported the monarchy and benefited from the political and economic rewards of loyalty. It was famine in 1972 and the international oil crisis of that period that provided the context or "preceding conditions" for discontented civilians who had called for revolution since 1960 to rise against a conservative governing elite and promote their sectional grievances in the name of liberating the peasants.[10]

A combination of events emboldened the soldiers. Pressure from the protesting soldiers and masses of civilians forced the Imperial cabinet to resign on February 27, 1974. The resignation of the cabinet was accompanied by the reduction of fuel prices, increases in the salaries of soldiers and the withdrawal of an education reform proposal which teachers and university students had criticized. These rapid concessions suggesting capitulation by the Emperor's government encouraged the soldiers to form "committees" or "councils" to highlight more grievances and lobby the weakened government for solutions.[11] The Airbone Corps formed the first "committee" (*Dergue* in Ethiopia's *Amharinya* language) headed by Colonel Alem Zewd. His committee consisted of randomly selected non-commissioned officers (NCOs) and young officers. Many of its members came from Ethiopia's "elite" military academy (the empire's Sandhurst or West Point), located in Harar province. Alem Zewd's committee pledged support for the successor cabinet headed by the aristocrat Endalkatchew Makonnen. Disagreements between Alem Zewd's "committee" and other units of Ethiopia's armed forces led to the establishment of a second Dergue (committee) on June 28, 1974 to coordinate the grievances of the Armed Forces, Police and Territorial Army. Majors Atnafu Abate, Sisay Habte and Tefera Tekle Ab, its leading figures, had defected from Alem Zewd's "committee."[12] Atnafu

Abate's "dergue" now consisted of junior officers below the rank of major. Unlike the first committee led by Alem Zewd, many of the members of the second committee (hereinafter called Dergue), founded by Atnafu Abate, had their training at the less prestigious Holeta Military Academy in Shoa province. Herein lies an important, but often neglected element, context or preceding condition that brought the Mengistu clique to power: the unexplored sour relationship between the Holeta soldiers and the Harar Academy graduates. That relationship transcended differences over Marxist and Communist ideology.

Like the first committee, the hundred-odd members of the new Dergue were randomly selected. They came from the Army, the Navy, the Air Force, the Territorial Army, the Prison Guards and the Police Force. There is no evidence that the Dergue intended to overthrow the monarchy and launch a Marxist revolution in Ethiopia. In fact none of its members was a known "radical," "progressive," "socialist" or "revolutionary." The Dergue considered itself a temporary pressure-group whose main objective was to consult with the Emperor to address the mainly economic grievances of the military. The military units that sent representatives to the Dergue expected those representatives to return after presenting their grievances to the Emperor in Addis Ababa, the capital city.

Not well-equipped to seize power themselves, students and other civilian radicals attempted to manipulate the Dergue. As Dawit Wolde Giorgis has accurately observed, the Dergue "might never have sponsored a revolution had the political ingredient not been added by the radical students and teachers, particularly those from abroad. . . ."[13] Many of these radical civilians had rushed home from Europe and North America to direct and fuel the urban insurrection against the Imperial Government. It was Ethiopian marxists from abroad such as Haile Fida and Senaye Likke, and other civilian socialists who associated with the Dergue, with the intention of influencing and eventually supplanting it, who provided key members of the Dergue their rudimentary knowledge of Marx and Lenin.[14] It was also these civilians from abroad who, according to Dawit, strongly urged some members of the Dergue to demand radical reforms including the deposition of the Emperor.[15]

The Dergue worked its way into power gradually and tactfully. The Committee's diverse members could not even reach a consensus to overthrow the Emperor and his government when they discussed the subject in early July 1974 and again from September 6–9.[16] Amid the rapidly changing political circumstances at the barracks and on the streets in the capital city, some of the Dergue's members arrested a number of the Emperor's officials for concealing the famine. They delivered the officials to the Emperor as "enemies of Ethiopia" to be prosecuted.[17] It was the Dergue's more ambitious members, namely Mengistu Haile-Mariam (from the Konso minority ethnic group), Sisay Habte (Amhara) and Debele Dinsa (Oromo) who initiated the process of deposing the Emperor by first pressuring the new Imperial cabinet under Endalkatchew Makonnen to resign on July 22, 1974. By September 10, 1974, the ambitious and radicalized faction led by Mengistu had reached a conclusion that they, rather than a civilian group, should become the leaders of a new Ethiopia.[18] This suggests that despite taking advice from Marxist civilians, the radical faction of the Dergue had its own agenda.

The faction led by Mengistu Haile-Mariam, however, needed a spur. The Dergue's sub-committee headed by Mengistu caused to be shown on Ethiopian Television, a documentary film which British journalist Jonathan Dimbleby had made in early 1974 about famine in Ethiopia for a British television program. Ethiopians watched an edited version of Dimbleby's film, *The Hidden Famine*, on September 11, 1974, depicting the agony of death from starvation in Wollo, in northeastern Ethiopia. Ethiopian Television, now free from censorship, contrasted the harrowing images of the dead and starving with old footage of the Emperor feeding his dogs from silver plates. As Dawit confirms, many Ethiopians "turn[ed] against the Emperor" after watching the film.[19] A group of Dergue members, allegedly instigated by Mengistu Haile-Mariam, entered Haile Selassie's palace on September 12, 1974, read out a proclamation of deposition to the frail monarch, and took him away in a Volkswagen Beetle to detention. He was, reportedly, suffocated to death on August 27, 1975 in the presence of Majors Mengistu Haile Mariam and Atnafu Abate, then secretly buried in Addis Ababa.[20] Haile Selassie, the only modern leader Ethiopia had known, who had ruled uninterrupted since 1941, was murdered nearly eight months before the Khmer Rouge forced Norodom Sihanouk, who had also reigned from 1941, to retire as Cambodia's monarch.

The Dergue converted itself into a Provisional Military Administrative Council (PMAC), on September 12, 1974 to take over the reins of government. But the PMAC (also to be referred to as the Dergue) did not entirely abolish the Ethiopian monarchy. It replaced the title of "emperor" with "king" and named the Emperor's son, Crown Prince Asfa Wassen, then recovering from a stroke in Switzerland, as the constitutional monarch. The PMAC dissolved Parliament, suspended the Constitution and banned the legend by which the Ethiopian monarch claimed descent from King Solomon of Israel and divine right to rule.[21]

The PMAC's proclamation of deposition of Haile Selassie revealed the reformist objectives of the soldiers who had seized power in contrast to the revolutionary aims of the civilians. The soldiers intended to accomplish three objectives. First, to revive Ethiopia's bruised international image by improving the peasant economy and reducing the recurrence of famine which the monarchy had neglected. This objective was not different from that of the December 1960 coup plotters. Second, to build national unity threatened by secessionist politics in Eritrea and the Ogaden region. Third, to defend Ethiopia's territorial integrity threatened by the growing military strength of neighboring Somalia.[22] The establishment of the PMAC ended a corrupt and anachronistic monarchical regime. However, a new government led by soldiers who had propped up the defunct imperial regime drew mixed responses from the civilian elite. The new political reality left many intellectuals wondering whether the old era had really ended and the revolution they had anticipated since 1960 began.

Whereas the military-led revolution in Ethiopia happened by an accidental convergence of factors, the Cambodian revolution led by well-known Khmer communists happened by a well-thought-out design. The Communist Party of Cambodia, a civilian organization which had established its own guerilla army and consisting of a group of people who had long opposed the monarchy, seized power on April 17, 1975, seven months and five days after the Dergue seized power in Ethiopia. The Khmer Rouge rode to power in Phnom Penh from the rural areas where it had amassed peasant support. With its peasant soldiers, and aided by the North Vietnamese, the communists achieved overwhelming victory over Marshall Lon Nol's Khmer Republic in a bloody civil war which had destabilized the Cambodian society and economy since the major warfare began in 1970.[23] With the collapse of the Khmer Republic, the

Khmer Rouge gained uncontested political power. In fact the Khmer Rouge had achieved that degree of power since 1970 by using the prestige of Cambodia's ousted monarch, Norodom Sihanouk, in rural areas. The Khmer Rouge moved to abolish the monarchy in 1976.

NATURE OF THE REVOLUTIONARY REGIMES

Arguably, the different circumstances that brought the Khmer Rouge and the Dergue to power imbued the two revolutionary regimes with different perceptions of their mission. The Khmer Rouge translated its total victory in a civil war into a determination to rapidly transform Cambodia. Given the circumstances surrounding its acquisition of power, the Dergue was not as confident as the Khmer Rouge of its ability to change Ethiopia. However, both regimes shrouded their initial structure and decision-making processes in great secrecy. Not much was known about the Dergue and the Khmer Rouge until after their fall or when some of their members who defected wrote about their activities. After the fall of the Khmer Rouge, in January 1979, it became clear that only "a standing committee of approximately ten men and women," trusted by the Secretary of the Communist Party, Pol Pot, exercised supreme power in Cambodia after April 1975. In its first two years in power, the standing committee exercised authority behind a curtain of code names such as *Brother Number One, 870* or simply *Angkar*, the Khmer word for "Organization."[24] The latter often meant the Cambodian Communist Party or, sometimes, Pol Pot himself. The Dergue acted in a similar fashion. It kept the total number of its membership and the sources of its early decrees secret.[25] It was only after his defection in 1985 that Dawit Wolde Giorgis, an official of the revolutionary government in Ethiopia, revealed that the Dergue consisted of "43 officers and 65 NCOs, and private soldiers."[26] Underneath its motley composition was a key characteristic. None of the Dergue's members had previously held any political office, knew the functions of government, or was familiar with Marxism. The convenor of the Dergue, Major Atnafu Abate, an Amhara from the 4th Infantry Division of the Ethiopian Army, and a Christian, staunchly opposed the adoption of Marxism as the ideology of the incipient revolution. He was later purged by Mengistu and the clique that evolved around him. Unlike the Khmer

Rouge, the Dergue was multi-ethnic in its composition. Its predominantly non-Amhara members were of average educational level below the rank of major and between ages 28 and 35. A few of them such as Major Mengistu Haile Mariam had completed military training in the United States.[27]

By contrast when the Angkar was unmasked, scholars discovered an organization of veteran Communists. Unlike the Dergue's members, those of the Khmer Rouge knew some Marxism and even how government worked. The Khmer Rouge-led revolutionary government included a former Minister, Khieu Samphan (alias Comrade Hem), as president of the state presidium, and former teachers Ieng Sary (Comrade Van) as Deputy Prime Minister responsible for foreign affairs, Son Sen (Comrade Khieu) as Deputy Prime Minister in charge of National Defense, and Pol Pot (Comrade Pol) as Prime Minister. They had run large rural areas during the 1970–75 war. A distinguishing feature of the Khmer Rouge that set it apart from the Dergue was that the Cambodian regime was bound together by collegial, blood and marriage ties as well as by ideological commitment. Four members of the Khmer Rouge—Ieng Sary, Pol Pot, Son Sen and Khieu Samphan—had been friends and students in Paris in the 1950s. Pol Pot married Khieu Ponnary, the sister of Ieng Sary's wife, Khieu Thirith.[28]

Ethiopia's revolutionary regime lacked the social and ideological bonds that united the top leadership of the Khmer Rouge. The Dergue initially sought that critical bond in bloodshed. Its decision, in November 1974, to execute 59 officials of the Emperor's government, plus Aman Andom, the Dergue's figure-head, was neither the product of panic nor an ideological commitment to destroy the old political class. It arose from a perceived political necessity to bind the diverse group of soldiers together in a common guilt by shedding blood in a "revolution" initially committed to avoiding bloodshed.[29]

MENGISTU, POL POT AND REVOLUTIONARY LEADERSHIP

Foreign observers of the incipient revolution in Ethiopia saw Mengistu as the "strong man" in the Dergue, ideologically less radical than many of his colleagues, but one who was unwilling to countenance Eritrean secessionist nationalism.[30] As Dawit argues, many members of the Dergue considered Mengistu the "best choice" for a leader of post-Imperial Ethiopia. For them, Mengistu embodied "the spirit of the revolution and symbolized the change which [the junior military officers] wanted" in a post-Imperial Ethiopia. Mengistu came from a poor family background. He was not an Amhara, the hegemonic ethnic group. Rather he was a poorly-educated soldier of the minority and often derided Konso ethnic group. He was rumored to be a son of a palace servant. Mengistu combined a humble social status and an affable demeanor which endeared him to the junior officers who wanted to end Amhara ethnic-chauvinism or, as Dawit put it, "class arrogance and racism."[31] But despite his social background, Mengistu had been brought up as a soldier in the Amhara traditions of nationalism, which emphasized respect for state authority and national unity. The national unity ideology which he and his colleagues in the Dergue upheld was not different from the pre-revolutionary conception of national unity which the Haile Selassie regime championed.

Pol Pot also grew up in the palace, but lacked the military training which Mengistu had. But like Mengistu, Pol Pot's amiable personality concealed a penchant for eliminating anyone who stood between him and power. While historian David Chandler dismisses any connection between the boyhood experiences of Pol Pot and his adolescent radical ideas, Ethiopian political scientist Paulos Milkias sees a subtle interplay between Mengistu's social background and his political views. Mengistu harbored a strong feeling against social hierarchies and aristocratic privileges. He, reportedly, vowed at the first meeting of the Dergue on June 28, 1974 to punish or eliminate those in Ethiopian society who looked down upon others because of their menial occupation and dark complexion.[32] The social vindictiveness of Mengistu and Pol Pot must have stemmed from humiliations they absorbed and viewed at the palace where they had their boyhood experiences.

Unlike the Khmer Rouge, Ethiopia's military council had to struggle for leadership of the revolution against intense domestic opposition. The Dergue's domestic opponents included those intellectuals who cooperated with the soldiers to hasten the downfall of the Haile Selassie regime. Left-wing civilian groups such as the All Ethiopian Socialist

Movement (MEISON) which had been organized at the time of the political crisis in 1974 initially opposed the Dergue "cit[ing] the emergence of . . . military dictators in Cambodia, Zaire, Sudan, and other
Latin American countries" as a reason for Ethiopians to reject a military
government.[33] Students of Addis Ababa University and the leaders of
the Confederation of Ethiopian Labor Unions (CELU) demanded the
return of the soldiers to their barracks and the replacement of the military council with a Provisional People's Government. CELU's demand,
four days after the Dergue seized power, received support from sections
of the military, especially the Army Corps of Engineers, the Air Force
and the Army Aviation Unit.[34] Under this intense pressure, struggle for
political survival became more important to the Mengistu faction of the
Dergue than considerations of its potential to transform Ethiopian society into a Communist utopia. Political survival also made the Dergue
even more ruthless.

The Dergue and the Khmer Rouge used political killings to achieve
internal ideological uniformity. Between 1974 and 1977, the Mengistu
faction killed Aman Andom, Teferi Bante and Atnafu Abate. Aman Andom was eliminated for urging rapprochement with Eritrean secessionists. Atnafu, "a nationalist" was killed for advocating moderation in the
treatment of political opponents and the use of "tradition, culture and
religion" to foster "unity" in Ethiopia rather than "alien values" such as
Marxism and Communism. As Dawit notes, Atnafu's ideas were deemed
"contradictory to the mood and thinking" of the radical civilians who
manipulated the Dergue after September 1974.[35] Teferi Bante, a moderate Oromo officer from outside the Dergue, who had been chosen to
succeed Aman Andom as its chairman on November 28, 1974, was
purged by the Mengistu faction for advocating cooperation with opposition groups in a public speech on January 30, 1977.[36] Similarly, in Cambodia, between 1977 and 1978, Pol Pot's forces killed the leaders of the
pro-Chinese group of Khmer communists, and the notable members of
the Vietnam-trained group such as Keo Moni, So Phim, Non Suon and
Chou Chet.[37] Khmer Rouge purges were aimed at resolving the conflict
over ideology in the Communist Party, and not necessarily its leadership.
The assassination of Teferi Bante, and the emergence of Mengistu
Haile-Mariam as leader of the Ethiopian revolution, was, however,
meant to resolve the dissension in the Dergue over revolutionary lead-

ership. The purges did not resolve the issue of ideology for the Ethiopian revolution.

REVOLUTION IN SEARCH OF IDEOLOGY

The Mengistu and Pol Pot regimes both described themselves as Marxist-Leninist and dedicated to building socialism. In fact they both spoke of creating a new socialist man. But the answers to whether they were genuinely Marxist, purely Communist, or whether the revolutions they led constituted the classic form of peasant revolutions vary.[38] While the Dergue paid lip-service to Marxism and communism, the strength and determination of the Khmer Rouge leadership to rapidly transform Cambodia along marxist and communist lines ran very deep. The Dergue's Marxism was a form of populist and pragmatic opportunism made necessary by the need to survive in a political culture where the vanquished had little chance of living. The Dergue's inadequacies in Marxist philosophy, but strong interest in nationalism and populism, had been clearly demonstrated in its adoption of "Ethiopia *tikdem*" (Ethiopia First) as its guiding principle on July 28, 1974. According to Rene Lefort, the slogan had been coined by an editorial writer of the state newspaper, the *Ethiopian Herald*, to appeal to the noblest sentiments of Ethiopians—unity—to end the political unrest of the period and avoid bloodshed.[39]

The Dergue appropriated the slogan partly to indicate its distaste for foreign ideologies. which did not reflect the more popular nationalist and patriotic sentiments of the military. As the Dergue explained to its more Marxist political opponents who mocked the soldiers' ineptitude in Marxist and Socialist ideology, "Ethiopia *tikdem*" meant *hibresabaw-inet*, "a sort of Ethiopian socialism." For the soldier-revolutionaries, Ethiopian socialism meant "equality; self reliance; the dignity of labour; the supremacy of the common good; and the indivisibility of Ethiopian unity."[40]

It must be noted that the emphasis on "self-reliance" in the Dergue's "Ethiopian socialism" had no affinity with the Khmer Rouge's Maoist idea of self-reliance or the Pol Pot regime's pursuit of absolute sovereignty as a revolutionary objective. The Dergue's notion of self-reliance

was in part a bold aspiration to stamp out begging which was pervasive
in Ethiopia. The Dergue also wanted commitment to a "common good,"
in an indigenous "socialist ideology" to take precedence over the prevailing ethnic and regional interests which threatened to tear Ethiopia
apart.[41] In short, this opportunistic labeling of the Dergue's revolutionary ideology as Socialist was actually intended, at a strategic level, to
bridge the competing ideological visions which threatened the soldiers'
revolution. It was not surprising that the Dergue's explanation of its socialism as an ideology rooted in Ethiopia's orthodox Christian traditions
of justice, fairness, equality and sharing did not convince the regime's
truly marxist civilian opponents. The Dergue tried again. In a very desperate search for a fashionable ideology to establish the revolutionary
credentials of the soldiers, but also one that could link the patriotic nationalism of the military with the socialist aims of the civilian competitors for power, the Dergue sent delegations to Tanzania, Yugoslavia,
China and India, between September and December 1974, "to shop for
an ideology" for the Ethiopian revolution.[42]

     With its political legitimacy contested by many armed civilian and
ethnonationalist groups, the Dergue soon surrendered its *Ethiopian Socialism* philosophy for a more left-leaning and trendy ideology. It proclaimed "scientific socialism," on December 20, 1974, as the "ideology
of the Ethiopian revolution."[43] For convenience sake, the Dergue became officially socialist to appease left-wing groups and consolidate its
tenuous grip on power. The revolutionary regime's more ambitious members such as Mengistu Haile Mariam, Alemayehu Haile and Debele
Dinsa and many supporters of the Dergue "acquaint[ed] themselves
with Marxist terminologies without believing in the doctrine itself."[44]
The Dergue's ideological newsletter, *Meskerem*, revealed the private
thoughts of the Dergue more clearly when it argued that "Maoism and
Euro-Communism are manifestations of petit-bourgeois national chauvinism." The paper noted that "what should be cultivated in a revolutionary society is socialist patriotism." For the Dergue, "socialist patriotism" meant "true love for one's motherland . . . [and] . . . free[dom] from
all forms of chauvinism and racialism." The Dergue's slogan was "Revolutionary Motherland or Death."[45]

     It is, therefore, accurate to say that the Dergue members were na-
tionalists rather than socialists and communists. Their political rhetoric

and association with Marxists alone will not be convincing evidence for proving the military regime's communist nature and orientation. Their Marxist vocabulary was an ideological ornament, at best a form of political grammar or ideological opportunism which the time and the context of their revolution dictated. By opportunistically labeling itself as Socialist and openly parroting Marxist phrases, the Dergue sought, domestically, to win over leftist intellectuals such as Haile Fida and Senaye Likke and to use their fame in the student movement to build a political base for the Dergue.

The Somali invasion of Ethiopia on July 23, 1977 provided another reason for Ethiopia's revolutionary military regime to continue professing Marxism in its public pronouncements. By December 1977, Somali soldiers had occupied one-third of Ethiopian territory, leaving the Dergue in a precarious position. At the time the Somalis struck, the lethal power struggle between the Dergue and its civilian opponents had weakened national support for the military regime. The soldiers needed the support of every Ethiopian, including their civilian adversaries to repel the Somali invasion. The invasion also created opportunities for domestic opposition groups whose origins and objectives are examined in the next chapter to expand their political bases. In the course of the invasion, the Western Somalia Liberation Front (WSLF) attacked key areas in the Ogaden and Harar, in southeastern Ethiopia. The Eritrean Peoples Liberation Front (EPLF), a break-away faction of the Eritrean Liberation Front, occupied most of Eritrea leaving the Dergue with only tenuous control over the Eritrean capital and the port cities of Massawa and Assab. Similarly, the Tigrayan Peoples Liberation Front (TPLF), a break-away faction of the Ethiopian Peoples Revolutionary Party (EPRP), increased its control over Tigray, in northern Ethiopia. The Ethiopian Peoples Democratic Movement (EPDM) kept parts of Gondar, in northeastern Ethiopia, under its control while the Oromo Liberation Front (OLF) consolidated its authority over western Wollega, in western Ethiopia.[46]

Initial U.S. isolation of the Dergue also complicated the military regime's domestic political dilemmas. The killing of the 59 former officials of the Emperor's government in November 1974 and the volatile political situation in Ethiopia, made the Carter Administration refuse to deliver U.S. military equipment to Ethiopia. This equipment which the

Dergue desperately needed to repel the Somali attack had already been paid for by the Imperial Ethiopian Government before it fell. The U.S. decision had been based on Congressional discussions in August 1975 about the Dergue. Congress considered alleged bombardments of "Eritrean villages and food crops," by the Dergue and the military regime's "interference with food and medical relief" for Eritrean refugees as "verging on genocide."[47] In dire straits, Ethiopia's military regime sought Cuban, and later Soviet military assistance. Cuban and Soviet weapons and also military advice that the Dergue used to defeat Somali forces in March 1978 came with an ideological price as we shall soon see.

There is a larger comparative point to be made from the preceding long review of the Dergue's metamorphosis. While the Ethiopian regime opportunistically shopped for an ideology for its revolution, and reached for allies in its struggle for survival, the Khmer Rouge was already expressing its Maoist, Marxist and Communist inclinations through a confident and radical program of transformation of Cambodia. Total victory in the civil war and successful evacuation of all cities had removed potential urban and other domestic opposition to the ambitious revolutionary program of the Khmer Rouge.[48] Sustained domestic opposition to the Dergue's power made ambitious social transformation and a self-reliant foreign policy of the Cambodian type less attractive to Ethiopia's soldier revolutionaries. As we will see in chapter six, the Dergue's defeat of Somali forces did present an opportunity for Mengistu to cast himself as the only person capable of assuring Ethiopian unity.[49] But that turned out to be a costly opportunity. It hardened the political attitudes of the Dergue's domestic opponents.

THE THOUGHTS BEHIND THE POLICIES

The Dergue and the Angkar had a common and openly-expressed aspiration to build a new society by breaking with their feudal and monarchical past. The Angkar renamed the Kingdom of Cambodia as *Democratic Kampuchea* (DK) and the Dergue renamed the Empire of Ethiopia as *Socialist Ethiopia*. But the enormous scope, rapid pace and doctrinaire fashion of Khmer Rouge social transformation contrasts with the Dergue's more cautious and calculating approach. Building socialism "within four years" in Cambodia and transforming an entire nation "within ten to fifteen years" was the boldest and most confident expression of Khmer Rouge optimism about what it claimed as its "historically correct mission to influence the destiny of Kampuchea."[50]

The Khmer Rouge approach to social transformation had an ambitious and utopian ring. The Khmer Communists wanted to surpass their Chinese ideological mentors by making a "Super Great Leap Forward" that would tower over Mao's Great Leap Forward program of agrarian and industrial development in 1958. Pol Pot's Four Year Plan (1977–80), reminiscent of Stalin's development plans, exhorted Cambodians to produce three or more tons of rice from every hectare of rice land compared to one in the past. David Chandler has attributed the rapid pace of social transformation in revolutionary Cambodia to Khmer Rouge paranoia and fear of counter-revolution.[51] Elizabeth Becker disagrees. She argues that the Khmer Rouge "tried to revolutionize Cambodia overnight to prove the country's superiority" in the Southeast Asian region.[52] Both Chandler and Becker are correct. Given what Karl D. Jackson has called the "unconstrained political domination" the Khmer Rouge enjoyed after April 1975, its rapid transformation of Cambodia could only have come from a sense of confidence amid great insecurity.

With excitement and optimism, the Pol Pot regime came to view the socio-economic development of Cambodia as analogous to its successful military operations in the civil war. A party document put this confidently: "The preparations for offensives to build up the country are like our past military offensives and not even as difficult." Angkar strongly believed that all Cambodia needed were "revolutionary people, and revolutionary methods." Technology which the Khmer Rouge would have had to import from developed Western countries appeared less significant. The Khmer Rouge proclaimed that just as "Lenin carried out a revolution with empty hands," so could a determined people.[53] After all, the Khmer Rouge had beaten the U.S.-backed Khmer Republic with sheer determination.

The Dergue was not as confident, doctrinaire, and determined to build socialism quickly as the Khmer Rouge. The limited scope and slower pace of the Dergue's revolutionary policies, in comparison to the Angkar's, testified to the soldiers' sense of their own vulnerability. In many cases, the Dergue acted in response to the proddings of its armed and ideologically more competent opponents for the sake of survival. Policies such as land reform and collectivization appealed to the Dergue because these policies helped the soldiers to project themselves as "the real revolutionary force" in Ethiopia.[54] Besides reaping popular support from land reform, the Ethiopian regime also contracted political alliances with notable Marxist groups to solidify itself. But, the Dergue refused to pursue some radical policies similar to those of the Khmer Rouge that some of its political allies had urged. For instance, the soldier-revolutionaries in Ethiopia did not evacuate the inhabitants of the capital city and other towns to the rural areas for "retraining" as the MEISON, a Marxist civilian group which cooperated with the Dergue from 1975 to 1977 proposed. Neither did the Dergue "close the Ethiopian fence" (i.e., seal Ethiopia off from the outside world), eject the large foreign diplomatic community in the country nor pursue a revolution unique in Africa as the genuinely Marxist civilian opponents had suggested.[55]

The Dergue considered it politically safe to have students who posed a serious threat to its tenuous power leave their campuses in the capital and other towns for the rural areas to organize peasants. But that rural "development" campaign, the *Zemecha*, as it was called in *Amharinya*, which the Dergue inaugurated in December 1974, was based on a proposal which students themselves had made to the Dergue in February. Ethiopian University students had suggested that they be permitted to go to the rural areas to relieve famine and politicize the peasants. Faced with student opposition, the Dergue seized upon the students' proposal and made it mandatory for all university and high school students to participate in what the Dergue dubbed as *Development Through Cooperation, Enlightenment and Work Campaign* in rural areas.[56] This Dergue version of Maoism was different from the Angkar's Great Leap Forward evacuation of cities.

With unbridled power and an ideological commitment to break with the past and restructure society, the Khmer Rouge divided Cambodians into two distinct groups: the *new people* and the *old people*. The *new people* consisted of those evacuated from the cities, members of the prerevolutionary political class, former landowners, army officers, bureaucrats, merchants, teachers and people who had lived outside the control of the Khmer Rouge during the civil war. The revolutionary regime in Cambodia suspected the loyalty of this group of people who constituted about 30 percent of the national population. Condemned to a life of misery with limited or no rights at all to food, decent housing, wealth and property, many of the *new people* perished. The other category of people, *old people* consisted of the majority of Cambodians, mainly peasants, who by 1975 had already lived for several years under the control of the Khmer Rouge, and other people who had joined the revolution at its initial stages. It was this group of people who had "full rights" in the new society. Having full rights meant having a right to adequate food and the privilege of joining the Communist Party and the army.[57] There is no doubt then that the Dergue and the Khmer Rouge had different views of revolutionary social order. One thing they had in common was their view of agriculture and food self-sufficiency as the key to a successful revolution.

AGRICULTURAL POLICY AND REVOLUTIONARY POLITICS

The Khmer Rouge believed that its revolution was "a new experience" in world history. That attitude shaped the agricultural policies of the regime. On the other hand, despite placing higher emphasis on agriculture, the pace at which the Dergue pushed its "socialist agricultural programs" was much slower than the Khmer Rouge. In terms of scope, the Dergue did not turn Socialist Ethiopia into a gigantic labor camp as the Khmer Rouge did in Cambodia.

The approach of the Khmer Rouge to agriculture broke new ground. Before it seized power, the Khmer Rouge had put some of its ideas of agrarian change into practice in the areas it controlled in southwestern Cambodia. These ideas included cooperative farms, forced relocation of populations, and formation of youth and work brigades whose members were taken from their families.[58] The Khmer Rouge took the idea of collectivization farther than the Dergue. The Cambodian regime dispossessed peasants of their land and even the freedom to pursue their vocations. That was because the Pol Pot regime viewed collective agriculture as the engine of social transformation and the most effective means of abolishing private property and capitalistic tendencies in the new society.

Although the situation differed from one region to the other, the majority of Cambodians worked about ten hours every day without pay or rest. Some had adequate food, but the majority subsisted on a ration of two ounces of rice gruel and salt.[59] The collectivization of houses, basic cooking utensils, cutlery and farm animals and even enforced collective eating from 1976 onwards fulfilled the regime's ideological objective of eliminating individualism which the Khmer Communists associated with capitalism. State regulation of dining prevented those who resisted state policies from secretly obtaining food from their families. Collective working also compelled Cham Muslims in cooperatives to dress like ethnic Khmers and to do the same work which every Khmer did, often involving the raising of pigs. Communal eating forced the Cham to eat the same food which every Khmer ate, often mixed with pork in violation of Islamic practice.[60] At the heart of the policy was an ultra-nationalist ideology of social conformity and ethnic uniformity. The Khmer Rouge intended to create a new society in which everyone pursued an agrarian vocation and became ethnically Khmer in dress code and eating habits. The consequences of this policy were lethal.

In Ethiopia, the Dergue had such a weak grip on power that it could not pursue any novel agricultural policy. Its major agricultural policy, land reform, drew upon the pre-revolutionary student ideas on agrarian reform which emphasized the nationalization and redistribution of land. The Dergue's *Land Reform Proclamation* of March 4, 1975 nationalized all rural lands and granted only usufructuary privileges to their tillers. It did not completely dispossess peasants of their land, but limited the amount of land that any individual peasant could own to ten hectares (24.71 acres), the perceived maximum amount which individual peasants could cultivate using their traditional farm technology. Perhaps, the Dergue's most revolutionary agricultural policy was freeing Ethiopian peasants from their outstanding debt obligations to their former landlords and granting the peasants the authority to use the oxen and farm implements of those landlords for a period of three years without compensation.[61] The Dergue's land reform proclamation laid the foundation for the type of socialist economic system that the soldiers wanted to build. In this economic system, the Dergue abolished private property as the Khmer Rouge did, but for different reasons. By limiting land holdings to ten hectares, too small for successful private farming, the

Mengistu regime created an incentive for peasants to join state or collective farms.[62] It is important to note that collectivization in Socialist Ethiopia became a means of controlling the political loyalties of peasants, not a way to create a gigantic agrarian utopia and enforce ethnic uniformity as the Khmer Rouge did.

Collectivization in Socialist Ethiopia highlighted the Dergue's pragmatic approach to socialism. In theory, any three peasants who lived in the same area could form a producer cooperative or cooperate to produce food. A producer cooperative or collective farm became eligible for registration and state support only when it had a minimum of 30 members. Members of registered collective farms had access to credit from the banks and could, if they wished, move from their individual homesteads to build their own centralized villages elsewhere.[63] To make collective forms of production more attractive, the Dergue decreed that peasants who lived closer to collective farms, but had not yet joined them as members, offer periodic free labor to those collective farms. These privileges did not endear collective farming to many peasants. By 1986, only 225 out of a total of 2,323 collective farms had attained the minimum membership required to obtain registration. That low rate of participation demonstrated the difficulties which the Dergue faced, and the reasons for the moderate measures it adopted, urging peasants to set up full-fledged collective farms with the ulterior motive of making them submissive allies of the state.[64]

The Dergue's collectivization policies also revealed the military regime's dual strategy of placating the civilian socialists as well as advancing the soldiers' key political interests: national unity and ethnic pluralism. To encourage peasants to produce collectively, the Dergue granted them the resources to form peasant associations (PA's). Membership was limited to the more vulnerable peasants who had no land or who owned less than 10 hectares of land. When collective farms served as the visible symbols of social interaction transcending the boundaries of class, gender and ethnicity, they enhanced the national unity and ethnic pluralism revolutionary objective of the Dergue. The Peasant Associations also helped to recruit peasant militias to help the Dergue to deal with armed resistance by aggrieved former landlords who formed the Ethiopian Democratic Union, in 1975, to overthrow the military regime and reverse its land reform measures.

One of the essential similarities and also greatest ironies of the Cambodian and Ethiopian revolutions was their failure to prevent famine despite their emphasis on agriculture. But even here, the Khmer Rouge bears more responsibility than the Dergue for famine because famine was not a traditional problem in Cambodia as it was in Ethiopia. Before 1970, Cambodians ate "on average about 600 grammes of rice per day." During the civil war (1970–75) Cambodians in refugee camps had a daily ration of 150 grammes of rice. But from April 1975, Cambodians reached "the brink of starvation."[65]

Poor natural conditions did not cause the starvation. The Khmer Rouge made the situation worse. No one had the incentive to produce food in a state where collectivization and regimentation robbed peasants of control over their produce. Forced labor on dams and irrigation in Pol Pot's Cambodia delayed planting in the rainy season. The city-people whom the Khmer Rouge set to work on the farm did not know how to grow rice. Prohibitions on free foraging for food intensified hunger. The extent of starvation was all too clear in the rice gruel and salt rations in some zones. Peasants in other districts ate "poisonous plants" to survive lethal famine. Yet, the Khmer Rouge exported rice—the staple food of Cambodia—to China in 1976 while *new people* in northwestern Cambodia starved to death. The human condition deteriorated in 1977 when thousands more starved to death or became ineffective because of illness and insufficient food.[66]

A combination of factors caused famine in revolutionary Ethiopia. They included recurrent drought, lack of peasant incentive to produce food as a result of low prices for food crops, state extractions of food from peasants in the form of quotas, peasant association political meetings during planting seasons, and fear of engaging in agricultural activities in a period of war.[67] The Dergue's extractions of food from peasants impoverished them. Taxation and collectivization also bred resentment.[68] The recruitment of peasants as soldiers by the Dergue, and its armed opponents, also undermined peasant food production.

As we will observe in chapter six, both the Dergue and the Khmer Rouge had opportunities to seek foreign aid to relieve starvation. But the Cambodian regime pushed its ideology of absolute self-reliance to the suicidal length of refusing famine relief aid. The situation was different in Ethiopia. The Dergue recognized the limits of self-reliance, swallowed its pride and accepted foreign aid, but on its own terms.[69] Here, the Dergue showed that it was less ideological and more pragmatic than the Angkar.

EDUCATION AND LITERACY

On education, the Dergue and the Khmer Rouge proved to be different revolutionary regimes. The soldier-revolutionaries in Ethiopia improved education and literacy while the Khmer Rouge placed a much lower priority on them. While the Dergue coopted intellectuals and other professionals to boost its Socialist pretensions and made peasant associations the vehicles for promoting literacy, the Khmer Rouge took literacy backwards. The Cambodian regime put many of the highly educated in the fields to grow vegetables, clear forests and break rocks with peasants as a means of facilitating its social leveling policies. As David Chandler put it, the Khmer Rouge preferred the production of food to "the learning of reading, writing and arithmetic."[70] Many of the intellectuals died of overwork, hunger and poor medical attention. Spurning academic pursuits and turning doctors into peasants formed part of a doctrinaire policy of absolute self-reliance. That policy was stretched to the point of using locally-made concoctions for the treatment of diseases. Chean Phanna, an eyewitness of the Cambodian revolution, put it more succinctly: "As for public health, there were no real hospitals or medications. . . . The doctors were children 12 or 13 years old. . . . The midwives did not observe proper hygiene. They would cut the umbilical cord [of new-born babies] with unsterilized scissors."[71] For the leaders of revolutionary Cambodia, the building of an agrarian society mattered more than the training of doctors. True to its revolutionary creed, the Khmer Rouge closed universities and burnt their libraries and turned many schools into warehouses for fertilizer.[72] That the Khmer Rouge closed schools and discouraged literacy and the Dergue received UNESCO's special literacy award for raising the literacy rate in Ethiopia "from 9 percent in 1974 to 37 percent by 1986," testify to the different visions of revolution which the Cambodian Communists and the Ethiopian soldier-revolutionaries had.[73]

RELIGION

The Cambodian and the Ethiopian revolutions reveal that not all revolutions make a sharp break with past values and institutions as Huntington has argued. Mocking religion as a social narcotic and a tool of feudalism has been a common theme in the revolutionary language of intellectuals in Africa and Asia. But no revolutionary regime since Lenin went as far in abolishing religion, desecrating its sacred monuments and texts and killing and disrobing its clergy as the Khmer Rouge did. The Khmer Rouge officially abolished Buddhism, the national religion of Cambodia, and Islam in 1975, forcing monks and nuns to abandon their religious vocations and join the peasantry. Desecration of Buddhism in revolutionary Cambodia went beyond disrobing monks to forcing them to raise pigs and cattle, in violation of their beliefs. The destruction of statues of Buddha in many Buddhist temples and the storage of cow dung in the temples offer extreme examples of Khmer Rouge contempt for religion—an ancient social institution in Cambodian society.[74]

The Dergue's policies on religion are distinguished by the respect the soldier-revolutionaries accorded religious symbols. Neither the Dergue nor its more radical civilian advisors and competitors converted the Ethiopian clergy into peasants or destroyed and desecrated the nation's many temples and monasteries. The execution of *Abuna* Tewoflos, head of the Ethiopian Orthodox Church, was the only vicious attack which the Dergue mounted against the Church in Ethiopia.[75] This execution has its grisly parallel in the killing of Imam Haji Res Los, the Grand Mufti of Cambodian Islam, by the Khmer Rouge.[76] Given the fact that the *Abuna* posed no political threat to the Dergue, his execution constituted an act of desecration. But otherwise, religious observance was tolerated in revolutionary Ethiopia.

To prevent secret religious observances, the Pol Pot regime closed all churches, mosques, Islamic schools and Buddhist *wats*. It also prohibited prayer and tore down the Catholic Cathedral in Phnom Penh, "stone by stone until no trace remained. . . ."[77] More egregiously, the Khmer Rouge forced Muslims to eat pork against their religious beliefs. This desecration of the religious faith of Muslims ended in death for those who resisted or disobeyed Khmer Rouge secularization of the clergy and the entire revolutionary society. Assault on religion in Cambodia had a deeper ideological motive. Unlike Ethiopia, where the religious class had served as the ideological bastion of monarchical power, some Cambodian monks had long been advocates of change—in some sense revolutionaries themselves. The anti-colonial movement in Cambodia was initially led by monks. The destruction of religion in revolutionary Cambodia and the disdainful treatment of monks could only have formed part of a deeper ideological inclination to change the dominant values of Cambodian society that were fostered by Buddhism.

The Dergue promoted religion and used its symbols to buttress the power of the revolutionary leadership. Mengistu always appeared at public functions with the heads of the Orthodox Christian church and the Islamic faith, ignoring even the voices calling for the separation of church and state.[78] Whereas the Pol Pot regime banned Islam, the Mengistu government put the Islamic religion on equal footing with Orthodox Christianity in Ethiopia, thus reversing the pre-revolutionary state policy of making Islam a subordinate faith. What historian Charles Maier would call "the wider historical process at work" here is that the Mengistu regime's policy on religion betrayed the Dergue's insecurity. In the case of Cambodia, attacks on religion reaffirmed the confidence of the Pol Pot regime in its radical social change mission.

Certainly, the Dergue had no alternative but to pursue a pragmatic policy on religion in an incurably religious society in order to build popular support for the regime in the midst of overwhelming domestic armed opposition. Building that popular support required a pragmatic policy on religion that appeased the Dergue's political opponents but did not alienate the peasants. The Dergue nationalized the lands of the Orthodox Church and the urban assets of the Grand Mosque in 1975. Given the popular consensus in Ethiopia about the redistribution of wealth, and giving land to its tillers, this policy of the Dergue had a favorable reception. But it was an economic policy, not an ideological one. Paradoxically, the Orthodox Church in Ethiopia gained more followers on "an unprecedented scale" at its moment of partial persecution. Violence and terror, as we shall later observe, so characterized the Ethiopian revolution that many found in religion a tranquil haven from social despair.[79] The underlying comparative lesson here is that the Dergue did not prevent Ethiopians from continuing to practice their religion. Indeed, churches remained open throughout the 17 years of revolution in Ethiopia.

TREATMENT OF ETHNIC MINORITIES

The different approaches of the Dergue and Khmer Rouge to revolution can again be discerned from how they treated ethnic minorities. Two hundred and fifty thousand Chams, who were predominantly Muslims, lived in Cambodia in 1975. In the course of the revolution, the Pol Pot regime cleansed Cham villages, banned the Cham language and forced Cham women to cut their hair as short as Khmers' rather than wear it long, as was customary. The Khmer Rouge also banned traditional Cham clothing and festivals. The Cham were persecuted on grounds of their ethnicity and of their faith as Muslims. It is important to emphasize that the Cham as a minority religious and ethnic group had been persecuted in Cambodia long before the Khmer Rouge seized power. As Kiernan notes, many Khmers had viewed the Cham with a "mixture of awe and fear" bordering on "contempt" because of the latter's reputation as sorcerers and diviners. During the revolution, the "distinct language and culture" of the Cham people, their "large villages" and sense of independence posed a threat to the fragmented and "closely supervised" new society that the Pol Pot regime wanted to create.[80] Furthermore, as Muslims who prayed five times a day and devoted significant time to religious rituals, the Chams, in the eyes of the Khmer Rouge, threatened the success of collectivized agriculture. Khmer Rouge persecution of the Cham also reflected the revolutionary regime's quest for a new and "pure" society purged of all ethnic groups except the Khmer willing to conform to Khmer Rouge ideological dictates.[81] Beside the Cham, the Chinese and Vietnamese lost their identity through Khmer Rouge prohibitions on their language and dietary habits.

The Khmer Rouge ideal of a revolution in which everyone became Khmer, in an ethnically pure or homogenous Cambodia, contrasted sharply with the Dergue's goal of a revolution in which every ethnic group retained its identity in a united, but ethnically diverse Ethiopia. *Amharinya*, the dominant language in pre-revolutionary Ethiopia, became just one of many officially recognized and promoted languages in revolutionary Ethiopia.

PEASANT REVOLUTION OR
REVOLUTION IN SEARCH OF PEASANTS?

There were different modes of peasant involvement in the Ethiopian and the Cambodian revolutions. In Cambodia, the Khmer Rouge had fought its way into power from its rural bases with the assistance of peasants. There was no comparable peasant involvement in the Dergue's acquisition of power. Peasants watched the Dergue, an urban group which had no firm roots in rural Ethiopia, depose an Emperor peasants revered.

With dogmatic determination, the Khmer Rouge tried to recreate the supposed agrarian powerhouse which Khmer intellectuals (not peasants) dreamed of and associated with the ancient kingdom of Angkor. The determination of the Khmer Rouge to triple rice production over four years meant harder work "at a furious pace" for peasants.[82] Under state compulsion, Khmer peasants hacked rice fields, dug canals and built dams with their bare hands.[83] Tens of thousands of Cambodian peasants died of malnutrition, disease and overwork. Peasants who resisted were executed. The robust desire to build socialism rapidly without capital, machinery, technical skill or material incentives could only have arisen from ideological dogmatism as well as "ignorance and wishful thinking." As Chandler notes, "hardly any of the leaders of the [communist] party had ever planted, transplanted, or harvested rice to feed a family."[84] Ethiopian peasants resented the intrusions of the state too. Wielding Mao's *Little Red Book*, student revolutionaries who helped to implement the Dergue's land reform policy, in 1975, lectured peasants on class struggle and the importance of collective farms much to the amazement of peasants who kept asking the students more practical questions about when and where they could get the oxen and fertilizer to produce food.[85]

In short, the two revolutions were not peasant revolutions, but revolutions that sought peasant support when and where expedient for legitimacy and survival. Although the Mengistu clique that controlled the

Dergue courted peasant support, it did not depend on peasants to survive mounting armed opposition. In fact, unlike the Khmer Rouge, the Dergue placed greatest emphasis on soldiers and urban dwellers as the vanguard of the revolution.

CONCLUSION

The revolutionary military regime in Ethiopia sought to build a post-Imperial society in which rural land previously monopolized by feudal landlords was equally redistributed to the peasants who tilled it. The regime pursued its limited objectives at a gradual pace and expected them to advance the Dergue's main aspiration: national unity and ethnic and religious equality. By contrast, under a civilian communist leadership, the Khmer Rouge sought to restructure Cambodian society, purge it of Western influence and build a closely-supervised state and army. The top party leadership intended to accomplish these broader objectives at a rapid pace—within ten to fifteen years nationally, and in some zones within four years. The Khmer Rouge was determined not only to turn Cambodia into a unique socialist utopia by sheer human will, but also to strengthen the Khmer ethnic group by purifying it and even enlarging its living space.

Arguably, the swift acquisition of power and the decisive control the Khmer Rouge exercised, and the need the Pol Pot regime felt to respond to the imperatives of total control, motivated it to transform Cambodia more broadly, comprehensively and rapidly than the embattled Dergue attempted in Ethiopia.

Unlike the doctrinaire and utopian Khmer Rouge, the pragmatic and opportunist Dergue showed eagerness to modify and even surrender ideology when politically expedient. This became even more apparent as anti-Dergue groups mastered the art of using peasant grievances as the foci of their resistance. In March 1990, fifteen months before his government was overthrown, Mengistu denounced Marxism, ended collective agriculture and introduced "free market pricing." He gave members of collective farms the liberty to abolish them. And the Workers Party of Ethiopia (WPE), which the Dergue had opportunistically formed in 1984, to project a Communist inclination as the price for Soviet arms delivery, was renamed the Democratic Unity Party of Ethiopia (DUPE).[56] This volte-face came amid significant internal and external developments. First, mounting domestic opposition to the Dergue. Second, the fall of the Soviet Union. Third, the predominance of the World Bank's structural adjustment principles in the foreign policies of the Dergue's Western aid donors.

Despite the anti-Western sentiments that existed among the educated elite in pre-revolutionary Ethiopia, the Dergue was not so anti-Western as to make the eradication of Western influence a feature of its idea of revolution and socialism. In fact, it had resisted pressure from civilian mentors to act as the Khmer Rouge did. Therefore, class analyses of social relations helped the Dergue to promote its national unity ideology by countering appeals to ethnicity by its opponents in the national debate on social justice. Promoting racial and ethnic equality also helped the Dergue to rally many Ethiopians around the patriotic need to secure their nation's borders against Somali irredentism. Thus, the Ethiopian regime did not subscribe to "radical social transformation" as sociologist Heinz Kaufeler has wrongly argued in his book *Modernization, Legitimacy, and Social Movement*. But he is correct that the Dergue, like the Khmer Rouge, practiced ruthless power politics and terror. Their aim was to secure total power.

NOTES

1. Quoted in Theda S. Skocpol, "France, Russia, China: A Structural Analysis of Social Revolutions, " *Comparative Studies in Society and History* 18, no. 2 (April 1976): 175.

2. Testimony of Tep Vung given at Siem Reap on June 1, 1979 in *Genocide in Cambodia: Documents from the Trial of Pol Pot and Ieng Sary*, ed. Howard J. De Nike, John Quigley and Kenneth J. Robinson (Philadelphia: University of Pennsylvania Press, 2000), 152.

3. Jean Louis Margolin, "Cambodia: The Country of Disconcerting Crimes," 633.

4. Yves Santamaria, "Afrocommunism: Ethiopia, Angola, and Mozambique," in *Black Book of Communism*, 684.

5. Ben Kiernan, "Pol Pot and Enver Pasha: A Comparison of the Cambodian and Armenian Genocides," in *Studies in Comparative Genocide*, ed. Levon Chorbajian and George Shirinian (New York: St Martin's Press, 1999), 167–71.

6. Kiernan, *The Pol Pot Regime*, 55.

7. Kiernan, *The Pol Pot Regime*, 26.

8. Kiflu Tadesse, *The Generation, Part II: The History of the Ethiopian People's Revolutionary Party* (New York: University Press of America, 1998), 60.

9. Helen Fein, "Revolutionary and Antirevolutionary Genocides: A Comparison of State Murders in Democratic Kampuchea, 1975 to 1979, and in Indonesia, 1965 to 1966," *Comparative Studies in Society and History*, 35, no. 3 (July 1993): 797, 799.

10. For a discussion of the grievances of the protesting soldiers, see Dawit, *Red Tears*, 13, and Rene Lefort, *Ethiopia: An Heretical Revolution?* (London: Zed Books, 1983), 52.

11. Andargachew Tiruneh, *The Ethiopian Revolution, 1974–1987: A Transformation from an Aristocratic to a Totalitarian Autocracy* (Cambridge: Cambridge University Press, 1993), 41.

12. Lefort, *Ethiopia: An Heretical Revolution?*, 56, 61.

13. Dawit, *Red Tears*, 12.

14. Interview with Tesfaye Mekasha Amare.

15. Dawit, *Red Tears*, 12–14.

16. Andargachew, *The Ethiopian Revolution 1974–1987*, 66. See also Lefort, *Ethiopia: An Heretical Revolution?*, 80.

17. Interview with Tesfaye Mekasha.

18. See Edmund J. Keller, *Revolutionary Ethiopia: From Empire to People's Republic* (Bloomington: Indiana University Press, 1988), 186. Keller argues that the Dergue forced the Endalkatchew cabinet out of office because of the cabinet's unresponsiveness to calls for reform, and the Dergue's suspicion that Endalkatchew was plotting against it. But according to my confidential sources, the demand for the resignation of the cabinet was a strategy which the Dergue used to test how the public might react to the overthrow of the Imperial Government. Dawit reinforces this point in *Red Tears*, 15.

19. Dawit, *Red Tears*, 15, 260.

20. Paulos, "Mengistu Haile Mariam," 52.

21. See *The Ethiopian Herald*, September 28, 1974, 1–5.

22. Lefort, *Ethiopia: An Heretical Revolution?*, 78–79.

23. Chandler, *Brother Number One*, 87.

24. Kiernan, *The Pol Pot Regime*, 33; Chandler, *Brother Number One*, 108.

25. The Ottaways, and Edmund Keller, put the Dergue's numerical composition at 120. See Marina and David Ottaway, *Ethiopia: Empire in Revolution* (New York: Holmer and Meier Publishers Inc., 1978), 7, and Keller, *Revolutionary Ethiopia*, 192. Andargachew Tiruneh, a law professor at Addis Ababa University, believes the figure of 120 included the clerical staff of the Dergue

but "the actual number . . . was 106." See Andargachew, *The Ethiopian Revolution, 1974–1987*, 64. Christopher Clapham put the number at 108. See Clapham, *Transformation and Continuity*, 40.

26. Dawit, *Red Tears*, 18.

27. Kirk John Miller, "An Analysis of the Ethiopian, Iranian and Nicaraguan Revolutions from the Perspective of United States Involvement," (diss., The University of Texas at Austin, 1985), 105–7. See also Dawit, *Red Tears*, 18, 33.

28. David Chandler, Ben Kiernan and Chanthou Boua, *Pol Pot Plans the Future: Confidential Leadership Documents from Democratic Kampuchea, 1976–1977*, Monograph Series 33 (New Haven: Yale University Southeast Asia Studies, 1989), 7; Kiernan, *The Pol Pot Regime*, 11, 100, 124, 259.

29. The author has preserved the confidentiality of the source, a former official of the revolutionary government.

30. World Bank, Office Memorandum, "Ethiopia: Recent Political Developments and Bank Operations," December 13, 1974, *Ministry of National Resources Development and Environmental Protection Archives*, Addis Ababa. See also Dawit, *Red Tears*, 50–51.

31. Dawit, *Red Tears*, 17.

32. Paulos, "Mengistu Haile Mariam," 46. Mengistu elaborates on his view of Ethiopian society in his "Report Delivered to the First Congress of COPWE," Addis Ababa, June 16, 1980, 7–8.

33. Wudu Tafete, "MEISON: From Opposition to Critical Support, 1974–77," (Paper Presented for the Departmental Seminar of the Department of History, Addis Ababa University, June 29–July 2, 1995), 5.

34. Marina and David Ottaway, *Ethiopia: Empire in Revolution*, 59.

35. Dawit, *Red Tears*, 33.

36. Halliday and Molyneux, *The Ethiopian Revolution*, 114; Dawit, *Red Tears*, 22.

37. Kiernan, "Conflict in the Kampuchean Communist Movement," 24.

38. For a summary of the various perspectives on the Cambodian revolution as a "peasant revolution," see Kiernan, *The Pol Pot Regime*, 163–69; Chandler, *Brother Number One*, 3, 122. For a view of the Ethiopian revolution as a Marxist revolution, see Halliday and Molyneux, *The Ethiopian Revolution*; and as a communist revolution, see Stephen L. Varnis, *Reluctant Aid or Aiding the Reluctant: U.S. Aid Policy and Ethiopian Relief* (New Brunswick, NJ: Transaction Publishers, 1990).

39. Lefort, *Ethiopia: An Heretical Revolution?*, 78.

40. Marina and David Ottaway, *Ethiopia: Empire in Revolution*, 8, 63. See also Dawit, *Red Tears*, 14, and Halliday and Mollyneux, *The Ethiopian Revolution*, 88.

41. Donald L. Donham, *Marxist Modern: An Ethnographic History of the Ethiopian Revolution* (Los Angeles, CA: University of California Press, 1999), 27.

42. Dawit, *Red Tears*, 14; Tefera Haile Selassie, *The Ethiopian Revolution, 1974–1991: From a Monarchical Autocracy to a Military Oligarchy* (London: Kegan Paul, 1997), 153.

43. Dawit, *Red Tears*, 23.

44. Kiflu Tadesse, *The Generation, Part II: The History of the Ethiopian People's Revolutionary Party* (New York: University Press of America, 1998), 60. See also *Abyot* (Information Bulletin of the EPRP) 1, no. 3 (February–March 1976): 25.

45. *Meskerem*, Inaugural and Special Issue (September 1980): 25; Marina and David Ottaway, *Ethiopia: Empire in Revolution*, 59, and Halliday and Mollyneux, *The Ethiopian Revolution*, 93.

46. Edmund J. Keller, "Constitutionalism and the National Question in Africa: The Case of Eritrea," in *The Political Economy of Ethiopia*, ed. Marina Ottaway (New York: Praeger, 1990), 105; Dawit, *Red Tears*, 309–10.

47. See Osman Saleh Sabbe, Spokesman of ELF/PLF, to Henry S. Reuss, Congress of the United States, and Henry S. Reuss, Member of Congress, to Hon. Dick Clark, Chairman, Subcommittee on Africa, Committee on Foreign Relations, U.S. Senate, Washington, D.C., 3 August 1976, in Congress, Senate, Committee on Foreign Relations, *Ethiopia and the Horn of Africa: Hearings Before the Subcommittee on African Affairs*, 94th Congress, 2nd Session, 4–6 August 1976, 61–62, 66, 68.

48. Jackson, *Rendezvous with Death*, 9.

49. Merahehiwot Gebremariam, "Ethio-U.S. Relations," *Ethioscope* 1, no. 2 (January 1995): 15; Dawit, *Red Tears*, 41, 48, 49, 108.

50. Chandler et al., *Pol Pot Plans the Future*, 43, 45; Chandler, *Brother Number One*, 114–115.

51. Chandler, *Brother Number One*, 114–115. See also Chandler et al., *Pol Pot Plans the Future*, 43, 45.

52. Becker, *When the War Was Over: Cambodia and the Khmer Rouge Revolution*, xvi.

53. Chandler et al., *Pol Pot Plans the Future*, 20, 21, 25, 27.

54. Dawit, *Red Tears*, 24. See also Marina and David Ottaway, *Ethiopia: Empire in Revolution*, 10.

55. Author's interview with Kifle Wodajo, former Dergue foreign minister, Addis Ababa, April 22, 1999.

56. Donham, *Marxist Modern*, 29. See also Teferra, *The Ethiopian Revolution, 1974–1991*, 102–3.

57. Kiernan, *The Pol Pot Regime*, 175–76, and Jackson, *Rendezvous with Death*, 52.

58. Chandler, *Brother Number One*, 96.

59. See testimony of Pen Bun Tiv, "Pol Pot Methods of Killing: The Yoke of Men," in De Nike et al., *Genocide in Cambodia*, 141.

60. Kiernan, *The Pol Pot Regime*, 78, 258, 269, 274–75.

61. Provisional Military Government of Socialist Ethiopia (PMGSE). Ministry of Agriculture and Settlement, and Institute of Development Research, "Agrarian Reform and Rural Development in Ethiopia," Addis Ababa, August 1978, 59. See also Dessalegn Rahmato, "Cooperatives, State Farms and Smallholder Production," in *Ethiopia: Rural Development Options*, ed. Siegfried Pausewang et al. (London: Zed Books, 1990), 100.

62. PMGSE. Ministry of Agriculture Planning and Programming Department, "General Agricultural Survey: Preliminary Report 1983–1984," vol. 1, *Ministry of Agriculture, Documentation Centre*, Addis Ababa, October 1984, 1.

63. Solomon Bellette, "Ethiopia's Agricultural Production Strategy: An Overview," in Proceedings of the National Workshop on Food Strategies for Ethiopia Held at Alemaya University of Agriculture, Ethiopia, December 8–12, 1986, 81. See also Dessalegn Rahmato, "Cooperatives, State Farms and Smallholder Production," 102.

64. Marina and David Ottaway, *Ethiopia: Empire in Revolution*, 102.

65. Kiernan, *The Pol Pot Regime*, 163–64. See also George C. Hildebrand and Gareth Porter, *Cambodia: Starvation and Revolution* (New York: Monthly Review Press, 1976), 19–22.

66. Haing Ngor with Roger Warner, *A Cambodian Odyssey* (New York: Warner Books, 1987), 162–3, 172; Chandler, *Brother Numbers One*, 117; Kiernan, *The Pol Pot Regime*, 177–78, 182–83, 187–88, 193.

67. For detailed analyses of the causes, impact and relief of famine in revolutionary Ethiopia, see Edward Kissi, "Famine and the Politics of Food Relief," chapter 7.

68. Mesfin Wolde-Mariam, "Ethiopia's Food Security: Problems and Prospects" (Paper Presented at the National Workshop on Food Strategies for Ethiopia, Alemaya, December 1986), 13.

69. Kissi, "Famine and the Politics of Food Relief," chapters 7 and 8.

70. Chandler, *Brother Number One*, 121.

71. Testimony of Chean Phanna, former fourth-year student of the Pharmacy Faculty, in *Genocide in Cambodia*, 119.

72. Testimony of Mr. Proum Douch Boranann, Phnom Penh, May 28, 1979, in *Genocide in Cambodia*, 85.

73. Dawit, *Red Tears*, 27.

74. "Report by Kampuchean Clergy on the Situation in Kampuchea After April 17, 1975," in *Genocide in Cambodia*, 145.

75. Author's interview with Andreas Eshete, former EPRP political activist, Addis Ababa, May 10, 1999. Andreas Eshete is now President of Addis Ababa University.

76. Kiernan, *The Pol Pot Regime*, 270–71.

77. Jackson, *Rendezvous with Death*, 49.

78. Author's conversation with Tekalign Wolde-Mariam, Historian, Addis Ababa University, Ethiopia, April 28, 1999.

79. Interview with Andreas Eshete.

80. Kiernan, *The Pol Pot Regime*, 256, 260.

81. Kiernan, *The Pol Pot Regime*, 269. See also Eric D. Weitz, *A Century of Genocide: Utopias of Race and Nation* (Princeton, NJ: Princeton University Press, 2003), 150, 164, 170–71.

82. Chandler et al., *Pol Pot Plans the Future*, 29, 38.

83. Statement of Ung Sam On, Phnom Penh, May 23, 1979, in *Genocide in Cambodia*, 124.

84. Chandler, *Brother Number One*, 116, 118.

85. Marina and David Ottaway, *Ethiopia: Empire in Revolution*, 74.

86. Workers Party of Ethiopia, "Report by Mengistu Haile Mariam: Resolutions Adopted by the Plenum," Addis Ababa, March 6, 1990, 42–43.

STATE-TERROR AND THE
QUEST FOR TOTAL POWER

Like sociologist Heinz Kaufeler, political scientist John Dunn is correct in arguing that the Ethiopian and Cambodian revolutions were characterized by "brutal domestic repression." Some analysts would add, from an ideological perspective, that the terror of the Pol Pot and Mengistu regimes offers yet another example of the prevalence of murder in the history of Marxist revolutions. But, the terror of the two revolutionary regimes also offers different lessons in the study of the relationship between revolution and genocide.

What happened in revolutionary Cambodia lends empirical support to Hannah Arendt's theory that "the effectiveness of [state] terror depends . . . entirely on the degree of social atomization."[1] The intensity of state terror in revolutionary Cambodia could be attributed to the submission of a fragmented and subdued society to the control of the Angkar. Events in revolutionary Ethiopia provide an alternative theory. There, the intensity and ruthlessness of state terror were not the result of submission of subdued groups in an atomized society, but rather the determined resistance of many organized and armed groups to the Dergue's quest for total power.

When one compares the nature and outcome of organized terror in Cambodia under Pol Pot and Ethiopia under Mengistu, one cannot resist the conclusion that despite the differences in their visions of revolution, the Dergue's ideology of absolute national unity and the Angkar's ideology of racial purity and territorial expansion had a common thrust. They were both exclusionary in nature and had an inherent capacity for mass violence. By proclaiming the "indivisibility of Ethiopian Unity" as its idea of scientific socialism, the Dergue totally rejected ethnic secessionism as an alternative mode of political organization. To enforce this nationalist ideology (what it called "socialist patriotism"), the Dergue issued a penal code on November 16, 1974 mandating the death penalty for anyone who opposed the military regime or challenged the existing national boundaries of Ethiopia.[2] The Penal Code made absolute obedience to the Dergue and the state ideology of national unity the necessary conditions for inclusion in the revolutionary society. Under these circumstances, moderates, secessionists and their sympathizers fell outside the Dergue's conception of those Ethiopians the revolutionary regime felt morally and legally bound to protect. A frustrated Dergue official in charge of press relations, Lt. Tamarat Ferede, declared in the mid-1970s that "it is the duty of every government to ensure that anarchists and political murderers are kept under control." The Dergue drew an arbitrary line between "anarchists" and "political murderers." Any Ethiopian opposed to the Dergue or "suspected of being lukewarm to the revolution" could be branded as either an anarchist or a political murderer.[3]

Similarly, by claiming that only the Khmer people and the Khmer language mattered in revolutionary Cambodia, the Khmer Rouge leadership excluded many groups of people from the state's definition of who among the Cambodian people deserved to live or be destroyed in the new society. As Eric Weitz has observed, "if race is a form of identity based on supposed biological ties among a group of people, then the [Khmer Rouge] view of the Khmer people as one extended family constituted a form of racialization."[4] In this racialized construction of group identity, only Khmers with the mind and attitude desired by Pol Pot's French-educated group of Communists had a place in the new Cambodia. Thus, the Khmer Rouge leadership marked for annihilation all Khmers it defined as having only the body and not the mind of the authentic new Khmer. Those marked for extermination included non-Khmer ethnic groups such as the Chams, Chinese, Thai and Vietnamese who wanted to maintain their distinctive ethnic identities.

Apart from their exclusionary ideologies of Ethiopian national unity and Khmer racial purity, the Dergue and the Khmer Rouge had other things in common with totalitarian regimes in human history. The Dergue and the Khmer Rouge appeared convinced that their policies and even terror served a nobler purpose. Pol Pot asserted in 1977 that he strongly believed Cambodia was under threat from internal enemies within the Khmer Rouge and external enemies from Vietnam. Therefore, by killing suspected enemies, his regime preserved Cambodia.[5] Mengistu had a similar conviction. He strongly believed that Ethiopia was under serious threat from internal enemies within the Dergue itself and from Eritrean secessionists and other domestic armed political groups. Like Pol Pot, Mengistu saw extermination of perceived enemies as necessary to ensure the unity of the Ethiopian nation.[6]

TOTAL POWER AND DOMESTIC OPPOSITION

Cambodia's peasants who had welcomed the revolution with hope and enthusiasm showed a willingness to accept sacrifices in the short term. Their hopes were dashed when the Khmer Rouge rapidly transformed their lives. When forced labor, communal eating, widespread malnutrition, executions and prohibitions on family life, movement, religious worship and traditional foraging for food became part of daily life, the Cambodian revolution lost its appeal and meaning to them. As one Khmer peasant eyewitness to the revolution put it, "people became unhappy with the revolution [and] . . . changed their minds about it because life was so tough. . . ."[7] But discontented Cambodians could not organize themselves into armed groups to oppose the Khmer Rouge because the Pol Pot regime effectively muzzled the society. That did not happen in Ethiopia.

Given the opposition it faced, the Dergue could not atomize Ethiopian society by controlling family life, prohibiting religion or communalizing eating and other forms of life as the Khmer Rouge did. But its enforced national unity ideology, collectivization of food production, oppressive taxation, and food delivery quotas imposed on peasants bred resentment. Ethiopia's "demoralized peasantry" did not organize an armed movement to express their dissent as urban students, intellectuals and workers did.

However, rural disaffection with intrusive state policies made Ethiopian peasants ready supporters of the armed groups that opposed the Dergue.[8]

The principal political groups that opposed the Mengistu regime were the Eritrean Peoples Liberation Front (EPLF), the Ethiopian Peoples Revolutionary Party (EPRP), the Tigrayan Peoples Liberation Front (TPLF), the Oromo Peoples Liberation Front (OLF), the Ethiopian Democratic Union (EDU), the Afar Liberation Front (ALF), the Western Somalia Liberation Front (WSLF) and the All Ethiopian Socialist Movement (ME'ISON). Each group had an independent armed force and laid effective claim to a particular territory in Ethiopia.

The EPRP, the most radical and ideologically Communist of the opposition groups, formed in August 1975, sought to integrate the ethnic-based opposition to the Dergue into a broad-based "class struggle" against the military regime.[9] The EPRP drew its leadership from the Amhara and Tigrayan educated and urban elite, especially Marxist civilians who had opposed the military regime through student demonstrations and industrial strikes in September 1974.[10] But the EPRP's cadres and followers were mainly high school students, thousands of whom perished in the party's ideological and power struggles with the Dergue and the TPLF.

Unlike the Dergue whose rhetoric and other pronouncements obscured an opportunist labeling of itself as Marxist, the EPRP's pronouncements betrayed the party leadership's Marxist convictions. The EPRP intended to "establish a socialist state" in revolutionary Ethiopia under "the leadership of the proletarian party (EPRP)." It denounced what it called the "imperialist" (pro-American) ideological orientation of the Dergue and favored the arming of peasants and workers to "take over state power." The EPRP advocated "revolutionary violence" against the Dergue and its supporters. It urged all Ethiopians to "do away with pests" (a reference to the Dergue and EPRP's ideological enemies) and "erase the dust of Ethiopia's history through [a] national democratic revolution [as] China . . . , Albania . . . , Vietnam . . . , Cambodia and Laos have done. . . ."[11]

The *Me'ison*, a group of left-wing Amhara and Oromo elites, severed its initial "cooperation" with the Dergue in August 1977, opposed the military regime afterwards and became a victim of the Dergue's terror.

Me'ison had initially thought that by offering the Dergue "critical sup-port," because of their common distaste for Amhara and Tigre ethnic chauvinism, it could push the military regime "farther to the left."[12] Eventually *Me'ison's* grievances against the Dergue featured accusations against the military junta for monopolizing state security decisions and harboring "pro-American" and "reactionary forces."[13]

Intensification of Eritrea's demands for independence provoked other regions and ethnic groups to revive or initiate their own political demands. A group of Marxist intellectuals from the largest ethnic group in Ethiopia—the Oromo—formed the Oromo Liberation Front (OLF) in October 1974. By supporting Eritrea's demands for an independent state, the OLF affirmed the right of the Oromo people to determine their future in a "Peoples Democratic Republic of Oromia," an inde-pendent state to be carved out of the existing borders of Ethiopia.[14] The more pan-Ethiopian members of the Dergue, including Mengistu, op-posed ethnic nationalism and considered accession to the Oromo and Eritrean secessionists' demands as endorsement of the break-up of Ethiopia. The Dergue's Penal Code on November 16, 1974 mandating death for any opposition to its rule and any challenge to the traditional borders of Ethiopia constituted an official order authorizing the killing of the Dergue's political opponents.

The TPLF, formed in February 1975, initially aspired to form a state combining the northern provinces of Tigray and Eritrea. Later, the TPLF leadership abandoned secessionism for armed struggle intended to overthrow the Dergue. The TPLF attracted Tigrayan peasants and young and educated Tigrayans. Its leaders combined Marxism-Leninism and Maoism with their northern nationalism.[15] The TPLF's political aim inevitably brought it and the Dergue into a protracted and bitter power struggle. Besides opposition from the OLF in the southwest, the EPLF, in the north, and the TPLF in the northeast, the Dergue faced renewed threats, in southeastern Ethiopia, from the Western Somalia Liberation Front (WSLF). The WSLF reaffirmed demands it had made since 1962 for an independent state to be known as Western Somalia for ethnic-Somalis inhabiting Ethiopia's southeastern Ogaden region. Arguably, the Dergue's ethnic pluralism revolutionary objective created an atmo-sphere of ethnic-self-assertion in revolutionary Ethiopia in a manner that was impossible in Pol Pot's Cambodia.

Some of the Dergue's opponents such as the EPRP, TPLF and the *Me'ison* liked, initially, the Dergue's reformist program, but opposed military leadership of the revolution. The EPRP, for instance, claimed that soldiers are incapable of leading socialist revolutions. EPRP newsletters insisted that the "Dergue's revolution [was] not socialist, but fascist." The party urged its followers to launch a "relentless mass offensive" against the "reactionary military junta."[16] Other armed groups such as the EPLF and OLF promoted the ideology of ethnic-self-determination and secessionism to counter the Dergue's national unity ideology.

There was some limited and sporadic opposition to the Khmer Rouge inside Cambodia and within the Communist Party. Between June and November 1978, Cham Muslims clashed with Khmer Rouge soldiers in a series of rebellions in Krauchmar district, in the Eastern Zone of Cambodia. The soldiers had attempted to seize copies of the Koran and enforce other cultural prohibitions against the Cham. In these rebellions, according to Kiernan, the Cham "slaughtered half a dozen of [Khmer Rouge soldiers] with swords and knives."[17] Here, the Cham resisted systematic attempts by the Khmer Rouge to undermine the foundations of their faith and livelihood as a group. But the Pol Pot regime responded by massacring the entire inhabitants of several Cham villages and razing others to the ground. Despite these pockets of Cham resistance, the substantial control and perpetual surveillance that the Pol Pot regime exercised over Cambodian society stifled any organized opposition of the kind that the Dergue faced.

Domestic disaffection with their regimes bred paranoia and fears of assassination in Pol Pot and Mengistu as leaders. People were strip-searched before going into their presence.[18] Pol Pot's recurring gastric problems led him to believe that his cooks were trying to poison him. He, reportedly, had maintenance workers in one of his many residences executed when power failures occurred. In that state of fear and paranoia, the distinction between friend and foe or service and subversion blurred. Between 1977 and 1978, many of the people killed by the Khmer Rouge were close friends of the leaders of the revolutionary regime. They included high-ranking cadres such as Siet Chhae, Regiment Staff Member; Ruos Mau, Northwest Zone Party Chief of Staff; Sua Va Sy, Party Secretary of the Commercial Branch; Mau Khem

Nuon, Deputy Chief of Staff of S-21 Security Office and Sien An; the Cambodian Ambassador to Hanoi. They were killed "along with their relatives" and close friends.[19] In July 1977, Pol Pot ordered the execution of well-known Cambodian moderates Hu Nim and Hou Yuon. Hu Nim had advised the Khmer Rouge "to have mercy on people . . . [and] carry out democratic actions" and also accept foreign aid to alleviate suffering. Hou Yuon had opposed the radical policies of the Khmer Rouge, especially the evacuation of cities.[20]

The Mengistu regime shared with the Pol Pot regime the desire to liquidate moderates within the revolutionary regime. But Mengistu and the Dergue did not adopt the Khmer Rouge method of collective punishment or wholesale murder of moderates, political opponents and their family members. The executions of General Aman Andom, the Dergue's first nominal chairman, on November 23, 1974; of General Teferi Bante, Aman Andom's successor on February 3, 1977; and of Major Atnafu Abate, a founding member of the Dergue, on November 13, 1977, were the most dramatic of the Dergue's earliest political killings of moderates.[21] Aman, an Eritrean non-member of the Dergue, and former commander of the Third Infantry Division of the Ethiopian Army, wanted a peaceful settlement with the EPLF on the issue of an independent state for Eritrea. Mengistu wanted to crush the Eritrean secessionist movement militarily.

Teferi Bante, a moderate Oromo senior army officer, a non-member of the Dergue who was chosen to succeed Aman Andom as chairman in November 1974, was purged for advocating moderation in the treatment of civilian opposition groups in a public speech he made in January 1977. Atnafu Abate, an Amhara senior army officer, co-founder of the Dergue and its second vice president, was purged under Mengistu's orders for his "conservative" ideological inclinations. A nationalist, Atnafu had opposed the adoption of Marxism, which a faction of the Dergue led by Mengistu and some left-wing civilian advisors, wanted to promote as the official ideology of the Ethiopian revolution. Atnafu had also opposed the "bloodshed which the extremists [within and outside of the Dergue] insisted was necessary" for the revolution.[22] A newsletter of the EPRP opposition group also reported on January 30, 1976 that the Dergue had secretly executed 103 "opposition elements" mainly military officers and men from the Army Engineering Corps (AEC) "in the first week of January" 1976. The AEC, according to this publication, had called for the replacement of the Dergue with a popular government. The EPRP newsletter further charged that the Dergue had executed soldiers "who had refused to go to war in the Afar and Eritrean regions" against Afar and Eritrean insurgents.[23]

Fear of sabotage and counter-revolution distorted the Dergue's and Angkar's perceptions of reality. Virulent fear of enemies led the Khmer Rouge leadership to order and encourage arrests, intensely examine the life-histories of suspected "enemies," relocate populations to different zones, enforce communal eating and purge minority groups. Pol Pot exhorted cadres at a "study session" in December 1976, to "cleanse" the party of "microbes," "enemies" and "traitors." He also blamed lower food productivity not on the unrealistic scope and rapid pace of his government's agricultural policies, but rather on the machinations of "capitalists." The party leadership considered cadres who failed to galvanize *new people* to triple food production or showed laxity in executing party policy as "wreckers," "enemies" and "traitors" to be eliminated.[24] The Dergue also encouraged arrests and relocated populations to government-controlled areas in resettlement programs, as we shall observe in chapter five.[25] Dawit has argued that the Dergue, on Mengistu's orders, jailed or executed managers of state farms who failed to motivate their workers to increase production. Mengistu regarded them as saboteurs and counter-revolutionaries.[26]

A key difference between the Angkar and the Dergue was the scope of their reaction to insecurity and perceived sabotage. The Pol Pot regime reacted to insecurity by fragmenting Cambodian society, establishing total control over it and surging ahead with purges of particular ethnic and religious groups. Communal eating, for instance, represented the greatest rupture of the fabric of social life in the Khmer Rouge program of total control.[27] Khmer Rouge methods of control such as the separation of families, encouragement of children to spy on their parents, relocation of populations and closely-supervised forced labor were so devastating that, unlike Ethiopia, Cambodians remained "unchallenging subjects."[28] Even while they cursed inwardly, for many Cambodians servitude in tranquillity, suicide, and the "parroting [of] Khmer Rouge ideology and slogans" became the only means of survival and escape from state terror in an atomized society.[29] A survivor of the Khmer Rouge revolution put it succinctly: "nobody liked the Khmer Rouge but they did not know where to run."[30]

Ethiopians had several choices. Those who did not like the Dergue could more easily turn to the numerous anti-Dergue groups to express their dissent. This was due to the fact that social fragmentation and state surveillance of the kind that the Khmer Rouge established in Cambodia never really existed in revolutionary Ethiopia. Hence, given the political atmosphere in which the two revolutions took place, the Dergue, more than the Khmer Rouge faced the greater counter-revolutionary challenge. But, in comparison to the Angkar, the Dergue acted cautiously to solidify ethnic unity. In the process of doing that, the Mengistu regime slaughtered opponents of its pan-Ethiopian ideology and quest for total power. The purges of people who spoke against the Dergue's national unity ideology and policies, between 1974 and 1977, revealed the intent of the Dergue to use terror and political mass murder to induce compliance with the military's leadership of the revolution and the soldiers' ideology of absolute national unity.

PRECONDITIONS FOR GENOCIDE?

Almost all of the Dergue's opponents attracted significant external and kindred support and sympathy. The Tigrayans in the TPLF received arms and logistical support from their allies, the Eritreans in the EPLF. The EPLF operated in Eritrea, a territory bordering Tigray. EPLF offered military assistance to the TPLF because the TPLF supported Eritrean independence and resolved to overthrow the Dergue, the chief enemy of the two political groups.[31] The ethnic Somali armed secessionist group, the WSLF, also received military and diplomatic assistance from the Somali government, Ethiopia's closest neighbor to the east.[32] With support from Somalia, the Afar Liberation Front (ALF) also kept Afar marksmen in eastern Ethiopia active in ambushes of government traffic on the road to Assab port—one of only two ports in Ethiopia. The ALF sabotaged rail traffic from Addis Ababa to Djibouti as it passed by the abodes of Afar nomads in Hararghe, in eastern

Ethiopia. The Gambella Peoples Liberation Movement (GPLM), an armed group of Ethiopians with ethnic affinity with the Anuak of the Sudan, opposed the Dergue from southwestern Ethiopia with the help of the Sudanese government, Ethiopia's closest neighbor to the west.[33] What took place in Ethiopia, therefore, sustains Barbara Harff's and Ted Robert Gurr's argument that opposition activities intensify, and the potential for genocide and politicide increases, when external actors, especially "kindred groups . . . who hold power in neighbouring states" offer support and sanctuary for rebel fighters in ethno-nationalist rebellions.[34]

The Dergue was backed, in its domestic political struggles, by Cuba and the Soviet Union. That shift of international alliances from Ethiopia's traditional ally, the United States, to new partners, Cuba and the Soviet Union, enmeshed state-organized terror and the quest for total control in revolutionary Ethiopia in Cold War politics.[35] As we will observe in the next chapter, terror in revolutionary Ethiopia was also a contest of group egos fueled by lingering personal antagonisms.[36]

Lack of unity within the Ethiopian opposition groups, and the settling of personal scores between them, made the political opponents vulnerable to the Dergue's terror. Perhaps more important, by conducting their opposition to the military regime in the Leninist context of ethnic self-determination up to and including secession from Ethiopia—an unpopular idea for many Ethiopians—the TPLF, EPLF, OLF and WSLF handed the Dergue a popular basis for justifying state-terror against them. The Dergue succeeded in convincing many Ethiopians to regard the purges of its moderate members advocating rapprochement with the TPLF and EPLF, the extraction of food from peasants, taxation and drafting of the youth into the national army as necessary measures to defend Ethiopia against those who sought to dismember it.[37]

GLORIFYING TERROR

The Dergue and the Angkar permitted and glorified violence against their enemies. In a permissive environment of state-sanctioned terror, the selective appropriation of folk wisdom by the Mengistu and Pol Pot regimes proved an effective technique for lowering moral standards and justifying mass murder. The Dergue glorified the executions of those it called "counter-revolutionaries" in chilling radio announcements. Those announcements were always preceded by a popular folksong: *fiyel wotete*. The song delivers a story about a pompous, overfed and useless young goat that dared the leopard to a fight only to perish together with its kids at the hands of its ferocious and much more powerful adversary.[38] Similarly, those who have survived to tell the horrors of the Khmer Rouge revolution speak of similar justifications of murder in revolutionary Cambodia. Group supervisors and high Angkar officials relieved themselves of the moral trauma of killing with the popular Khmer aphorism, *tuk kor min cham-nenh, dork-chen kor min khart* (To spare you is no gain. To remove you is no loss).[39]

The Dergue and the Angkar went beyond the glorification of murder to trample upon basic social norms. They barred any form of mourning for those they killed regarding such basic cultural rites as expressions of disapproval of the death of the state's "enemies." The Dergue's killing squads justified this outrage against basic social norms by pinning notices on the dead bodies, many of which had been left exposed on the streets for days, denouncing them as "counter-revolutionaries" who deserved their fate. Bereaved families lucky enough to secure the bodies of their murdered relatives for burial had to pay for the bullets used in killing them. The families were also warned by government urban associations (*kebelles*) "not to mourn counter-revolutionaries."[40] In Cambodia, Khmer Rouge cadres conserved bullets by using clubs, bamboo sticks, pick axes and other crude implements to kill. The available evidence indicates that the leaders of the Dergue and the Khmer Rouge knew about these outrages.[41]

TERROR BY IMITATION?

The common patterns of terror in revolutionary Ethiopia and Cambodia should not suggest that the Dergue and the Khmer Rouge learned their killing and other revolutionary methods from each other. No concrete evidence exists to indicate that the Khmer Rouge exported its revolution to Ethiopia and vice-versa. No form of relationship, political or diplomatic, existed between the Mengistu and the Pol Pot regimes. In fact their foreign policies, examined in detail in chapter six, were poles apart. Therefore, the similarities of state-terror in revolutionary Ethiopia and Cambodia may be a matter of accident. They could also suggest influences on the Dergue by left-wing groups with ideologies similar to the Khmer Rouge or highlight opportunistic adoption by the Dergue of the methods of the EPRP, which had contact with the Khmer Rouge. There is evidence that the EPRP had some contact with the Khmer Rouge. There were some Dergue officials who were also members of the EPRP.

The EPRP—one of the Dergue's key political opponents—was the only Ethiopian political group to condemn Vietnam for overthrowing the Khmer Rouge.[42] Kiflu Tadesse, a member of the EPRP, and the party's biographer, has revealed that:

> [d]uring one of the [EPRP's] earlier trips to China, the EPRP delegation had also visited the Kampuchian [sic] Khmer Rouge which had given the EPRP some assistance. At that time, the Khmer Rouge was still in power and the discussion with the EPRP was conducted in Phnom Penh . . . , this was the period that the Khmer was deporting urban dwellers to the countryside for what it called a "rehabilitation" process.[43]

No details of this meeting exist and Kiflu Tadesse does not mention the nature of the "assistance" which the EPRP received from the Khmer Rouge. Melaku Tegegne, a member of the EPRP's central committee, who knew about the meeting, has disclosed to the author that the meeting with the Khmer Rouge took place on the advice of the Chinese government from which the EPRP had requested arms to confront the Dergue. According to Melaku, the purpose of the visit was not to take cues from the Cambodian revolution, but to "please the Chinese" for the sake of facilitating arms delivery.[44] Melaku asserts that the EPRP and the Khmer Rouge had "ideological differences" about the importance of peasants and the centrality of agriculture in socialist revolutions. Ideologically, the EPRP favored urban political and military struggle, with intellectuals, not peasants, at the helm of the revolution and the state.

Other Ethiopians have different opinions. Kifle Wodajo, who served as a foreign minister under the Dergue, argues that given the pronouncements of some EPRP members and the advice their surrogates in the Dergue offered to the military council, the EPRP must have admired the Khmer Rouge idea of revolution and visited Democratic Kampuchea to take cues. The "anti-urban bias," of the civilian opposition groups and their advice to the Dergue "to close the Ethiopian fence" (seal off Ethiopia from the international public), bore some resemblance to Khmer Rouge revolutionary ideas and methods.[45] Given the contact with the Khmer Rouge, the ideological preoccupations of the EPRP such as its anti-American sentiment, its denunciation of the Dergue for not being radical enough and its condemnation of Vietnam for overthrowing "the legitimate government of Kampuchea" (the Khmer Rouge), it would not be unreasonable to suppose that had the EPRP acquired power in the turbulent days of 1976, it could have become more radical than the Dergue in its socialist programs and equally as murderous as the Dergue and the Khmer Rouge. Either the EPRP was grossly naive about the Cambodian revolution or it took Khmer Rouge propaganda too seriously.

OTHER FORMS OF TERROR

Arbitrary killings took place in Cambodia and Ethiopia. True, the Dergue's slogans such as "Revolutionary Motherland or Death," "Build the Revolution on the Graves of the Reactionaries" and the Khmer Rouge's categorization of real and imagined foes as "microbes," as well as the utterances of Pol Pot, motivated people to kill. But individuals took advantage of the permissive atmosphere of terror to settle old scores and kill as a form of momentary sport. In Ethiopia, men who were married to beautiful women, had the largest herds of cattle, owned expensive villas and cars became the chief targets of gun-totting peasants, party cadres and *kebelle* members.[46] In the Dergue's infamous detention center, *Bermuda*, one revolutionary cadre, Ayalew, found it personally gratifying to select individuals and groups for mock and actual executions. Similar things happened in Cambodia. There, it was dangerous to possess American dollars, to be well-educated, to own a car, a wrist watch or even a pair of sunglasses. These attributes of a better life came to be associated with the bourgeois tendencies that the Khmer Rouge intended to destroy.[47] Elizabeth Becker, however, cautions uncritical acceptance of these reports.

She views them as exaggerated suggestions of pervasive and irresistible state control over people's lives in revolutionary Cambodia.[48] However untrue many of these reports may appear, one cannot deny the fact that the permissive atmosphere of terror which the Khmer Rouge created led its loyal cadres to kill and intimidate without restraint and remorse.

Furthermore, Cambodian and Ethiopian students abroad transported their disagreements home when the revolutions took place and resolved them by extra-judicial killing.[49] Pol Pot's purging of Hou Yuon, with whom he had disagreed on ideological issues in their student days in France, mirrors the assassinations of former student leaders such as Haile Fida, Senaye Likke and Berhane Meskal during the White and Red Terror campaigns in Ethiopia in February 1977. Some of the people whose corpses literally choked the streets of Addis Ababa during the Ethiopian revolution were actually members of the student movement who had returned from France and the United States. Former student revolutionaries such as Haile Fida and Senaye Likke were killed in the 1970s, possibly by the EPRP. An EPRP newsletter described pro-Dergue intellectuals such as Haile Fida as "long a leader of the reformist wing of the Ethiopian Student Movement in Europe"; Mesfin Kassu as "a person very much known for betraying the Student Movement"; Senaye Likke as having stayed "for long period in USA where he stood in constant opposition to the Eritrean struggle"; Dr. Kedir Mohammed as "a reactionary who divided the students in the Middle East."[50]

The EPRP marked these former student-revolutionaries for elimination. Their killers were, possibly, their own colleagues with whom they had disagreed on aspects of Marxist ideology, Maoist revolutionary strategy, and on domestic policies such as the Eritrean secessionist question and foreign relations such as interaction with the Soviet Union, China and Albania. Khmer Rouge cadres and ordinary Cambodians killed Lon Nol soldiers in 1975, possibly without official permission. As Kiernan notes, in Battambang, in northwestern Cambodia, people took vengeance on "former landgrabbers."[51] In a manner similar to what happened in Battambang, Ethiopian peasants arbitrarily executed their former landlords without state authority in Wollo, in northeastern Ethiopia.[52]

CONCLUSION

Both the Dergue and the Khmer Rouge used extreme methods to achieve their revolutionary objectives. Their exclusionary ideologies and the nature of the resistance to them (poorly or well-organized) conditioned in different ways the course and outcome of terror in the two revolutionary societies. Failure to accommodate groups which did not share their worldviews meant that the Dergue and Angkar could only maintain security and pursue their brands of revolution by imposing their rule. But they differed in the manner in which they sought total control of their revolutionary societies. While the Pol Pot regime surged ahead with racial purges and rapid transformation of the fabric of social life, the Mengistu regime gave up radical social transformation for enforced national unity. But in the process of solidifying ethnic-unity-in-diversity, the Dergue annihilated its political opponents. Did the "ruthless power politics" and the "brutal domestic repression" that characterized the Ethiopian and Cambodian revolutions, and led to the deaths of many, constitute genocide and crimes against humanity? How can such crimes be proven and even be prosecuted?

NOTES

1. Quoted in Becker, *When the War Was Over: Cambodia and the Khmer Rouge Revolution*, 205. See also Kaufeler, *Modernization, Legitimacy, and Social Movement*, 12–13; Dunn, *Modern Revolutions*, xxiii–xxiv.

2. Marina and David Ottaway, *Ethiopia: Empire in Revolution*, 59, and Halliday and Mollyneux, *The Ethiopian Revolution*, 93.

3. Guillebaud, "Dergue's red terror," 11.

4. Weitz, *A Century of Genocide*, 163.

5. De Nike et al., *Genocide in Cambodia*, 11.

6. Interview with Tesfaye Mekasha, July 30, 1995.

7. Ben Kiernan, "Wild Chickens, Farm Chickens, and Cormorants," in *Revolution and Its Aftermath in Kampuchea: Eight Essays*, ed. David P. Chandler and Ben Kiernan, Monograph Series no. 25 (New Haven: Yale University Southeast Asia Studies, 1983), 141, 142–46, 147.

8. Author's interview with a group of 8 peasants at Wegel Tena, North Wollo Administrative Region, Ethiopia, October 12, 1995. See also Dawit, *Red Tears*, 269, 272.

9. *Abyot* (Information Bulletin of the EPRP) 1, no. 2 (January 30, 1976): 25.

10. John Markakis and Nega Ayele, *Class and Revolution in Ethiopia* (Nottingham: Spokesman, 1978), 154.

11. See *Abyot* [*Special Issue*] (February 1978): 4; *Abyot* 2, no. 3 (April 1977): 63.

12. Author's interview with Yeraswork Admassu, former *Me'ison* member and "middle-level militant," Addis Ababa, May 4, 1999.

13. Halliday and Molyneux, *The Ethiopian Revolution*, 133.

14. Halliday and Molyneux, *The Ethiopian Revolution*, 93, 198, and Marina and David Ottaway, *Ethiopia: Empire in Revolution*, 59.

15. Dawit, *Red Tears*, 115–16. See also Marina and David Ottaway, *Ethiopia: Empire in Revolution*, 87.

16. *Abyot* 1, no. 2 (January 30, 1976): 25.

17. For a detailed account of the Cham rebellions against the Khmer Rouge, see Kiernan, *The Pol Pot Regime*, 262–67.

18. Chandler, *Brother Number One*, 132, and also interview with Yeraswork Admassu.

19. Chandler, *Brother Number One*, 128, 131.

20. Anthony Barnett, Chanthou Boua and Ben Kiernan, "Bureaucracy of Death," *New Statesman* 99 (May 1980): 674; Kiernan, *The Pol Pot Regime*, 33.

21. Dawit, *Red Tears*, 18–19, 33.

22. Dawit, *Red Tears*, 33.

23. *Abyot* 1, no. 2 (January 30, 1976): 6.

24. Chandler, *Brother Number One*, 129, 130.

25. For detailed analysis of the Dergue's resettlement policies, see Kissi, "Famine and the Politics of Food Relief," 267–71, 280–85.

26. Dawit, *Red Tears*, 274.

27. Anthony Barnett, "Democratic Kampuchea: A Higher Centralized Dictatorship," in *Revolution and Its Aftermath*, 226.

28. Kiernan, *The Pol Pot Regime*, 250.

29. Kiernan, *The Pol Pot Regime*, 193, 213, 465, and Joanne Criddle and Teeda Butt Mam, *To Destroy You is No Loss: The Odyssey of a Cambodian Family* (New York: Atlantic Monthly, 1987), 162, 169.

30. Kiernan, *The Pol Pot Regime*, 193.

31. Clapham, *Transformation and Continuity*, 246.

32. Dawit, *Red Tears*, 117. See also Markakis and Ayele, *Class and Revolution*, 171.

33. Kissi, "Famine and the Politics of Food Relief," 242.

34. Barbara Harff and Ted Robert Gurr, "Systematic Early Warning of Humanitarian Emergencies," *Journal of Peace Research* 35, no. 5 (1998): 560, 567.

35. Author's interview with David Korn, former U.S. Chargé d'Affaires in Ethiopia, Washington, D.C., June 12, 1994.

36. Medhane Tadesse, "EPRP vs. TPLF: The Struggle for Supremacy Over Tigray, 1975–1978" (Paper presented for the Departmental Seminar of the Department of History, Addis Ababa University, June 29–July 2, 1995), 2, 5.

37. Canadian Broadcasting Corporation, "Interview with Ethiopia's Head of State [Mengistu Haile Mariam]," February 27, 1985, *World Food Programme Archives, Incoming Cables*, Addis Ababa, Ethiopia, April–July 1985.

38. I thank Tekalign Wolde Mariam, Department of History, Addis Ababa University, for sharing this information and translating the song for me.

39. Author's conversation with Kong Peng, Cambodian student, University of Oregon, USA, November 1999. See also Chandler, *Brother Number One*, 117, and Criddle and Butt Mam, *To Destroy You is No Loss*, 153.

40. Guillebaud, "The Dergue's red terror," 11, 12.

41. Criddle and Butt Mam, *To Destroy You Is No Loss*, 137; Ben Kiernan, "Implication and Accountability," *Bangkok Post* (Guest Column/Cambodia), January 31, 1999, and Ethiopian News Agency, *State-Terrorism On Trial: Genocide and Crimes Against Humanity, 100 Prosecution Eye-Witness Accounts* (Addis Ababa: Ethiopian News Agency, 1998), iv.

42. For EPRP statements on the Vietnamese invasion of Cambodia and the fall of the Khmer Rouge, see *Abyot* 4. no. 1 (January 1979): 32, and also *Abyot*, "Kampuchea: Extermination of A Nation," 4, no. 4 (December 1979): 1.

43. Kiflu, *The Generation, Part II*, 312.

44. Author's taped interview with Melaku Tegegne, former EPRP leader, Addis Ababa, May 3, 1999.

45. Author's taped interview with Kifle Wodajo, Addis Ababa, April 22, 1999.

46. Author's interview with Merera Gudina, former *Me'ison* member, Addis Ababa, April 17, 1999.

47. See Criddle and Butt Mam, *To Destroy You is No Loss*, 50, 149, 161.

48. Becker, *When the War Was Over: Cambodia and the Khmer Rouge Revolution*, 162.

49. Bahru, *A History of Modern Ethiopia*, 225–26; Kiernan, *The Pol Pot Regime*, 11; Becker, *When the War Was Over: Cambodia and the Khmer Rouge Revolution*, 202.

50. See *Abyot* 1, no. 3 (February–March 1976): 13.

51. Kiernan, *The Pol Pot Regime*, 212.

52. Author's taped interviews with 8 farmers including ex-peasant association leaders at Kutaber, North Wollo Administrative Zone, October 20, 1995.

5

DETERMINING AND
PROSECUTING GENOCIDE

Legal scholars and social scientists who study genocide distinguish between "genocide" and other atrocious crimes which are legally characterized as "crimes against humanity." The United Nations Genocide Convention (UNGC) of December 9, 1948 specified that genocide means:

> any of the following acts committed with intent to destroy, in whole or in
> part, a national, ethnical, racial or religious group . . . (a) by killing mem-
> bers of the group; (b) causing serious bodily or mental harm to members
> of the group; (c) deliberately inflicting on the group conditions of life cal-
> culated to bring about its physical destruction in whole or in part; (d) im-
> posing measures intended to prevent births within the group; [and] (e)
> forcibly transferring children of the group to another group.[1]

The intent to destroy a group is at the heart of the crime of genocide.
Genocide may overlap crimes against humanity. But Crimes Against
Humanity are legally defined, as in the 1998 Rome Statute of the Inter-
national Criminal Court, as:

> any of the following acts when committed as part of a widespread or sys-
> tematic attack directed against any civilian population, with knowledge of
> the attack: a) murder; b) extermination; c) enslavement; d) deportation or
> forcible transfer of population; e) imprisonment or other severe deprivation

of physical liberty in violation of fundamental rules of international law; f)
torture; g) rape, sexual slavery, enforced prositution, or any other form of
sexual violence of comparable gravity; h) persecution against any identifiable group or collectivity on political, racial, national, ethnic, cultural, religious, gender, . . . or other grounds that are universally recognized as im-
permissible under international law: . . . i) enforced disappearance of
persons; j) the crime of apartheid; [or] other inhumane acts . . . causing
great suffering, or serious injury to body or to mental or physical health.[2]

Systematic and organized persecution of civilians because of the victims'
alleged politics, race, or religion—and without the necessary genocidal
intent to destroy the victims' group—constitutes the essence of crimes
against humanity.

The UN Genocide Convention obliges its signatories to undertake to
prevent and punish genocide as the greatest crime against humanity. Having been a victim the use of poison gas against civilians, perpetrated by
Italy under Benito Mussolini in 1935–36, it is not surprising that Ethiopia
became sensitive to the need for international criminal law and was
among the first nations to ratify the UN Genocide Convention of December 1948 in July 1949. In 1951 Cambodia also assumed the obligations of the Genocide Convention by ratifyng it. But Ethiopia went further than Cambodia to redefine the legal concept of genocide broadly to
protect political groups left unprotected in the UN Genocide Convention.

GENOCIDE AND LAW: THE POLITICS OF JUSTICE

Eight years after ratifying the UN Genocide Convention, Ethiopia incorporated the basic ideas of the Convention into its national Penal
Code of 1957. In Ethiopian law, *Genocide and Crimes Against Humanity* are defined as acts committed "with intent to destroy, in whole or in
part, a national, ethnic, racial, religious or political group." Under the
Ethiopian Penal Code, individuals and groups may be guilty of "genocide or crimes against humanity" if, "in time of war or in time of peace,"
they organize, order or engage directly in:

1. killings, [or causing] bodily harm or serious injury to the physical
   or mental health of members of the [protected] group, in any way
   whatsoever; or

2. measures to prevent the propagation or continued survival of its members or their progeny; or

3. the compulsory movement or dispersion of peoples or children, or . . . placing [them] under living conditions calculated to result in their death or disappearance.[3]

Since ratifying the Genocide Convention, Cambodia and Ethiopia have joined those countries that have attempted to apply the provisions and ideas of that international legal instrument in domestic trials. In 1979, Cambodia, under a new leader Hun Sen, tried Pol Pot and Ieng Sary, two key leaders of the Khmer Rouge, for genocide and condemned both to death in a judicial process that made a mockery of justice and accountability. The "trial" appropriately characterized by international human rights law scholar William Schabas as "an exercise in public denunciation of a pair of brutal despots [Pol Pot and Ieng Sary]" was orchestrated by Vietnam, the Southeast Asian nation that had invaded Cambodia and ousted the Khmer Rouge.[4] This public denunciation took place at a time when the ousted Khmer Rouge government still controlled parts of Cambodia.

Since the 1979 show trial of Pol Pot and Ieng Sary for genocide, the pardoning of Ieng Sary by King Sihanouk in 1996 and the death of Pol Pot in 1998 by natural causes, there has been renewed interest in a serious international prosecution of senior and surviving leaders of the Khmer Rouge regime for crimes they committed between 17 April 1975 and 6 January 1979.[5]

The United States and the United Nations have championed this quest for an international criminal tribunal similar to those established for prosecuting perpetrators of genocide in Rwanda and the former Yugoslavia for the prosecution of the Khmer Rouge. Toward that end, the United States Congress passed the Cambodian Genocide Justice Act of 1994 making it "the policy of the United States to support efforts to bring to justice those accused of crimes against humanity in Cambodia."[6] U.S. support for an international trial of the Khmer Rouge initially came in the form of financial aid to Yale University's Cambodia Genocide Program headed by Ben Kiernan, and later Susan Cook, to document evidence of Khmer Rouge crimes for a future genocide trial.

Notwithstanding the problems posed by the amnesty already granted to some senior leaders of the Khmer Rouge including Ieng Sary by King Sihanouk, there are other serious impediments on the road towards justice in post-Khmer Rouge Cambodia. The current leaders of Cambodia, including Prime Minister Hun Sen, were themselves members of the defunct Khmer Rouge. The Hun Sen government demonstrated its reluctance to cooperate with an international tribunal by imposing certain conditions. It wanted prosecution of the crimes of the Khmer Rouge to be left to Cambodian prosecutors in Cambodian courts. But the United Nations insisted that any trial chamber, earning its support, be "international in nature."[7] The Hun Sen administration had wanted "international" participation to be limited to an "advisory" role.

The Hun Sen government even threatened to drag the United States into the judicial process should the UN insist on an "international" trial with more than an advisory role for itself. The post-Khmer Rouge Cambodian government initially wanted any international trial of the crimes of the Khmer Rouge to take account of the U.S. secret bombing of Cambodia, in the early 1970s, that many scholars agree aided the Khmer Rouge into power and also U.S. support of the Khmer Rouge at the United Nations and in the field even after Vietnam overthrew the Khmer Rouge regime in 1979. But, Washington wants any international trial of the Pol Pot regime to be limited to the period 1975–79, the time when the Khmer Rouge was in power. China, which provided the Khmer Rouge regime with financial and military aid when it was in power, and on the Thai frontier as we will note in the next chapter, had threatened to veto and impede the establishment of an international criminal tribunal for the prosecution of the crimes of the Khmer Rouge.[8] Beyond the politics, some Cambodians see a genocide trial, domestic or international, as setting a bad precedent that would not only inflame the passions of millions of Cambodians who lost relatives during the Khmer Rouge period, but also jeopardize "national reconciliation" considered necessary in a post-genocide society. However, on June 6, 2003, the United Nations and the Royal Government of Cambodia, Under prime Minister Hun Sen, agreed to establish a mixed tribunal known as "Extraordinary Chambers" to try surviving members of the Khmer Rouge. That agreement came into force on April 28, 2005. Thus, it has taken 27 years, since the Khmer Rouge was overthrown, for the post-Khmer Rouge government of Cambodia and the "international community" to negotiate a mutually acceptable legal framework for prosecuting the crimes of the Khmer Rouge. The tribunal has been described by UN Secretary-General Kofi Annan as a trial chamber that would meet both "Cambodia's needs for justice" and the UN's interest in "international standards" of prosecution.[9] Unlike the Ethiopian High Court, as we shall soon see, which consists mainly of Ethiopian lawyers, the proposed genocide tribunal for Cambodia would have Cambodian lawyers, to be appointed by the United Nations. To the extent that the Cambodian mixed tribunal bears any similarity to its Ethiopian counterpart, it is that the proposed tribunal in Cambodia would operate "within the existing court structure of Cambodia." But unlike the Ethiopian genocide court, the Cambodian mixed genocide tribunal would limit the scope of its investigation and trial to only "senior leaders of democratic Kampuchea and those who were responsible for the crimes . . . committed during the period from 17 April 1975 to 6 January 1979." And the maximum penalty the Cambodian tribunal can impose for convictions of crimes within its jurisdiction is life imprisonment and not death as in the Ethiopian court.

The proposed mixed tribunal for the Khmer Rouge crimes is expected to begin in 2006 and operate for a period of three years. But its operations are contingent on the availability of funds to pay for the tribunal's staff and other related activities. Staffing and other trial expenses, for the three-year session of the tribunal, are estimated to cost about $56.3 million. That huge cost is to be borne by the government of Cambodia and the United Nations. The Cambodian government would contribute $13.3 million and the United Nations would raise $43 million through "voluntary" donations from its member states. From a comparative perspective, there have been more vigorous international and monetary assistance for a genocide trial in post-Khmer Rouge Cambodia than there have been for a similar trial in post-Dergue Ethiopia. As of March 2005, several countries including Japan, Canada, Germany, Luxembourg, Austria, the United Kingdom and France had pledged $38.48 million as the UN's contribution towards the establishment and operation of the Cambodian mixed tribunal. The United States has, so far, not pledged any money toward the tribunal, but U.S. government officials have pointed to the $7 million that Washington has spent since 1994 toward research and documentation of the crimes committed by the Khmer Rouge. In terms of Cambodia's financial contributions to the setting up of the tribunal, not much progress has, so far, been made. In March 2005, the Cambodian government announced that it will not be able to pay its 13.3 million contribution to the total cost of the tribunal. The government is hoping to be able to meet that financial obligation under the tribunal agreement through domestic and international fund-raising campaigns. Arguably, the Cambodian government, which had wanted to drag the United States into the trial process in the hope of embarrassing it for American policies that aided the Khmer Rouge, would not be looking to Washington for financial donations. That is because in its Foreign Assistance Appropriation Act of 2005, the U.S. congress has tied any further American financial aid for the Cambodian tribunal to certification by the U.S. State Department that "Cambodia's judiciary is competent, independent, free from . . . corruption, and its decisions are free from interference by the executive branch.[10] Thus, as Etcheson put it "the politics of achieving justice in Cambodia" has "intersected" with the interests of Cambodians as well as international actors.[11] The situation is a bit different in Ethiopia, but equally complicated.

Unlike Cambodia, the defendants in Ethiopia are no longer active and do not control any part of the country. In May 1991, when Ethiopia's repressive military junta was ousted, the successor regime, the Ethiopian Peoples Revolutionary Democratic Front (EPRDF), a coalition of former armed groups that opposed the Dergue organized by the TPLF, established a Central High Court to try Ethiopia's former head of state Mengistu Haile Mariam, who fled into exile in Zimbabwe, thirty-seven of his top officials, and many supporters and mid-level bureaucrats of the ousted regime, for "genocide" and "crimes against humanity."

The genocide trial in Ethiopia is not being conducted under the international law of genocide which excludes protection of political groups, but under Ethiopia's domestic law on genocide and crimes against humanity which criminalizes the destruction of groups on grounds of their political beliefs. The charges against the Dergue are contained in eight-thousand pages of legal documents. In them, the Ethiopian Court alleges that the Dergue jailed, tortured and ordered the killing of members of opposition political groups and caused "bodily harm or serious [physical and mental] injury" to their leaders and supporters. The Court has further charged the Mengistu regime with placing members of the targeted political group "under living conditions calculated to result in their death or disappearance" and "under confinement that caused them social harm."[12]

Ethiopia's genocide trial is a significant test case of the evolving domestic and international law on the prosecution and punishment of the crime of genocide. It also has broader implications for the definition of genocide in the twenty-first century. The trial could also answer questions that scholars of genocide studies continue to raise about the relationship between broader state objectives and the specific conduct of state officials. Ethiopian domestic law on genocide and crimes against humanity holds criminally responsible for genocide the following categories of people. First, higher government officials who authorize extrajudicial killings. Second, lower-level bureaucrats who carry them out or kill on their own without state authority. Third, ordinary people who openly support extra-judicial killings even if they did not directly or actively participate in them.[13]

As of June 2004, nearly 6,426 defendants, including Ethiopia's ousted head of state Mengistu Haile Mariam, thirty-seven of Mengistu's higher government officials and a large number of ordinary citizens have been charged with genocide and crimes against humanity. Mengistu and nearly 3,000 indictees are being tried in absentia. All the defendants are answering charges that they ordered, participated in or supported the Dergue's infamous Red Terror assassination campaign of the mid-1970s against opposition political groups. In Ethiopian law, the crime of genocide is punishable by imprisonment from five years to life or, in cases of exceptional gravity, death.

While a credible trial of the surviving members of the Khmer Rouge has become a casualty of domestic and international politics, the ongoing trial of the leaders of the Dergue has become a major problem in the domestic politics of post-Mengistu Ethiopia. It is not the 1,569 decisions so far handed down, the 1,017 convictions that led to various prison terms or even the six death sentences passed that have stirred up emotions among the defendants, human rights activists and scholars of genocide studies about the trial. Rather, it is the length of time that this ten-year-old trial has taken. In the course of the ten years, forty-three of the accused persons have died in prison. The trial has also proceeded at an erratic pace. It was suspended in 2002 and resumed in November 2003. The prosecutors attribute the suspension and the slower pace of the trial to the arduous task of gathering evidence on crimes committed nearly thirty years ago.

What further complicates this particular trial is the fact that not only the Dergue but also its opponents—the surviving victims of those political killings including former TPLF leaders now in power in Addis Ababa—engaged in the same atrocities under prosecution. They killed unarmed civilians they perceived as assisting their enemies (the Dergue, *Me'ison* and EPRP). In February 2004, thirty-three surviving members of the Dergue in detention and awaiting trial wrote to Ethiopia's Prime Minister Meles Zenawi, a former leader of the TPLF, requesting state funds to prepare their defense. The accused former officials pointed to the thirty-year time lapse of their alleged crimes, the deaths of some of their witnesses and the irony that only "surviving . . . supporters of one side" in a political conflict over power are facing prosecution as reasons for seeking clemency or abrogation of their trial.[14] Herein lies the problem that Robert Cribb has identified. That in considering and prosecuting politically-motivated killing as genocide, students and scholars of genocide studies would face the unpleasant moral dilemma of assessing the roles of both victims and perpetrators in precipitating the conflict or power struggle that resulted in large scale massacres.

SCHOLARS AND GENOCIDE

The application of domestic law in the Ethiopian genocide trial reinforces the views of sociologists Leo Kuper, Helen Fein and Kurt Jonassohn, historian Frank Chalk and psychologist Israel Charny that the United Nations erred by excluding the protection of political groups from the Genocide Convention, and creating negative implications for the protection of human rights.

Kuper has noted that "political affiliation can be as permanent and as immutable as racial origin," hence political differences in human societies are just "as significant a basis for . . . annihilation as racial, national, ethnic or religious differences." After all, as Kuper observes, it is political conflicts that trigger genocide against the ethnic, racial, national and religious groups that the Genocide Convention protects. Therefore, separating political victims from ethnic and racial victims is "impossible."[15] Kuper is not alone in seeking a broader definition of genocide that protects political groups. Frank Chalk's and Kurt Jonassohn's research definition of genocide as "a form of one-sided mass killing in which a state or other authority intends to destroy a group, as that group and membership in it are defined by the perpetrator" is significant for understanding what happened in Cambodia.[16] Chalk and Jonassohn argue that it is the perpetrator's definition of the victim group that should matter in determining and prosecuting genocide because quite often the perpetrator's ideology or worldview redefines and converts ethnic, national, racial and religious groups into political enemies which the perpetrator then targets for destruction. Their classification of genocide according to the motives of the perpetrators: "to eliminate a real or potential threat, to spread terror among real or potential enemies, to acquire economic wealth or to implement a belief, a theory, or an ideology" is very instructive.[17]

Helen Fein offers a nuanced position on the scholarly debate on genocide that reinforces Kuper's point, but raises questions about Chalk and Jonassohn's formulation. Fein agrees with Kuper that political beliefs, like ethnic and religious identities, are also stable and permanent attributes or characteristics that can be inherited or passed on from generation to generation. Helen Fein cautions scholars who study genocide about how far they should go to broaden their conception of victim groups. As Fein argues, by seeking to include perpetrators' arbitrary and changing criteria for defining victim groups in the discussion of what constitutes victim groups, Frank Chalk and Kurt Jonassohn overlooked the stable and definite criteria of victim group membership and, therefore, missed the key difference between genocide (the destruction of "real collectivities") and state-terror (the "intimidation" of "groups constructed by the paranoid imaginations of despots"). Fein concludes that victims of genocide are selected by perpetrators because they "are members of a collectivity" that is stable and identifiable. The victim groups in a genocide situation are often defenseless and persecuted on a sustained basis regardless of whether they resist or surrender. Helen Fein calls the killing of political opponents during revolutions by perpetrators for the sake of preserving their unchallenged as "despotic genocide."[18]

For psychologist Israel Charny, determining genocide is a moral judgement that human beings should make and not a legal battle to be waged by lawyers and scholars. Charny has suggested that the sanctity of every human life requires a broader definition of genocide that treats all cases of mass murder as genocide. For this moral purpose, Charny has proposed a "generic definition of genocide" as "the mass killing of substantial numbers of human beings, when not in the course of military action against the military forces of an avowed enemy, under conditions of the essential defenselessness and helplessness of the victims."[19] Similar to Helen Fein's description of political mass murder as a form of despotic genocide, Charny has argued that each instance of mass murder should be assigned to one or more subcategories so that over the course of time new categories of genocide can be created.

Political scientists Barbara Harff, and Ted Robert Gurr have created the word, "politicide" to distinguish "political mass murder" or deliberate annihilation of political groups (which in my view occurred in Ethiopia) from intentional killings of ethnic, racial, national and religious groups or genocide (which occurred in Cambodia).[20] The relevance of Harff's and Gurr's conception of politicide for a comparative study of what happened in Ethiopia and Cambodia lies in the most recent expansion of the concept of politicide by Barbara Harff. As she now acknowledges, the state is not the only perpetrator of genocide or politicide. That, indeed, "non-state actors can and do attempt to destroy rival ethnic and political groups." Thus, Harff's revised definition of genocide and politicide sees both crimes as "the promotion, execution, and/or implied consent of sustained policies by governing elites or their agents—or in the case of civil war, either of the contending authorities—that are intended to destroy, in whole or part, a communal, political or politicized ethnic group."[21] This is important for understanding the Ethiopian case.

Like Chalk and Jonassohn, Harff and Gurr contend that a clear distinction between "genocide" and "politicide" is very difficult to make. That is because very often the victims of both crimes are "ethnically defined and politically active; or defined in terms of political affiliation or class but not necessarily active."[22] For example, in revolutionary Cambodia the murder of defenseless groups of people on grounds of their political beliefs and socio-economic class accompanied the killing of equally defenseless groups because of their ethnicity and religious beliefs. But in Ethiopia, the distinction was clear. Racial or ethnic killings did not accompany the targeting of active, organized and armed political opponents. Hence, Chalk's and Jonassohn's research definition of genocide as "a one-sided mass killing" does not fit the Ethiopian situation of mutual massacres by well-armed opponents struggling for power in the context of war and revolution. Neither the Dergue nor its armed opponents were "defenseless" and "helpless." Here is where a clearer definition of political groups (active and inactive) can make an important contribution to genocide studies.

There are other scholars who accept the standard definition of genocide in the UN Genocide Convention as adequate and reasonable and argue against broadening it. These scholars include historian Ben Kiernan who has consistently applied the UN definition of genocide to his studies of the crimes of the Khmer Rouge. International human rights law scholar William Schabas is even more emphatic in his view that "undesirable consequences" might result from "enlarging or diluting the definition of genocide." As Schabas argues, "[t]he broader and more uncertain the definition [of genocide], the less responsibility States will be prepared to assume."[23]

The Vietnam-orchestrated public denunciation of Pol Pot and Ieng Sary in 1979, the proposed, mixed tribunal for the Khmer Rouge and the ongoing genocide trial in Ethiopia, as noble as they are, have generated intense controversy. The controversy revolves around the nature of the crimes (genocide or otherwise) that occurred in Ethiopia and Cambodia, and whether the UN Genocide Convention is the sole authority for determining genocide and punishing its perpetrators. Besides examining these controversies, the task of a comparative study of the Ethiopian and Cambodian cases of organized killing of groups should also include a resolution of other controversies raised in the literature on the Mengistu and Pol Pot regimes.

THE CONTROVERSIES

The historiography of the Cambodian revolution is plagued by three controversies. The first is a disagreement over the intent of the killings in Cambodia, that is, whether or not the Khmer Rouge deliberately planned to kill the 1.7 to 3 million Khmers and other ethnic, religious and national groups who are estimated to have been killed during the revolution as part of a declared or disguised official policy of annihilation. The second is a disagreement over state involvement in or direction of the killings, that is, whether the central government was even aware of the killings. The third is the nature of these atrocities, that is, whether they constitute genocide as strictly defined in international law or just random acts of murder.

Michael Vickery, Serge Thion and David Chandler do not believe that the Khmer Rouge leadership knew about or ordered the terror and killings in Cambodia. Therefore, they question the charge of genocide against the Pol Pot regime. Vickery argues that the conventional characterization of revolutionary Cambodia as a "killing field" is grossly misinformed. He does not deny that political violence and killings took place in revolutionary Cambodia, but he challenges the "stereotype" that the Khmer Rouge intentionally committed these horrors as part of a planned program of genocide against particular groups. Vickery asks: "Was it objective natural conditions, caprice of individual cadres, or the result of [official] policy; if it were the latter, what was central policy, and how was it modified or distorted at lower levels?"[24]

Like Vickery, Chandler agrees that "a million Cambodians, or one in eight, died from warfare, starvation, overwork, misdiagnosed diseases, and executions." But he argues that "[m]ost of these deaths . . . were never intended. . . ."[25] David Chandler also contends that labeling Pol Pot as a "genocidal fascist," or a "genocidal communist," and comparing him to Adolf Hitler has no explanatory value beyond making Pol Pot "a household word synonymous with genocide, chaos, and everyone's worst fears of communism." Chandler attributes the terror and executions in Cambodia under Pol Pot to the "amateurism," "ignorance," and "wishful thinking" of the Khmer Rouge. For Chandler, the deaths in revolutionary Cambodia were the unintended consequences of a revolution in which:

> lower ranking cadres and officials fearful of reprisals, struggled to apply what they took to be the exigencies of [official plans and] made unworkable demands on the people under them on whose behalf the revolution was ostensibly being waged. The speed at which the plan was implemented led to the deaths of thousands of citizens.[26]

Like Vickery and Chandler, Serge Thion disputes suggestions of Khmer Rouge direction and supervision of the killings. He does not see the Khmer Rouge leadership as having wielded the kind of absolute control required for the commission of these atrocities. According to Thion, the entire Cambodian society was "riddled with political factions, military *camarillas*, regional powers, all contending for influence and the purging of rival forces." As a result of factionalism, the Pol Pot regime never came close "to having complete control over the national economy, the state power system, the army, the party, and . . . even the state security office, S-21 [Tuol Sleng]."[27] If the situation Thion describes were true and a struggle for power between armed political factions served as the context of the killing in Cambodia, the situation would be comparable to what happened in Ethiopia under the Dergue. Under those circumstances, the killing of active and armed opponents in a domestic war by the Khmer Rouge would not constitute genocide.

Anthony Barnett and Ben Kiernan disagree with Vickery, Chandler and Thion. They contend that revolutionary Cambodia was tightly controlled by the Khmer Rouge leadership. While Barnett and Kiernan acknowledge that not every single execution in Cambodia was planned, given the spontaneous actions that often occurred, they do not see spontaneity and arbitrariness or differences in zonal implementation of policy as evidence of a lack of central direction of affairs. In the view of Barnett, the differences in zonal implementation of policy which Vickery, Chandler and Thion point to were inevitable, because they demonstrated the varying degree of zeal with which cadres, invested with power by the center to act, acted. Beneath what appears to Serge Thion as "a bloody mess," Barnett sees a "remarkable degree of [order and] uniformity." And the uniform policies included the evacuation of towns, abolition of money, elimination of private property, restrictions on cultural practices and "enforced confiscation of food from the producers." The "killings and the starvation in Cambodia," in the view of Barnett, were "primarily the consequences of general regulations imposed successfully throughout the country, and of the deliberate extension of the state's absolute control on a sector by sector basis."[28] Kiernan sees Barnett's analyses as "closest to the truth." In Kiernan's view, the Khmer Rouge leadership achieved "unceasing and increasingly successful top-down domination" and accumulated power that was "unprecedented." He sees revolutionary Cambodia as a society that was "tightly organized and controlled" and a state that was "much more omnipotent" than Vickery, Thion and Chandler have observed.[29]

If Kiernan and Barnett are correct, then how does one characterize the killings in a tightly-controlled Cambodia under the powerful Khmer Rouge. Here too, the opinions differ. The editors of the *Black Book of*

Communism, a book that explores the bloody history of Communist ideologies, would equate the crimes of the Khmer Rouge, as well as the
Dergue, to the repression, genocide and terror that, in their view, have
"always been . . . the basic ingredients of modern Communism."[30] From
this theoretical premise, Vickery, Chandler and Thion would seem then
to have an ideological agenda in denying the prevalence of terror and
mass murder in Marxist and Communist philosophy and revolutionary
practice. The same agendas would also seem to color the interpretations
of other scholars about Mengistu's revolution in Ethiopia. But such con-
clusions would be more a partisan ideological judgment than an objective analysis of the facts. In the Cambodian case, Vickery, Chandler and
Thion are not alone in expressing skepticism about the characterization
of the crimes of the Khmer Rouge as genocide.

Human rights law scholar William Schabas has raised some serious
questions about the relationship between the crimes of the Khmer
Rouge and genocide as defined in international law. In his review of
Genocide in Cambodia, a compilation and analysis of documents from
the "trial" of Pol Pot and Ieng Sary, edited by Howard J. De Nike, John
Quigley and Kenneth J. Robinson, William Schabas argues that "the evidence of genocide," as presented by the editors of the volume, is "un-
convincing." Schabas sees "destruction of religious institutions" and
"forced assimilation of populations" in revolutionary Cambodia as "acts
of cultural, not physical, genocide." And since cultural genocide is not
part of the definition of genocide in the Genocide Convention, Schabas
concludes that from a strict legal interpretation of the UN Genocide
Convention, besides the persecution of the Muslim Cham and the Buddhist monkhood, "there isn't much left on which to hang the accusation
of genocide against the Khmer Rouge."[31] Legal scholars Steven Ratner
and Jason Abrams agree with Schabas. They have also concluded from
their study of the Pol Pot regime that "the bulk of the terror [in revolutionary Cambodia] did not qualify as genocide."[32]

The debate on the Ethiopian revolution is not over state involvement
or whether the central government deliberately planned and directed the
killing. That is viewed by many Ethiopians as undisputable. The disagreement is also over three issues. First, the overall intent of the Dergue's
killings. Second, the nature of the crimes in law. Third, the narrow definition of the perpetrators in court.

The U.S. Government which has offered legal and financial assistance to facilitate the "genocide" trial in Ethiopia, believes the Dergue's crimes have the requisite intent to constitute genocide under both international and Ethiopian law. The U.S. Senate Foreign Relations subcommittee on Africa reached that conclusion as far back as August 1976. At that time, Congress criticized the Dergue for burning villages suspected of having assisted the opposition movement, EPLF, and cited the interferences of the Dergue with food and medical relief, earmarked for about 400,000 Eritrean civilians in Sudan in 1975, as actions "verging on genocide." Congress also viewed the Dergue's torture of its political opponents, "summary executions," "mass arrests [of people] without cause," and "bombing of civilian marketplaces"—crimes that meet the legal definition of war crimes and crimes against humanity—as clear evidence of state-organized genocide.[33] The *Wall Street Journal* was even more emphatic in describing extra-judicial killings and other forms of persecution such as forcible resettlement of groups in Ethiopia as a "Holocaust," a charge that equated the Dergue to the Nazi regime.[34]

Those who dispute the characterization of the Dergue's crimes as "genocide" point to their implication as racial, religious or ethnic killing and the focus on the Dergue or the Ethiopian revolutionary state as the sole perpetrator. The American journalist, John Ryle, has argued that:

> on the face of it, the genocide charge seems odd. The Dergue was undoubtedly responsible for terrible crimes, but it was not, in any ordinary sense, guilty of genocide: it did not—at least not during the Red Terror [1976–1977] kill people on the grounds of race or creed.[35]

Merera Gudina, an Ethiopian of Oromo ethnicity and a former member of the opposition political group, Me'ison, who was arrested and tortured by the Dergue, agrees with Ryle. In his view, the Dergue's killing campaigns transcended the boundaries of ethnicity as well as class and gender. John Ryle, Merera Gudina, and a substantial number of Ethiopians who condemn the Dergue's atrocities, but reject the characterization of them as genocide, point to the arbitrary and shifting targets of state-terror in revolutionary Ethiopia. They argue that the Dergue did not discriminate in its killings. It targeted children as tender as ten and thirteen years of age—minors whom the regime considered as EPRP operatives.

Other commentators on the Ethiopian revolution see a mirror image of Democratic Kampuchea in Socialist Ethiopia. Robert Kaplan, the journalist, has argued that "the manner in which Ethiopians died evoked the well-known slaughter of millions of Cambodians by the Khmer Rouge. . . ."[36] Critics of such comparisons such as Merera caution that the Mengistu regime was similar to the Khmer Rouge only in terms of its ruthless annihilation of political opponents. Distinctly, the Mengistu regime was motivated more by a desire to stay in power than an intent to exterminate the ethnic populations of the political groups which opposed it. Although the war in northern Ethiopia took a toll on the Tigrinya-speaking populations in Eritrea and Tigray, in real ethnic terms, Merera argues, more Amhara people (members of the EPRP) died in the hands of the Dergue than any other ethnic group.[37]

Other critics of the charge of genocide against the Dergue focus their criticisms on the restrictive or narrow conception of the "perpetrators" in the Ethiopian case. They contend that the EPRP, the TPLF, and all the armed groups, which opposed and eventually overthrew the Dergue, killed deliberately, indiscriminately and ruthlessly as the Dergue did. Ethiopian scholar Hagos Gebre Yesus describes what happened in revolutionary Ethiopia as "national nihilism" in which the Dergue stands as guilty of murder against its political opponents as those opponents [EPRP, TPLF, OLF, ALF, WSLF, EDU and Me'ison] do against the Dergue.[38] Many Ethiopians the author spoke with in 1999 who share Hagos' view saw nothing but "vengeance" behind the motivations of the TPLF-led EPRDF's trial of the members of the regime it ousted for genocide.

The contentious debates over the intent of the killings, extent of state direction of them and the character of these crimes in revolutionary Ethiopia and Cambodia only highlight the efforts of scholars and other commentators to distinguish between genocide and other crimes against humanity. But what really are the facts?

THE FACTS: DEFINING THE EXPENDABLE

Chalk and Jonassohn contend that the perpetrators' definitions of the victims matter more than the definition of the victim groups in the UN Genocide Convention. In Ethiopia and Cambodia, the Khmer Rouge and the Dergue defined the boundaries of the groups to be destroyed. The process of destroying them was systematic and selective in Cambodia. Some random and arbitrary killings took place in Ethiopia, but most of the state-directed political murders were planned. The disparity could be attributed to the different degree of opposition and insecurity that the two regimes faced. The Dergue's Revolutionary Defense Squads (*nebelbals*) and Revolutionary Campaign Directorate (*Abyotawi Zemecha Memrea*) defined many of the people they murdered as "bandits," "puppets of imperialism," "counter-revolutionaries," "anti-unity" and "anti-Ethiopia elements."[39] These are what Helen Fein calls groups constructed by the paranoid imaginations of despots. In reality, these categories of "enemies" to be destroyed were broad and arbitrary enough to permit the Dergue's cadres the discretion to settle their own personal scores.

The first victims of the Angkar's vision of a "new" and "pure" revolutionary society were those Cambodians who had been associated with the Lon Nol regime. In late 1975 and early 1976, the Khmer Rouge hunted down and liquidated former soldiers, policemen and officials of the deposed military regime. These are clear cases of politically-motivated murder of opponents who were no longer active or in power. As the revolution progressed, the Khmer Rouge broadened the boundaries of the groups to be destroyed to include particular classes of Cambodians and specified national groups. Among them were the Communists trained in North Vietnam whose minds the Khmer Rouge leadership could not control, and foreigners it deemed undesirable in the new society.[40] Other targets were the city people, categorized as *new people*. This group comprised men, women, girls, boys, and babies who did not live in Khmer Rouge "liberated zones" during the civil war. Because they lived in enemy territory during the war, the Khmer Rouge did not only suspect their loyalty, but also regarded them as contaminated and, therefore, expendable in the new revolutionary society.

The *new people*, and Cambodia's peasants, bore the brunt of the Pol Pot regime's utopian objective of making a "Super Great Leap Forward" in agricultural production. This ideologically-defined group of Cambodians provided the labor force for building the massive irrigation dikes, maintaining rice fields and constructing dams and villages in malaria-infested areas. Many perished under these hazardous conditions. Others died of misdiagnosed and mistreated illnesses.[41] This is clear evidence of the imposition of conditions on groups calculated to bring about their eventual destruction. The peasants and the *new people* were

Cambodian citizens who could conveniently be viewed as the "national" group which the Genocide Convention protects. The expendable "national" groups also included Khmer "merchants" and "rich farmers" whom the Khmer Rouge perceived as having exploited Cambodia's peasants. The revolutionary regime did not spare intellectuals, doctors, lawyers, monks, teachers, and civil servants whose western education marked them, in Khmer Rouge anti-Western ideology, as impure class of Khmers. In short very few Cambodians escaped the determination of the Khmer Rouge to build the world's purest and most perfect society. From Chalk's and Jonassohn's research definition of genocide, one could argue that Khmer Rouge ideology of purity converted doctors, merchants and other members of the Cambodian ethnic group into political enemies to be destroyed. Only Pol Pot and his French-educated group of Cambodian communists escaped the slaughter of western-educated intellectuals, the supposedly contaminated.

The Khmer Rouge also targeted religious and ethnic groups such as Monks, Muslims, Christians, Chams, Chinese, Vietnamese, and foreign nationals "mainly Thai and Lao" for annihilation.[42] An intent to "wipe out religion" from the new society is evident in the persecution of Buddhist monks and Muslim clerics, the dominant religious groups. Through outright massacres, and other forms of persecution such as the disrobing of monks and closure of Buddhist temples, the Khmer Rouge succeeded in eliminating a substantial number of monks and undermining the bases of their faith. According to Ben Kiernan, by the end of the Cambodian revolution in January 1979, "fewer than 2,000 of Cambodia's 70,000 monks" had survived. Apart from the numbers killed, the timing of the killings was also suggestive of the intent of the Khmer Rouge leadership. The assault on the monkhood took place early in the revolution and the process of extermination was swift and massive, judging from a September 1975 party document which lauded the regime's "ninety to ninety-five percent" success in eradicating "the foundation pillars of Buddhism."[43]

The different scope of persecution of religious groups in Ethiopia, as compared to Cambodia, is instructive. The Dergue intimidated only a handful of religious groups, but did not zealously exterminate them as the Khmer Rouge did. On the issue of targeting religious groups, the Dergue proved to be more selective than the Khmer Rouge. The revolutionary regime in Ethiopia "requisitioned" the land and other property of the Orthodox Church in the insurgent province of Eritrea. The intent was political: to redistribute church property in the insurgent province to supporters of the Dergue's national unity ideology. The search for total power in Eritrea aimed at weakening support for the EPLF. In Wollo, in northeastern Ethiopia, overzealous local Dergue cadres intimidated, but did not kill, the clergy of the Mekane Yessus Church, a Protestant denomination. The cadres "feared [the Church] as an undesirable competitor . . . for peasant loyalty." Here, it was political power rather than anti-religious ideology that motivated the Dergue. Ironically, Ethiopia's Orthodox and Protestant churches "experienced unusual growth in membership" despite these isolated instances of harassment. More than 300,000 Christians took part in the famous Kulubi pilgrimage in honor of St. Gabriel and "ten times as many people participated in the Ethiopian Orthodox Church's Maskal festival" during the revolutionary period as compared to the decade preceding the revolution. Ulrich Meister is, therefore, correct in arguing that "it would be a gross exaggeration to speak of a general persecution of religion" in revolutionary Ethiopia.[44] In the same way, despite the fierce repression of ethnic insurgencies, it would be an exaggeration to speak of a general persecution of ethnic minorities in "Communist" Ethiopia. That certainly cannot be said of Cambodia under Pol Pot.

The physical fate of ethnic minorities under the Khmer Rouge was much worse than under the Dergue. The Khmer Rouge targeted for expulsion and directly massacred the entire Vietnamese population of Cambodia. Besides the Vietnamese who, undoubtedly, suffered a "campaign of systematic racial extermination," the Chinese suffered "the worst disaster ever to befall any ethnic Chinese community in Southeast Asia." By 1979, "only 200,000 Chinese" out of their population of 425,000, in 1975, had survived. Kiernan is very cautious in characterizing the Pol Pot regime's annihilation of the Chinese as racially-motivated. He suggests that the Khmer Rouge targeted the Chinese population in Cambodia because the party leadership viewed the predominantly urban Chinese as the "archetypal city dwellers" the revolutionaries intended to eliminate. Here, as Kiernan suggests, it was "geographic" origin more than racial identity that marked the Chinese as expendable enemies of a revolution that had an anti-urban ideology.[45]

Given the Pol Pot regime's ideological distaste for urban groups, viewed as an exploitative economic class, and the regime's abolition of money and markets, Kiernan is correct that the Chinese stood as the middlemen minorities who symbolized the kind of capitalism the Angkar intended to destroy in the new Cambodia. By profession, the Chinese were traders and money lenders. But it can also be argued that the Chinese population in Cambodia were targeted because they were Chinese. This is still racism, in my view. The Chinese were part of the racial groups whose existence the Khmer Rouge outlawed. Their language was banned and exposure of the Chinese in Cambodia to conditions of hunger and disease betrays an intent of the Khmer Rouge to stifle the survival and biological reproduction of the domestic Chinese as a racial and national group.

Like the Vietnamese, the Chinese and Buddhist monks, the Chams were targeted on grounds of their ethnicity and religion. About 100,000 of an estimated Cham population of 250,000, at the time the revolution in 1975, had perished by the time the Khmer Rouge was overthrown in January 1979. A decision of the Khmer Rouge leadership to "break up" the Cham people and impose upon them conditions inimical to their survival as an ethnic and religious group was made in early 1974. As Kiernan notes, "[t]heir distinct [Muslim] religion, language and culture, large villages, and autonomous networks threatened the atomized, [and] closely supervised society that the [Khmer Rouge] leadership planned."[46] Here was a religious group, as Barbara Harff and Ted Robert Gurr have pointed out, that was defined politically or seen by the Khmer Rouge as a political threat to the idea of a new, closely-supervised revolutionary society.

The Khmer Rouge regime attacked the communal characteristics of the Cham as a group, as well as the foundations of its faith as Muslims. The intent of the Khmer Rouge to destroy the Cham people by undermining their physical and spiritual well-being took such forms as forcing them to eat pork and raise pigs, collecting and destroying all copies of their religious text, the Koran, banning the Cham language, the traditional Cham sarong, the Islamic religion, closing of Cham schools and preventing Cham women from wearing their hair in the customary long style.[47] The Khmer Rouge used its overwhelming military might to crush the Cham people who resisted these policy impositions. It also "dispersed in small groups of several families" those who survived these overtly racial and religious assaults. Only 20 Cham community leaders, out of 113, survived the Cambodian revolution. And only 30 of the "more than one thousand Muslims who had made the pilgrimage to Mecca" survived. By the end of the Cambodian revolution, the Khmer

Rouge had also reduced the Thai minority population numbering 20,000 in 1975, "to about 8,000." And only 800 of the 1,800 families of the Lao ethnic minority group survived. The Khmer Rouge wiped out the entire 2,000 members of the Kola minority group.[48]

The overt racial killing that accompanied other politically-motivated murders in Cambodia went beyond the targeted individuals and groups to include members of their families. This is where the different social and cultural systems and also the political contexts in which the Cambodian and Ethiopian revolutions occurred shaped the choices that the Khmer Rouge and the Dergue made. In Khmer Rouge notions of justice and purity, those who associated with a "guilty person" were as equally tainted. Consequently, the targets for murder included the wives and orphaned children of the regime's "enemies." A compelling example was the murder of Cambodian Ambassador to Hanoi, Sien An and his wife.[49] Anthropologist Alexander Hinton has argued that Khmer Rouge determination to destroy whole families had its origins in "the Cambodian cultural model of disproportionate revenge." In the view of Hinton, the object of revenge in Cambodian culture is "to completely defeat the enemy." And the belief that "someone in the deceased foe's family [might] disproportionately avenge the death" encourages the killer to obliterate the line of the deceased. According to Hinton, the extreme violence of the Khmer Rouge period can be attributed to this "cultural model" of killing which the party leadership manipulated in its exhortation of cadres to settle their "class grudge." Here, a mixture of paranoia, and "emotionally salient" elements of Cambodian culture nurtured this excessive brutality.[50] Thus contrary to Vickery's arguments, Cambodia under Pol Pot earned its image in contemporary memory as a "killing field."

Ethiopia's revolutionary regime initially targeted a restricted class of political "enemies," mainly former officials of the Haile Selassie regime. The Dergue executed fifty-nine of them on November 23, 1974, after a general meeting at which the members of the Dergue "deliberated [and] agreed upon the execution."[51] In these early political killings, the Dergue spared the wives and family members of the officials. Where the Dergue thought family members of its political enemies posed a political threat as in the case of members of the imperial family, the military junta detained, but did not murder them. This is an important difference between the Dergue and the Khmer Rouge.

Ethiopian political scientist, Paulos Milkias has suggested that "[a]ltogether the number of people who were violently killed during the seventeen years of state terror in Ethiopia is no less than 2,000,000."[52] Here, it was not a social system or national culture of disproportionate revenge that spurred the killings. It was a political culture of unquestioned obedience to the state and its leader. With orders to kill, zealous state cadres took the extermination of the Dergue's political opponents as a heroic adherence to the regime's idea of "socialist patriotism." Violence and terror in revolutionary Ethiopia highlighted one fact. People were killed not for racial and religious reasons, but very often in the name of political slogans.

Ethiopia's "genocide" trial has overlooked one inescapable fact of the Ethiopian revolution and its relationship to mass murder. Jean-Claude Guillebaud, an eyewitness of the bloodiest period of the Ethiopian revolution, has accurately observed that although "the unprecedented repression unleashed by the military regime . . . [was] out of all proportion to the violence on the other side" of the power struggle, the "political murders" that took place in the course of the revolution were "not all the work of one side."[53] This is another distinguishing feature of the Ethiopian and the Cambodian revolutions. The killings in Cambodia were one-sided. Those in Ethiopia were not. Arguably, the *White Terror* campaign of assassination of Dergue officials and their supporters which the EPRP started in early 1976 partially triggered the Dergue's brutal *Red Terror* retaliatory killing spree. Certainly, the targets of the EPRP's infamous *White Terror* political murders were limited to Mengistu, who escaped several attempts on his life, officials of the Dergue, members of the Dergue's "revolutionary defence squads" (*nebelbals*) and officials of pro-Dergue "urban political associations" (*kebelles*) who had attained notoriety for their killing of EPRP sympathizers. The Dergue responded with what it called "Stalin's whip" or "a lesson in extermination" of the leaders, members and sympathizers of the EPRP.[54]

There is sufficient evidence about state authorization of political murders in revolutionary Ethiopia. The Mengistu regime officially sanctioned the Red Terror campaign of total liquidation of the EPRP as a political group in state Proclamation 121 of 1977. This was certainly the most systematic state-organized campaign of annihilation of political opponents in the history of Ethiopia. Between February 1977 and March 1979, the

Dergue issued "hundreds of orders" and "directives," to state agents and revolutionary cadres to kill. It also received "reports of summary executions," "torture and extra-judicial killings" of EPRP members.[55]

It is noteworthy that hundreds of the dead in Ethiopia did not fall at the hand of the Dergue alone, but also from that of political groups which opposed the Dergue. Again Guillebaud has accurately observed that part of "the terror and . . . encouragement to denunciation" that soaked the streets of Addis Ababa in blood between 1976 and 1977 stemmed from the settlement of private scores "which ha[d] nothing to do with the revolution."[56] The leaders and supporters of the EPRP labeled members of the TPLF as *tebaboch* (narrow nationalists) and "pass[ed] death sentences" on them. The TPLF in turn labeled the leaders and supporters of the EPRP as *Adisochu Neftengoch* (the new chauvinists) and marked them for annihilation. As Medhane Tadesse has observed, "killing and counter-killing" characterized the political relationship between the EPRP and the TPLF in 1976 and 1977. The TPLF "destroyed" the main EPRP political base in Assimba, in Tigray province, in northern Ethiopia. The EPRP also carried out death sentences on *Me'ison* members who cooperated with the Dergue labeling them as "bootlickers" and "*banda* intellectuals" (meaning collaborators and quislings).[57]

After eliminating the already weakened EPRP, the Dergue next turned its attention to the ethnopolitical groups. It imprisoned and tortured "hundreds of people belonging to the Oromo ethnic group" in Addis Ababa on grounds of being Oromo, and therefore, likely to have sympathies for the Oromo Liberation Front. The Dergue made similar arbitrary connections between Tigrinya-speaking people from the secessionist province of Eritrea and the Eritrean Peoples Liberation Front. By linking Tigrinya-speaking Ethiopians from Tigray—the closest linguistic kinsmen of the Eritreans—to the Tigrayan Peoples Liberation Front, the Dergue attempted to transform its persecution of political groups into mass murder of people on the basis of their biological affinity with members of ethno-political opposition groups.[58] The Dergue failed in this lethal enterprise.

Ethiopian historian Merid Wolde Aregay sees history and culture as the greatest obstacles to the Dergue's designs. He argues that historically, Ethiopians had known and accommodated murder on political and ideological grounds. Emperors Menelik, Tewodros and Haile Selassie had eliminated their opponents and used violence and coercion in their state-building enterprises without incurring popular wrath. But extermination of people on the grounds of their race and ethnicity in a multi-ethnic nation has been the moral threshold that Ethiopians have never crossed.[59] The idea of Ethiopia as a moral nation may be too much of a valorization of the ancient Christian monarchy. The Dergue failed to turn political mass killing (politicide) into genocide (ethnic, racial and religious killing) because of the political conditions, rather than the context of values, in which the soldiers conducted their revolution. Unlike the Khmer Rouge, the Dergue had no total control over Ethiopian society or monopoly over the instruments of terror to induce political compliance and societal acquiescence. Since the military junta faced intense domestic opposition to its power and legitimacy, consolidating political order required building alliances and popular support in Ethiopia's multi-ethnic society. Organized armed opposition limited the Dergue's scope of target groups to those who posed the greatest political threat to the military regime's quest for total control. That was a political decision and not a cultural choice.

BUREAUCRATIZING AND DOCUMENTING MURDER

Killing of the magnitude that occurred in Ethiopia and Cambodia could not have been accomplished without a coherent system of organization and documentation. The Dergue's and Khmer Rouge's killing machines had structures of command, methodologies of investigation and reporting mechanisms. The complex recorded mechanism of killing is significant proof of the intent of the Ethiopian and Cambodian states to destroy individuals and groups opposed to their ideology and power. Much of the terror and murder took place in state interrogation centers: clear evidence that the Khmer Rouge was just as aware of killing in Cambodia as the Dergue was in Ethiopia. The headquarters of the Dergue's terror was the well-known Central Investigation Organization in Addis Ababa, known as the Third Police Station. But the infamous and not well known torture center called *Bermuda* was where most of the killing of political opponents was done.[60] *Bermuda* reveals as clear evidence of state-directed murder as Tuol Sleng does in Cambodia.

Ethiopia's centers of interrogation functioned under the Ministry of State and Public Security (MSPS). The Dergue trained and armed local "revolutionary death squads" (*nebelbals*) and pro-Dergue Urban Dwellers Associations (*kebelles*). It also created a para-military group, the Dergue Special Forces (DSF), and put their activities under the Dergue Campaign Department (DCD). The DCD, which coordinated the affairs of the MSPS, the *nebelbals*, *kebelles* and the DSF, was itself under the command of the Dergue Standing Committee (DSC). The DSC was chaired by Mengistu himself. This elaborate bureaucracy of murder often worked effectively. On April 30, 1976, the Dergue Campaign Department ordered the Dergue Special Forces to eliminate anyone who participated in planned EPRP nation-wide protests against the Dergue on May Day. The DSF carried out this directive that led to the deaths of "hundreds" of young people in Ethiopia. The DSF also executed "fifteen to thirty youths" in each of the twenty-eight zones in Addis Ababa created by the Dergue to facilitate effective control of the capital city.[61] The Dergue's killing squads transported the corpses of the massacred to the morgue at the Menelik hospital in Addis Ababa and barred the families of the dead from claiming them unless they paid for the bullets used to kill the victims.

To perfect the state's killing machine, the Dergue brought trained interrogators from the former East Germany to assist in locating and crushing clandestine political movements and suspected dissidents. The Dergue Campaign Department specifically ordered its Ethiopian and German interrogators to torture EPRP members until they "confessed" or renounced their political beliefs.[62] Detailed files on prisoners and videotapes of torture and executions demanded from the death squads, and bureaucrats at torture centers, provided proof of implementation of state orders to torture or kill.

The Dergue demonstrated the intent to completely destroy its political enemies by following them across the borders of Ethiopia. Former Dergue Minister of the Interior, Colonel Tesfaye, has admitted that he headed state killing squads that followed political opponents who fled Ethiopia. One such killing squad named *Wolfgang* traced and murdered thirteen of the Dergue's political opponents exiled in the former East Germany. Another squad, *Umberto*, carried out similar assassinations of the Dergue's exiled political opponents in Rome.[63]

Although David Chandler disputes claims of state direction of the killing in Cambodia, he provides other evidence that appears to lend credence to Barnett's and Kiernan's view that the Khmer Rouge leadership directly ordered and tacitly encouraged mass murder. Chandler has noted that Pol Pot's speeches acquired "a more menacing tone" from 1977 onwards when he exhorted party cadres to eliminate "enemies," "traitors" and "ugly-microbes."[64] In the context of the culture of Cambodia described by Alexander Hinton, these exhortations could not have done anything less than incite murder or endorse it. There is also a link between the central government's determination to kill "traitors" and "ugly-microbes" and the rigorous documentation of "life histories" and "confessions" of enemies the party leadership sought and obtained from its bureaucrats.[65]

No evidence of central control and direction of the Pol Pot regime's campaigns of genocide is more compelling than David Chandler's study of the inner workings of the Tuol Sleng prison. Tuol Sleng was a former high school in the southern part of Phnom Penh which the Khmer Rouge turned into an interrogation and torture center. Chandler offers the most compelling evidence of the extent of awareness of the Khmer Rouge leadership about mass murder in revolutionary Cambodia. According to Chandler, Tuol Sleng was "an essential part of the [Khmer Rouge] regime" and "an officially supported operation" which generated the necessary documents and "confessions" to feed the "leadership's paranoia."[66] As the Dergue did, the Khmer Rouge required its bureaucrats at Tuol Sleng to compile lists of "confessions," type and tape record others and file them for verification. Kaing Kek Ieu (alias Deuch), director of Tuol Sleng, kept Pol Pot and other leaders of the Khmer Rouge informed about tortures, interrogations and executions at Tuol Sleng. The harrowing processes of torture at Tuol Sleng forced many victims to make false admissions of offenses against the state. That happened in Ethiopia too. The intent of bureaucratized murder in Ethiopia and Cambodia was to destroy every form of resistance and dissent. The Khmer Rouge succeeded in muzzling dissent. The Dergue could not.

THE KILLING METHODS: A CASE
OF INFLICTING BODILY HARM

Those interned at state interrogation centers in Ethiopia and Cambodia had a common experience of torture, on a substantial scale. Interrogation procedures were the same throughout Ethiopia and resembled some of the methods used at Tuol Sleng. Blindfolding, gagging of suspects, shackling of arms tied behind the back, suspending tied and shackled suspects on a table or from a ceiling were popular torture methods in revolutionary Ethiopia. Victims bound and suspended were beaten and left hanging for hours. If the victims did not die in this contorted position, their persecutors lashed the soles of their feet and later forced them to run on gravel or stones with their bruised feet to intensify the pain and suffering. Many collapsed and died or chose suicide to end physical agony. Others developed gangrened feet and slowly perished.

Dergue interrogators put other victims in barrels of dirty water or suffocated them with plastic bags over their heads, tied at the neck. Some were forced to lie on their backs and gaze directly at the sun and into bright lamps. Mock executions, removal of finger- and toenails, crushing of wrists with tightened handcuffs formed part of the string of torture methods. Prison guards frequently raped women suspects or killed them for rebuffing their sexual advances. Other interrogators inserted sticks and metal bars into the genitalia of women prisoners and suspended bottles of water from the testicles of male prisoners.[67] Those who were lucky to escape execution did so with permanent physical damage to parts of their body.

Democratic Kampuchea surpassed Socialist Ethiopia in its torture-methods. Some of the practices at Tuol Sleng appear to have had a more sinister motive than merely torturing victims to obtain "confessions." Three extraordinary torture methods recorded by Tuol Sleng bureaucrats border on bizarre experiments with human bodies:

"A 17-year old girl, with her throat cut and stomach slashed, put in water from 7.55 p.m. until 9.20 a.m., when the body begins to float slowly to the top, which it reaches by 11.00 a.m."

"A large old woman stabbed in the throat and her stomach slashed, put in water at 9.34 p.m., rises at 5 p.m. the next day."

"A young man, hands tied, put in water, rises to the top as the big woman
does. If his hands are not tied and he has been bashed to death, the body
rises to the top and turns over."[68]

These horrors are compounded by recent revelations that Khmer
Rouge cadres burned the people they killed and ground their charred
bones "with urine to make manure for the fields."[69] The Khmer Rouge
leadership knew and encouraged these atrocities. A Tuol Sleng memorandum which David Chandler cites, authorizes interrogators "to use
the hot method for prolonged periods," and even "if it kills . . . this
wouldn't be a violation of the Organization's rules."[70] Subordinates at
Tuol Sleng meticulously documented their killing methods and reported
their adherence to the Organization's rules. Chum Rithy, a 25-year-old
eyewitness to murder in Pol Pot's Cambodia, has testified that "the authorities [possibly the leaders of the Khmer Rouge or those who acted
of their behalf] bragged" about daily executions of people whom they regarded as tainted and, therefore, undesirable in the new Cambodia.[71]

EVACUATIONS AND RESETTLEMENT:
CASES OF TRANSFER OF GROUPS?

The Dergue and the Khmer Rouge both used evacuation and resettlement of people to achieve total control. The deaths which resulted from
the process of resettlement in Ethiopia and Cambodia have attracted
some comparisons. In January 1986, the *Wall Street Journal* characterized mass death of Ethiopians from the Dergue's resettlement program
as "government-organized group murder" which "shape[d] up as a mass
extermination on the order of the Khmer Rouge killing fields. . . ."[72]
While the process of resettlement in Ethiopia and Cambodia was similar, the scope and intent of the program in both countries was different.
The Dergue did not evacuate urban areas and relocate their populations
in the countryside with disastrous results as the Khmer Rouge did in
April 1975. However, it did resettle masses of perceived political dissidents from northern Ethiopia to the Southwest as the Khmer Rouge did
to the people of Cambodia's Eastern Zone which shared a boundary
with Vietnam.

There is a consensus among those who study Cambodia that the Eastern Zone—comprising the former provinces of Svay Rieng, Prey Veng, Eastern Kompong Cham, and the Chhlong district of Kratie—was the only place in revolutionary Cambodia where the 1.7 million inhabitants practised their religion, worked without control, ate a normal meal and dressed well.[73] Khmer Rouge cadres in the Eastern Zone had demonstrated a sense of independence during the evacuation of cities in April 1975 by treating evacuees more kindly. They had offered them medicines and food in contrast to the brutal and bellicose conduct of cadres from the Southwest. Demographically, the Eastern Zone had one of the largest populations. Economically, it was pivotal because of its rubber plantations and important rice-growing areas. The strategic location of the Zone as a border post gave it immense political significance as "the center of Vietnamese-Cambodian contacts."[74] In a revolutionary society where the Khmer Rouge wanted to achieve uniformity of policy, the distinctive character of the Eastern Zone caused the party leadership enormous displeasure. Pol Pot demonstrated that displeasure by sending loyal Southwestern troops to the Eastern Zone in May 1978 to bring the region in line with central government policies. The pacification or purification of the Eastern Zone, in 1978, took the form of direct massacres of cadres, heavier work schedules and deportations of "tens of thousands" of the inhabitants to the northwestern provinces.

Pol Pot's treatment of people from the Eastern zone differed and bore the closest resemblance, in recent memory, to the Holocaust. The Khmer Rouge leadership gave each Eastern Zone cadre evacuated to the northwestern province of Pursat a blue scarf, not as a token of honor or of loyalty to the state, but as a "sign" to distinguish them from other Khmers. The object of this unusual identification was to make cadres of the Eastern Zone more visible as the dissident and impure Khmers to be exterminated. Kiernan has estimated that in six months the Khmer Rouge wiped out more than 100,000 people, about one-seventeenth of the population of the Eastern Zone.[75]

The situation was different in Ethiopia. Certainly, resettlement formed a crucial part of the Dergue's methods of social control, but the soldiers did not invent it. Between 1957 and 1961, the Haile Selassie government settled people on "unused lands" as a means of expanding food production. Those resettlement programs, carefully managed by the state, had been supported and funded by the World Bank and USAID. They were voluntary in nature and involved moving peasants only a short distance from where they lived.[76] By contrast, the Dergue pursued a unique resettlement policy in the modern history of Ethiopia. The policy began early in the revolution, in 1975, and involved moving peasants and non-peasants over long distances and far away from where they lived. Due to the financial and political costs of resettling people amid mounting armed opposition to the Dergue, and the outrage of the resettlees over collectivization in the settlements, the military regime decelerated the program in 1979. But it resumed resettlement at the height of a nationwide famine in September 1984. Now, the Mengistu regime resolved to move 1.5 million people from northeastern Ethiopia, the hotbed of EPLF and TPLF opposition to the Dergue, to southwestern Ethiopia.[77] Mengistu gave the reasons for reviving and enforcing resettlement at an emergency meeting of party officials in February 1985:

> Almost all of you here realize that we have security problems. The guerrillas [EPLF, OLF, TPLF] operating in many of these areas do so with great help from the population. The people are like the sea and the guerrillas are like fish swimming in that sea. Without the sea there will be no fish. We have to drain the sea, or if we cannot completely drain it we must bring it to a level where they will lack room to move at will, and their movements will be easily restricted.[78]

Mengistu's rationale for moving people from northeastern Ethiopia to the southwestern regions sounds like Pol Pot's reasons for moving people from the Eastern Zone to the Northwestern Zone. But the meaning intended in Mengistu's rationale was not to brutally exterminate the ethnic populations of those guerrilla areas, but to forcibly relocate those perceived to be assisting anti-Dergue groups. By putting "people who . . . [had] accepted the revolution along sensitive parts" of the country and removing those who had not and were accessible to opposition groups to distant lands, in the southwest, the Dergue hoped to deprive its armed opponents in northern Ethiopia of potential recruits and gain intelligence information from its loyalists on the activities of the OLF in southwestern Ethiopia.[79] The Dergue succeeded in these latter goals.

Mengistu's personal interest in resettlement, in a political culture in which the leader commanded popular reverence, turned the program into the pet project of revolutionary cadres. State radio propaganda promised resettlees private land, schools, grinding mills, clinics, and free agricultural inputs. These promises induced some people to voluntarily register for resettlement.[50] But when news of unfulfilled promises and accounts of death from malaria in some resettlement sites filtered back to Tigray and Wollo, peasants became more reluctant to emigrate. What made resettlement in revolutionary Ethiopia especially lethal was the zeal of soldiers and party enthusiasts to enforce the program despite the refusal of the peasants to resettle. Government soldiers and revolutionary cadres picked people from the streets, markets and even farms and resettled them. The Dergue rewarded keen participation. Party cadres and peasant association chairmen competed to earn state medals and Mengistu's praise for resettling the largest number of people. Mengistu personally endorsed the coercive measures that peasant association officials used including the execution of peasants who resisted resettlement.[51]

The human cost of resettlement in Ethiopia was enormous. A study commissioned by the German NGO Berliner Missionswerk estimated that about 100,000 people died in the resettlement process or after their arrival in resettlement camps.[52] Clashes between the ethnic groups already living in resettlement locations and the newly-arrived resettlees as well as attacks on settlements by anti-Dergue groups, increased the death rate in the settlements. The EPRP, for instance, attacked and killed many resettlees in the settlement camp in Pawe, in Gojjam. Far from being the well-meaning response to hunger which the Dergue claimed, resettlement was a human rights disaster. Neglecting its responsibility to provide prophylactic medicines to assist resettlees to combat diseases such as malaria, the Dergue condemned hundreds of thousands of people to death. RRC field workers witnessed the death of "hundreds" of infants, the elderly, and the weak through this state resettlement program which Dawit has characterized as tantamount to "genocide of helpless people."[53]

Did the Dergue perpetrate genocide by resettlement? If the Special Prosecutor in the Ethiopian genocide trial can construct intent from the results of the resettlements, showing that the Dergue intended to destroy all or a part of the 100,000 estimated victims of resettlement because of their membership in a particular ethnic or religious group by resettling them in places where their survival would be jeopardized, the Dergue would be guilty of genocide under the UN Genocide Convention, the Ethiopian Penal Code and the Chalk and Jonassohn definition of genocide.

Jason Clay and Bonnie Holcomb believe that this can be easily demonstrated. They have argued that the Dergue purposefully used resettlement, aided by Western relief aid, as a tool to stifle the survival of the Oromo, the largest ethnic group in Ethiopia which had posed "the most serious threat" to Ethiopian governments since the nineteenth century.[54] Clay and Holcomb are right in situating the Dergue's resettlement program within a long-standing Ethiopian state strategy of relocating people for security reasons. However, people who were forcibly resettled between 1978 and 1986 in Ethiopia were not relocated on the basis of their ethnicity but by their material condition and perceived political affiliations.[55] The resettlement of Oromos and Amharas from Wollo, Tigrayans and other ethnic groups from Tigray, in the north, Amharas and Oromos from Shoa, in central Ethiopia, Beta Israel (Ethiopian Jews) from Gondar, in the northeast, Kembatas and Hadiyas from Keffa province in the southeast and vagrants in Addis Ababa and other urban areas undermines Clay and Holcomb's argument that resettlement in revolutionary Ethiopia was deliberately designed to destroy a particular ethnic group.

When a genocidal intent to exterminate an identifiable racial or ethnic group exists, the perpetrator usually blocks the flight of the target groups to safety. That is exactly what the Khmer Rouge did, but not the Dergue. The Khmer Rouge massacred ethnic Vietnamese whom they had ordered expelled from Cambodia and who were on their way to Vietnam. They also prevented other Vietnamese from fleeing Cambodia and later massacred them.[56] But in Ethiopia, once the victims of resettlement began to migrate toward government-controlled areas, the Dergue facilitated their movements, although it failed to help them with medicines and food. Similarly, anti-government armed political groups such as the EPLF and TPLF helped peasants and resettlees in government-controlled areas who wished to emigrate to territories held by the anti-Dergue groups. While in rebel-held territories, the relief organizations of the EPLF and TPLF assisted resettlees with food and medicine.[57] But it is also important to emphasize that in Ethiopia the Dergue and its opponents, especially the TPLF and EPLF, often used famine and relief food as weapons of war.

The Dergue's poorly-planned and hastily-implemented resettlement program, from October 1984 to February 1986, was intended as a counter-insurgency strategy to intimidate and isolate potential peasant-recruits of the TPLF and EPLF. It was not a tool of genocide against the Oromo ethnic group as Clay and Holcomb have suggested. The Dergue was motivated, in part, by suspicion that unpublicized international relief assistance and other support from foreign non-governmental organizations helped the TPLF and EPLF to recruit peasants as soldiers and escape state control. That suspicion was reinforced when the Mengistu government impounded an Australian ship, the *Golden Venture*, at Assab port in January 1985. The vessel, which was bound for Port Sudan, in the Republic of Sudan, and mistakenly berthed at Assab, in Ethiopia, contained relief cargo clearly marked for delivery to the EPLF and TPLF.[88] The incident confirmed long-held suspicions of Mengistu that international sympathy for anti-government groups increased the flow of resources to their relief organs, thus strengthening their resolve to overthrow his government. Here, Barbara Harff and Ted Robert Gurr are correct in arguing that violence and killing intensify when the perpetrators of politicide realize that assistance to their target groups is being furnished by external supporters and sympathizers.[89]

CONCLUSION

Unlike Cambodia where there was extensive genocide against ethnic and national groups like the Chams, Vietnamese and Chinese, and even what might be called "classicide" against urban-based middle and upper classes, such destruction was limited in Ethiopia to armed political groups that opposed the Dergue. Other intra-group killings intended to settle personal scores also took place in Ethiopia. As violent and immoral as they were, these overtly political killings on the part of the Dergue and its opponents do not add up to an attempt to destroy in whole or in part a national, ethnic, racial or religious group as such. Had the Dergue destroyed a defenseless or inactive group of people who only held political views different from the Dergue's, and had the revolutionary military regime broadened the killing of its political opponents to include members of their family and the ethnic groups from which those political opponents came, the Dergue would be guilty of genocide. But the empirical evidence indicates that that is not what happened. The Dergue committed crimes against humanity including politicide, and not genocide as strictly defined in the UN Genocide Convention.

On the other hand, the intent of the Khmer Rouge to commit genocide is very clear from the empirical evidence of its annihilation of ethnic

Chams, Chinese, Vietnamese and Buddhist Monks. These groups were targeted on grounds of their ethnicity, religious beliefs and national origin. The Khmer Rouge was able to commit crimes of that scope because of the unbridled power it exercised over a subdued and atomized society. The situation in Ethiopia was not as clear cut. Under the UN Genocide Convention, the crimes of the Dergue would not constitute genocide because the Dergue targeted those it killed because of their political affiliation and opposition to the revolutionary regime and not because of the religious faith or ethnicity of the target groups. But the Ethiopian case presents a challenge to scholars of genocide studies because in Ethiopian law, politicide is a form of genocide. The question is: which law should apply in determining and prosecuting the crime of genocide? There is no doubt, however, that the Dergue committed crimes against humanity under international law.

Like other crimes against humanity, politicide, that is the intentional destruction of political groups, even in the context of revolution, has the potential of spinning into genocide. But as the Ethiopian revolution demonstrates, not all politicides necessarily lead to genocide. Ethiopian law is itself confused over this important point. Again as the Ethiopian revolution demonstrates, not all revolutions lead to genocide.

Beyond the legal and scholarly debate on genocide, at a human and moral level, the crimes of the Pol Pot and Mengistu regimes are grave enough to deserve proper prosecution and appropriate condemnation. In Ethiopia, they deserve even more: impartial justice. Given the complex history of the Ethiopian revolution, and the history of political mass murder in Ethiopia, justice should not be blind to the atrocities of the EPRP, EPLF, TPLF, OLF and other armed anti-Dergue opposition groups. These were organized and heavily armed groups that also engaged in terror and committed political murder. The Dergue did not have an absolute monopoly over the instruments of terror as the Khmer Rouge had. But it is probably expecting too much to ask the Ethiopian government to prosecute its own members in the future.

It appears that the trial of Mengistu and his colleagues in post-Dergue Ethiopia is more symbolic than substantive. Ethiopia's Special Prosecutor sees in the trials a dual mandate. First, "to establish for public knowledge and for posterity a historical record of the abuses of the Mengistu regime." Second, "to bring those criminally responsible for human rights violations and . . . corruption to justice."[90] In a world of genocide denials and revi-

sionism, the trial in Ethiopia is worthy of praise and support. But it is significant for the Court to acknowledge that what happened in Ethiopia was
not a one-sided mass killing. The public record must reflect that in the
name of justice and accountability.

Cambodia's one-sided mass killing is yet to see any serious justice.
The complicated search for justice in post-revolution Ethiopia and
Cambodia demonstrate the difficulties of finding appropriate legal
mechanisms for the prosecution of genocide in post-genocide societies.
But as in Ethiopia and Cambodia justice becomes even more difficult
when the domestic prosecutors are themselves part of a government
which includes perpetrators of the crimes they are prosecuting. Justice
becomes even more complicated when those who are supposed to be
the impartial international arbiters of justice were themselves "accomplices" to the crimes under prosecution. Psychologist Israel Charny has
defined the concept of "accomplices" as "those who assist, prepare, or
furnish the mass murderers of the world with the means to exterminate
huge numbers of people."[91] But who were the international supporters
or accomplices of the Dergue and the Angkar?

NOTES

1. Convention on the Prevention and Punishment of the Crime of Genocide, Approved and proposed for signature and ratification or accession by
General Assembly resolution 260 A (III) of December 9, 1948.

2. See Article 7 of Rome Statute of the International Criminal Court, http://
www.icenow.org/romearchive/romestatute/rome=e.doc.

3. The Empire of Ethiopia, *Penal Code of the Empire of Ethiopia of 1957*
(Addis Ababa: Ministry of the Pen, 1957), 87.

4. William Schabas, "Cambodia: Was it Really Genocide?," *Human Rights
Quarterly* 23, no. 2 (May 2001): 477. See also Craig Etcheson, "The Politics of
Justice in Cambodia" (a talk at the Montreal Institute of Genocide and Human
Rights Studies, Montreal, Canada, September 12, 2003), 8. For a catalogue of
documents and analysis of the proceedings of the trial, see De Nike et al.,
Genocide in Cambodia.

5. Susan E. Cook, "Prosecuting Genocide in Cambodia: The Winding Path
Towards Justice,"<http://www.yale.edu/cgp>; Etcheson, "The Politics of Justice
in Cambodia"; George Chigas, "The politics of defining justice after the Cambodian genocide," *Journal of Genocide Research*, 2, no. 2 (June 2000).

6. Etcheson, "The Politics of Justice," 11; William Schabas, "Cambodia: Was it Really Genocide?," 475.

7. Chigas, "The Politics of Defining Justice," 260.

8. Etcheson, "The Politics of Justice," 3, 5, 10–11.

9. *Agreement between the United Nations and the Royal Government of Cambodia Concerning the Prosecution Under Cambodian Law of Crimes Committed during the Period of Democratic Kampuchea*, June 6, 2003, http://migs.concordia.ca/links/Cambodia.html. See also United Nations Press Release L/3082, "Governments Pledge $38.48 Million for Khmer Rouge Trials in Cambodia," March 23, 2005. http://www.un.org/News/Press/doc/2005/l3082.doc.htm.

10. For information on problems of meeting Cambodia's financial obligations to the tribunal, see Nathaniel Myers, "Khmer Rouge Tribunal Need More than Money." *Bangkok Post* July 19, 2005. On the Congressional bill imposing conditions on U.S. financial contributions to the tribunal, see "Gregory H. Stanton, "Seeking Justice in Cambodia: Realism, Idealism, and Pragmatism." http://www.genocidewatch.org.

11. Etcheson, "The Politics of Justice," 6–7.

12. See Transitional Government of Ethiopia, Central High Court, *Genocide and Crimes Against Humanity*, Part One, Unofficial Draft Translation, Addis Ababa, October, 1994, 8.

13. *Ethiopian Penal Code of 1957*, 11.

14. See "Letter written by jailed Derg officials to Prime Minister Meles Zenawi," *Ethiopian Reporter*. <http://www.ethiopianreporter.com/display english.php?id=614> (February 9, 2004).

15. Leo Kuper, *Genocide: Its Political Use in the Twentieth Century* (New Haven: Yale University Press, 1981), 139, 146. For further analysis of Kuper's thoughts on the necessity of including political groups in the legal definition of genocide, see Israel Charny, ed. *Encyclopedia of Genocide*. vol. 1 (Santa Barbara, CA: ABC-CLIO, 1999), 5, 12.

16. Frank Chalk and Kurt Jonassohn, *The History and Sociology of Genocide: Analyses and Case Studies* (New Havenm CT: Yale University Press, 1990), 23–26, 27–32.

17. Chalk and Jonassohn, *History and Sociology of Genocide*, 23, 29.

18. For the views of Helen Fein on genocide see, *Genocide: A Sociological Perspective* (London: Sage Publications, 1993), 23–27; "Genocide, Terror, Life Integrity, and War Crimes: The Case for Discrimination," in *Genocide: Conceptual and Historical Dimensions*, ed. George J. Andreopoulos (Philadelphia: University of Pennsylvania Press, 1997), 99; *Encyclopedia of Genocide*. vol. 1, 5.

19. Israel W. Charny, "Toward a Generic Definition of Genocide," in *Genocide: Conceptual and Historical Dimensions*, ed. George J. Andreopoulos (Philadelphia: University of Pennsylvania Press, 1997), 64, 75.

20. Barbara Harff and Ted Robert Gurr, "Systematic Early Warning of Humanitarian Emergencies," *Journal of Peace Research*, 35, no. 5 (1998): 560, 567.

21. Barbara Harff, "No lessons learned from the Holocaust?: Assessing risks of genocide and political mass murder since 1995," *American Political Science Review*, 97 (2003): 58.

22. Harff and Gurr, "Systematic Early Warning," 560.

23. For the views of Kiernan, and of Schabas on genocide, see Ben Kiernan, "The Cambodian Genocide: Issues and Responses," in *Genocide: Conceptual and Historical Dimensions*, 197–201; William A. Schabas, *Genocide in International Law* (Cambridge, MA: Cambridge University Press, 2000), 9.

24. Michael Vickery, "Democratic Kampuchea: Themes and Variations," in *Revolution and Its Aftermath in Kampuchea*," 101, 112,

25. David P. Chandler, *The Tragedy of Cambodian History: Politics, War, and Revolution Since 1945* (New Haven: Yale University Press, 1991), 1.

26. Chandler, *Brother Number One*, 115, 161.

27. Serge Thion, "The Cambodian Idea of Revolution," in *Revolution and Its Aftermath*, 28.

28. Anthony Barnett, "Democratic Kampuchea: A Highly Centralized Dictatorship," in *Revolution and Its Aftermath*, 212, 214, 216.

29. Kiernan, *The Pol Pot Regime*, 26–27.

30. See Stephane Courtois, "Introduction: The Crimes of Communism," in *Black Book of Communism*, 3.

31. Schabas, "Cambodia: Was it Really Genocide?," 472–74.

32. See footnote 8 in Schabas, "Was it Really Genocide?."

33. Congress, Senate, Committee on Foreign Relations, *Ethiopia and the Horn of Africa: Hearings Before the Subcommittee on African Affairs*, 94th Congress, 2nd Session, August 4–6, 1976, 66.

34. The *Wall Street Journal*, "Today's Holocaust," January 27, 1986, 24. The response of the Ethiopian government is contained in Berhane Deressa, Deputy Commissioner of the RRC, to The Editor of the Wall Street Journal, January 31, 1986, *Christian Relief and Development Association Archives*, Addis Ababa, File: RRC Reports and Minutes. January–December 1986.

35. John Ryle, "An African Nuremberg," *The New Yorker*, October 2, 1995, 52.

36. Robert Kaplan, "The African Killing Fields," *The Washington Monthly*, 28, no. 8 (September 1988): 32.

37. Author's interview with Merera Gudina, Addis Ababa, April 17, 1999.

38. Hagos Gebre Yesus, "The Bankruptcy of the Ethiopian Left—Meison-EPRP, A-Two-Headed Hydra: A Commentary on the Ideology and Politics of National Nihilism," in *Modern Ethiopia: From the Accession of Menelik II to the Present*, ed. Joseph Tubiana (Rotterdam: A.A. Balkena, 1980), 455.

39. Ethiopian News Agency, *Ethiopia: State Terrorism on Trial*, i, ii, 10, 20; Interview with Yeraswork Admassu, Addis Ababa, May 4, 1999.

40. Chandler, *Brother Number One*, 124.

41. Chandler, *Brother Number One*, 117; Kiernan, "The Cambodian Genocide—1975–1979," in *Century of Genocide*, 342.

42. Anthony Barnett, Chanthou Boua and Ben Kiernan, "Bureaucracy of Death," *New Statesman*, 99 (May 1980): 671.

43. Kiernan, "The Cambodian Genocide—1975–1979," 340; Chanthou Boua, "Genocide of a Religious Group: Pol Pot and Cambodia's Buddhist Monks," in *State-Organized Terror: The Case of Violent Internal Repression*, ed. Timothy Bushnell et al. (Boulder, CO: Westview Press, 1991), 235.

44. Ulrich Meister, "Ethiopia's Unfinished Revolution," *Swiss Review of World Affairs*, 33, no. 2 (May 1983): 17.

45. Kiernan, "The Cambodian Genocide—1975–1979," 340–41, 343.

46. Kiernan, "The Cambodian Genocide—1975–1979," 341, 342.

47. FBIS Daily Report, "Phnom Penh Radio Specifies New Tasks," April 28, 1975, H9.

48. Kiernan, "The Cambodian Genocide—1975–1979," 341–42. For a statistical table of the "approximate death toll" of the Cambodian revolution, see 343.

49. Criddle and Butt Mam, *To Destroy You is No Loss*, 147, 153; Kiernan, *The Pol Pot Regime*, 198, 243.

50. Alexander Laban Hinton, "A Head for An Eye: Revenge, Culture, and the Cambodian Genocide," (paper presented at the meeting of the Association of Genocide Scholars, Montreal, Canada, November 1997), 1–4. See also Alexander Laban Hinton, "The Dark Side of Modernity: Toward an Anthropology of Genocide," in *Annihilating Difference: The Anthropology of Genocide*, ed. Alexander Laban Hinton (Berkeley: University of California Press, 2002), 19.

51. The Ethiopian Special Prosecutor's Office (SPO) has the minutes of this meeting containing information about the Dergue members who were present, the comments they made and the "order" they gave which sealed the fate on the 60 ex-officials. See Ethiopian News Agency, *State Terrorism on Trial*, iv; Transitional Government of Ethiopia, *Genocide and Crimes Against Humanity*, 8–9; and also Mary Anne Weaver, "Annals of Political Terror," *The New Yorker*, (December 28, 1992/January 4, 1994): 106.

52. Paulos, "Mengistu Haile Mariam," 51.

53. Guillebaud, "Dergue's red terror," 11, 13.

54. Kiflu Tadesse, *The Generation*, Part II, 114.

55. Ethiopian News Agency, *Ethiopia: State Terrorism on Trial*, v; Dawit, *Red Tears*, 22.

56. Guillebaud, "Dergue's red terror," 13.

57. Medhane, "EPRP vs. TPLF," 8–9; Author's interview with Merera Gudina, Addis Ababa, April 19, 1999; *Abyot*, Information Bulletin of the EPRP, no. 3 (February–March, 1976): 25–26.

58. Ethiopian News Agency, *Ethiopia: State-Terrorism on Trial*, 19.

59. Author's interview with Merid Wolde Aregay, Professor of History, Addis Ababa University, Ethiopia, May 12, 1999.

60. Interview with Yeraswork Admassu.

61. Ethiopian News Agency, *Ethiopia: State-Terrorism on Trial*, iv.

62. Amnesty International Bulletin (Canadian Section) "File on Torture: Ethiopia," 14, no. 3 (April 1987): 2.

63. Ethiopian News Agency, *Ethiopia: State-Terrorism on Trial*, 26–27.

64. Speech quoted in Chandler, *Brother Number One*, 129.

65. For detailed analyses, see David Chandler, *Voices from S-21: Terror and History in Pol Pot's Secret Prison* (Berkeley, CA: University of California Press, 1999).

66. Chandler, *Voices from S-21*, 11, 17, 32, 51; *Brother Number One*, 124, 127, 131.

67. Amnesty International, "File on Torture: Ethiopia," 7.

68. I thank Ben Kiernan for sharing this source, dated 9/9/80, from his personal field notes with me. See also Chandler, *Voices from S-21*, 32.

69. Howard De Nike et al., "Reports of Field Investigators," in *Genocide in Cambodia*, 242. Read 227–49 for gruesome details about the use of burned bodies as fertilizer.

70. Chandler, *Brother Number One*, 128.

71. De Nike et al., *Genocide in Cambodia*, 243.

72. The *Wall Street Journal* [Editorial], "Today's Holocaust." See also Robert Kaplan, *Surrender or Starve: The Wars Behind the Famine* (Boulder: Westview Press, 1988), 106, 110.

73. Kiernan, *The Pol Pot Regime*, 205, 209; Chandler, *Brother Number One*, 127; Becker, *When the War Was Over: Cambodia and the Khmer Rouge Revolution*, 179–180; Vickery, *Cambodia, 1975–1982*, 132, 137–38.

74. Becker, *When the War Was Over: Cambodia and the Khmer Rouge Revolution*, 178.

75. Kiernan, "Genocidal Targetting: Two Groups of Victims in Pol Pot's Cambodia," in *State-Organized Terror*, 213–15, and "The Cambodian Genocide—1975–1979," in *Century of Genocide*, 343.

76. Arian P. Wood, "Spontaneous Agricultural Resettlement in Ethiopia, 1950–1974," *RRC Documentation Center*, Addis Ababa, Ethiopia. File No. A 6. 91.

77. Dawit, *Red Tears*, 287; RRC, "Interim Report: Assistance to Settlement," September 1980, *RRC Documentation Centre*, Addis Ababa, 24, and "Settlement Policy," July 1981, 1.

78. Statement attributed to Mengistu in Dawit, *Red Tears*, 298.

79. Dawit, *Red Tears*, 288–89. Dawit's point is confirmed in author's taped interview with Tesfaye Mekasha, former vice-Minister of Foreign Affairs in the Imperial Government, Addis Ababa, July 30, 1995.

80. Author's taped interviews with Amhara, Oromo and Kembatta settlers in Pawe, Gojjam Administrative Region, Ethiopia, October 1, 1995.

81. Author's taped interviews with Zegeye Asfaw, Minister of Settlement in the Dergue administration, Addis Ababa, May 29, 1995, and peasants at Mersa, North Wollo Administrative Zone, Ethiopia, October 20, 1995. See also Dawit, *Red Tears*, 271, 300–301.

82. Peter Niggli, *Ethiopia: Deportations and Forced Labor Camps: A Study by Peter Niggli on Behalf of the Berliner Missionswerk, 1986* (Berlin: Berliner Missionswerk, 1986. While it is true that many people died during and after the resettlement program, precise figures on the resettlement mortality may be difficult to obtain since no one kept accurate statistics. See Ethiopian News Agency, *Ethiopia: State-Terrorism On Trial*, v.

83. Dawit, *Red Tears*, 118.

84. Jason Clay and Bonnie Holcomb, *Politics and the Ethiopian Famine, 1984–1986* (Cambridge, MA: Cultural Survival, 1986), 25–26.

85. Author's taped interviews with Amhara and Oromo resettlees at Pawe resettlement villages 14 and 23, Pawe, East Gojjam Administrative Region, October 1, 1995 and with Tesfaye Mekasha Amare.

86. Kiernan, *The Pol Pot Regime*, 296.

87. Author's interviews with Kembatta resettlees in Pawe, Gojjam Administrative Region, Ethiopia, October 1, 1995.

88. Taye Gurmu, Deputy Commissioner of the RRC, to Brother Augustine O'Keefe, CRDA, May 29, 1986. *CRDA Archives*, Addis Ababa, RRC Files: Reports and Minutes, January 1985–December 1985. See also RRC, Addis Ababa, *Official Statement*, "A Frustrated Outcry," October 3, 1986. *FAO Archives*, Addis Ababa, IL 2/2 RRC Files February 1986–August 1987, January–December 1988.

89. Harff and Gurr, "Systematic Early Warning," 560.

90. Ethiopian News Agency, *Ethiopia: State Terrorism on Trial*, iii.

91. Charny, "Towards a Generic Definition of Genocide," 65.

6

FOREIGN RELATIONS AND TERRITORIAL POLITICS

The Dergue's slogan, "Revolutionary Motherland or Death" was a resolute call to arms to defend the borders of Ethiopia and to liquidate the political groups whose secessionist ideologies, in the view of the military regime, threatened national unity and security. Similarly, Khmer Rouge exhortation of every Cambodian to "kill thirty Vietnamese" was also the most forthright demonstration of the intent of the Pol Pot regime to expand the borders of Cambodia by recapturing "lost ancient territory." The leaders of the Khmer Rouge considered the Vietnamese as the "historical" and "hereditary" enemies of the Khmer people.[1] Here, the Khmer Rouge racialized view of a group (Vietnamese) as having common biological and dangerous traits appears to be rooted in a racist ideology of ethnic homogeneity and Khmer racial revivalism mixed with an imperial ethic of expansion that was very different from the Dergue's. But as Eric Weitz has argued "ideology alone is never a sufficient explanation for massive developments such as genocide." Ideological beliefs always "intersect" with "politics" and "international developments."[2] But who were the Dergues and Angkar's international backers?

This chapter examines the common and distinctive features of the foreign relations and frontier politics of the Dergue and the Angkar. It concentrates on the nature of the territorial problems that confronted the two revolutionary regimes, the foreign policy principles which guided their conduct of international affairs, and the strategies they adopted to achieve their foreign policy goals. The key argument of this chapter is that the differences between the Dergue and the Angkar become even more apparent in their foreign policies. Both regimes found the military and diplomatic tools they needed to address the issue of national borders that was central to the meaning of revolution in Ethiopia and Cambodia. Yet, it was the differences in their territorial problems that took the Dergue and the Angkar in different foreign policy directions. Democratic Kampuchea's territorial problems were mainly external. Socialist Ethiopia's were internal.

THE FRONTIER QUESTIONS: ETHIOPIA

Domestic support for a military leadership of the Ethiopian revolution revolved around the Dergue's success in eradicating the biggest threat to the unity and territorial integrity of Ethiopia: the secessionist nationalism of the WSLF and EPLF and the irredentism of neighboring Somalia. The Dergue's Penal Code of November 1974 had mandated the death penalty for any group that challenged the traditional borders of Ethiopia. Also the emphasis which the revolutionary military regime put on "the indivisibility of Ethiopian unity," in its concept of socialism, as we have already noted, affirmed the determination of the soldiers to rally a broad national and international opposition to any breakup of Ethiopia.

Somali irredentism posed the major external threat to the territorial integrity of Ethiopia, and the security of the Dergue. Since 1961, Ethiopia's eastern neighbor, Somalia, had sought without success, to annex the Ogaden region in southeastern Ethiopia where ethnic Somalis live. Dergue members such as Mengistu from the Third Division of the Ethiopian Army, stationed close to the Ethiopia-Somalia border, had reliable intelligence information, in the early 1970s, about Somalia's intentions to capture what it considered as its ancient lands under Ethiopia's occupation.[3]

CAMBODIA

The Khmer Rouge blamed French colonial administrators for giving land and rivers belonging to Cambodia to Vietnam, Laos and Thailand in the nineteenth century. Pol Pot's foreign ministry regarded that transfer of territory as a "violation of justice towards Kampuchea" in a secret draft history of Cambodia's borders. In that document, the Pol Pot regime also claimed that Vietnam had illegally acquired "Kampuchea Krom," a territory inhabited by ethnic Khmer, from an eighteenth century Cambodian monarch who, in desperation, sought Vietnamese help to retain power in Cambodia. But Kampuchea Krom was not the only "lost territory" which the Angkar wanted to regain. A survivor of the Khmer Rouge revolution, Lang Sim, told Kiernan in an interview in France, in December 1979, that Khmer Rouge cadres announced at a meeting held in her village in the Southwest province, at the end of 1977, that Cambodia "aimed to fight to recover Kampuchea Krom from Vietnam, as well as Surin and other provinces from Thailand." The Khmer Rouge also claimed Sisaket, in northeastern Thailand, and even parts of Southern Laos. For the Cambodian revolutionary regime, reclaiming all these "lost" historical territories was a significant patriotic duty.[4] The legitimacy of the revolution depended on success in territorial expansion. That locked Cambodia into a tense relationship with all three of its neighbors.

The Dergue's territorial objectives were mainly internal, very limited and not expansionist. Hence its frontier politics affected relations with only those opposition groups, such as the EPLF and the WSLF, that appealed to ethnic particularism to mobilize sectional support against the Dergue's pan-Ethiopianist project. Whereas the Khmer Rouge rejected negotiated settlement of its frontier problems and attacked its neighbors, the Dergue incorporated third-party mediation into its military solution of its border problems. Prior to the Somali invasion of Ethiopia in July 1977, the Soviet Union and Cuba attempted to "resolve the Ethiopia-Somalia [border] dispute by proposing a sort of federal or confederal solution." The Dergue appeared "willing," to accept the proposal, but Siad Barre, Somalia's president opposed the idea.[5]

PRINCIPLES OF FOREIGN POLICY

Again the different nature of the regimes in Ethiopia and Cambodia is reflected in their foreign policy principles. The Dergue had limited aims. The Khmer Rouge had ambitious objectives. Ethiopia's revolutionary regime did not deviate from the foreign policy principles of the monarchical regime it had ousted. It promised, soon after taking power in September 1974, to "be strictly nonaligned," "adhere to UN and OAU charters" and "respect all international obligations."[6] Circumstances later to be discussed caused the Dergue to surrender non-alignment for whatever alliance that helped the military junta to achieve the total power it never succeeded in attaining.

The Khmer Rouge was not as eager as the Dergue to modify or even surrender the principles guiding its foreign relations. The Cambodian regime's utopian ideals and doctrinaire views of society are evident in its perception of world politics and other international developments. It perceived the world as rigidly divided into three hostile blocs: the imperialist, revisionist and non-aligned blocs. The Khmer Rouge included the United States, Japan, West Germany, France, England and "the capitalist Europeans countries . . . including Canada" in the "imperialist bloc" of countries. It viewed them as "exploitative" and potentially hostile to the Cambodian revolution. The Khmer Rouge drew no distinction between the United States, which it called the "chief imperialist" country, and the former Soviet Union, which it considered as the "chief revisionist" power. For the Pol Pot regime, the Soviet Union was a socialist pretender. Moscow's opposition to socialism and revolution of the kind which the Khmer Rouge endorsed, put it in the same category as countries in the "imperialist bloc."[7]

The sympathies of revolutionary Cambodia resided with the third bloc of countries, the Non-Aligned Countries. The Pol Pot regime considered them as "victims of imperialists and revisionists." The Khmer Rouge leadership strongly believed that the "imperialist" and "revisionist" countries are in constant competition with one another to infiltrate and control the non-aligned countries, a situation that required "vigilance" from Cambodia and those countries in Southeast Asia, Africa and Latin America belonging to the Non-Aligned bloc.[8]

This view of international affairs influenced the Cambodian regime's choice of allies and its evaluation of their aid and attitude. For example, the Khmer Rouge saw foreign aid from the "imperialist bloc" as a subversive tool and a form of "interference" in Cambodia's internal affairs.[9] It was clearly self-destructive for the Khmer Rouge to perceive any foreign aid, even aid to relieve humanitarian crises such as famine as a tool of subversion. From the perspective of foreign policy thinking, the Cambodian regime showed that it was different from the Ethiopian revolutionary military government. In the late 1970s and throughout the 1980s, Ethiopia became the symbol of international famine-relief operations. While the Khmer Rouge regarded "independence," "self-reliance," "non-alignment," "socialism" and "communism" as serious ideological guidelines for the conduct of international affairs, the Dergue took them as slogans in revolutionary discourse.

Three key objectives flowed from the "political line of Angkar's foreign affairs." First, to gather "more friends around the world while reducing the number of enemies to a minimum."[10] The "enemies" included "imperialists" and "revisionists" beyond Cambodia's borders. Pol Pot cautioned Cambodians to be "friendly, but . . . careful all the time."[11] Second, "to get friends in Southeast Asia and the neutral countries of the world." This second foreign policy principle ideologically limited the perimeter of Cambodia's diplomatic engagement to Asia, Africa and Latin America and particularly to what the Khmer Rouge leadership called "the progressive forces in the Non-Aligned nations of the Third World." Disengagement of interaction with "the imperialist bloc" of countries in Europe and North-America could not have been clearer. Third, "to pay attention to close solidarity with the pure Marxist-Leninist forces, especially those with no conflicts with [Cambodia]" as well as "expand solidarity among anti-imperialist forces."[12] The purist and anti-imperialist ideology of the Khmer Rouge made it select for diplomatic relations only those countries Pol Pot called "friends with the best characteristics."[13]

In Asia, the Khmer Rouge counted only China and Korea among its "friends with the best characteristics." It viewed Burma (now Myanmar), Malaysia, Indonesia, Singapore, Taiwan, South Korea and the Philippines as "puppets of [American and Soviet] imperialism," and therefore potential enemies of revolutionary Cambodia. The Pol Pot regime considered Laos as "too weak to fight [Cambodia]" and Thailand as a country that would not "dare to send troops to fight us." From the perspective of the Khmer Rouge, Vietnam remained "the treacherous enemy." In Europe, the Khmer Rouge chose Albania, Yugoslavia and Romania as its key friends. Here, the Pol Pot regime was closer to the EPRP, a key armed opponent of the Dergue, in international relations philosophy than it resembled the Dergue. The Cambodian regime considered these countries, together with China and North Korea, as "friends" who have become "more and more understanding of us and have supported us more."[14] Revolutionary Cambodia's "friends" in Africa were Algeria and Senegal and not Ethiopia.[15]

Ethiopia was a founding member of the Non-Aligned Movement. It had no conflict with Cambodia. The Dergue publicly claimed to be "progressive" and "Marxist." Yet, no evidence exists, so far, that Socialist Ethiopia and Democratic Kampuchea had any diplomatic relations. Neither did the Dergue and the Khmer Rouge have any direct contact nor consider each other as friends. The unpublicized relations which the Khmer Rouge had with Ethiopia's opposition Maoist party, the EPRP, are an indication that the Dergue and the Khmer Rouge stood at opposite ends in their ideology and revolutionary practice. Realistically, the Khmer Rouge did not view revolutionary Ethiopia as a country with the "best characteristics" or the Dergue as a pure Marxist-Leninist, progressive and anti-imperialist government deserving the diplomatic affections of revolutionary Cambodia. In fact, the Dergue's opportunist use of Marxist vocabulary, its more moderate conception of Socialism and Communism and its relationship with the USSR and the United States troubled supposedly "pure Marxists" and "anti-imperialists" such as the Khmer Rouge and the EPRP deeply. In the worldview of the Pol Pot regime, the Dergue's lip-service to socialism was the worst characteristic of a regime in a non-aligned country. As Pol Pot emphasised: "We [DK] don't speak about Socialism. The essence of application is important not words."[16]

The Dergue had a different view. Its leadership took socialism and communism as words or slogans in revolutionary politics. The revolutionary theorists who published the Dergue's ideological newsletter, *Meskerem*, related communism to the Dergue's patriotic nationalism. The soldiers associated communism with patriotism or what they called "love of the Motherland [Ethiopia]." To be a true Communist, in the view of the Dergue, was to be willing "to protect [Ethiopia] vigilantly from its enemies." This view appears to be similar to one the Pol Pot regime had. But the real difference is that while the Khmer Rouge stoked racial and ethnic differences, and proved to be a racist revolutionary regime, the Dergue expected "true communists" to "realize that tribal, religious [and] racial . . . differences weaken national unity and socialist construction." The Dergue resolved to "fight against such tendencies."[17] The Khmer Rouge used them as tools of revolution. The larger point to be made here is that the Dergue had a different and non-traditional conception of communism from that of the Khmer Rouge.

MILITARISM AND NATIONALISM

Militarism, foreign alliances and aid, and anti-American rhetoric were the common strands in the foreign policy strategies of the Dergue and the Khmer Rouge. The differences resided in their objectives and application. Here, the Dergue's nationalistic and the Khmer Rouge's utopian and ethnic-expansionist nature come into sharper focus.

The application of Khmer Rouge foreign policy contradicted its pledges to "remain friendly" and "reduce tension." Cambodia's relations with Vietnam were hostile.[18] While the party leadership claimed that it would "avoid tension" with its neighbors and consider "friendship and solidarity with Vietnam as a sacred object," Son Sen, Deputy Prime Minister responsible for defence and security matters, wanted Cambodia "to be tough" and "chase back" Vietnamese who encroach on "our border [at Ratanakiri]." On May 14, 1976, the Khmer Rouge Standing Committee, comprising Pol Pot, Son Sen and Ieng Sary among others, discussed the reactions of Vietnam to two attacks launched against it by the Khmer Rouge army in Mondol Kiri a week before (May 7, 1976). The Vietnamese had complained that Khmer Rouge soldiers had attacked them "8 times" between March and May 1976 wounding and killing an undisclosed number of Vietnamese. The Vietnamese "asked [the Khmer Rouge] to avoid any more collision in order not to murk the color of our [border] negotiation." Kang Chap (Comrade Se), the Cambodian Communist Party's Secretary for the Northern Zone, articulated the basic Khmer Rouge position on Vietnam:

> they still think they are a big country with many people, they still want to oppress us and [think] we are scare[d] of them.[19]

Kiernan has argued that the Khmer Rouge abandoned all pretense of seeking a negotiated settlement of its border dispute with Vietnam,

Thailand and Laos. In December 1976, the party leadership ordered the divisional commanders of the Cambodian army to prepare for a guerrilla war. On January 27, 1977, Khmer Rouge troops killed "over thirty Thai villagers" in a raid on the border with Thailand. In that same month, Khmer Rouge soldiers clashed with Laos. As Kiernan notes, the most serious Khmer Rouge violence against Vietnam occurred on the border with Vietnam in March 1977. Khmer Rouge forces attacked the Vietnamese provinces of Kieng Giang and An Giang. Further raids took place in April 1977 on Vietnamese posts and villages resulting in the deaths of 222 civilians. Eyewitnesses of these persistent attacks on the Vietnamese admit that the Khmer Rouge provoked these border clashes.[20]

An individual "from Region 25," whom Kiernan interviewed, recalled the shift of Khmer Rouge policy objective from its 1975–76 focus on "gathering people and working" to the 1977 emphasis on "victory over Vietnam." In the summer of 1977, Khmer Rouge troops killed "hundreds of people" when they attacked forty villages in Vietnam. Sok, a Khmer, told Kiernan that he had witnessed the "shelling of markets on Vietnamese territory" by Khmer Rouge soldiers. A woman from Kirivong, in the Southwest Zone, had also observed Khmer Rouge attacks on Vietnam "all along the border, within fifteen minutes of each other" and the burning of Vietnamese houses on April 30, 1977.[21] The Khmer Rouge claimed that the Vietnamese had built those houses on Khmer land. Liberation of Khmer land was a typical Khmer Rouge justification of these attacks. But in reality, they amounted to militarism, crimes against humanity and the violation of international law.

The Dergue sought UN, U.S. and Organization of African Unity (OAU) arbitration to resolve, through application of international law, Ethiopia's frontier conflicts with Somalia and the Eritrean Peoples Liberation Front.[22] Those arbitrations secured a ceasefire between Somalia and Ethiopia and the withdrawal of Somali troops from Ethiopian territory. But they failed to end the domestic conflict between the Dergue and its armed opponents. The Khmer Rouge did not wish to submit to international resolution of its frontier disputes with Vietnam. The Khmer Rouge Security Chief, Son Sen, cautioned in May 1977 that Cambodia "could lose tremendously if [it] applied [international law]" in the border dispute.[23] By 1977, the Khmer Rouge had made it a central policy to retake Kampuchea Krom (southern Vietnam) from Vietnam by force and through raids and incursions across the border with Vietnam.

The Khmer Rouge leadership made this policy known throughout Cambodia. A peasant from Kirivong, in the Southwest (Mok's territory), confirmed to Kiernan that in 1978 party cadres who addressed party rallies stressed that "Vietnamese territory is Cambodian territory." Another interviewee, a Khmer student, recalled this official position. He heard Ta Mok's son-in-law, San, proclaim at "a mass meeting of four subdistricts," in February 1978, that "[t]he . . . aim of the revolution is to fight and take the territory of Kampuchea Krom back." At the meeting, Ta Mok's son-in-law exhorted peasants to "support the Revolutionary Army to get the territory back."[24] The leaders of the Khmer Rouge hoped that by adopting an aggressive attitude towards Vietnam, they could consolidate an image of themselves as the "ultimate nationalists and saviours of Cambodia."[25]

Another illuminating contrast between the two revolutions is the role that foreign invasion played in the fortunes of the revolutionary regimes. Khmer Rouge irredentism leading to attacks on Vietnam provoked the Vietnamese invasion of Cambodia in January 1979. That invasion brought the Khmer Rouge revolution to an abrupt end. But the Ethiopian revolution was strengthened, for a brief period, by an unprovoked invasion of Ethiopia by irredentist Somalia in July 1977. As we have already noted in chapter three, far from successfully weakening the Dergue and destabilizing Ethiopia, the Somali invasion of Ethiopia rather helped the Dergue and advanced its nationalist causes. An Ethiopian eyewitness of the invasion has recorded that the Somali invasion of Ethiopia transformed "a desperate situation" into "an emotional national cause" for the Dergue because:

> In an unprecedented surge of patriotism, Ethiopians [in] Addis Abeba [the hub of opposition to the Dergue] donated their labour, money and moral support to the war.[26]

Ethiopia's victory over Somalia in March 1978 did not necessarily help the Dergue to achieve total power. But it created an opportunity for the military regime to refocus its revolutionary priorities. It now laid

more emphasis on national unity at all costs—Revolutionary Motherland or Death—rather than the 1974–75 policy theme of eradicating
famine through land reform. Mengistu viewed himself, and many
Ethiopians now regarded him, as the savior of Ethiopia and the only
person capable of assuring national unity. Again Merahehiwot Gabremariam notes that the victory:

> inflated Mengistu's ego and strengthened the army man's proclivity for be-
> lieving that there were no problems that the country faced, including in
> Eritrea, which could defy military solution. Thus by default, Siad Barre
> [the leader of Somalia] strengthened Mengistu's hand in Ethiopian poli-
> tics and helped pave the way for Ethiopia's descent into military dictator-
> ship.[27]

After March 1978, Ethiopia's foreign relations more and more reflected
the search for military equipment and other forms of foreign aid, regardless of the source and the price, in part, to preserve the traditional
boundaries of Ethiopia. Agricultural development now took second
place to military mobilization in the Dergue's domestic politics. The
military regime ordered peasant associations to recruit more peasants
for military service with the predictable negative effects on rural food
supply.

SOURCES OF MILITARY AID

Israel Charny has argued that nations in the international system that
provide genocidal regimes with arms and other instruments to commit
mass murder are themselves "accomplices" to genocide. But are they?
Indeed, to what extent did "international developments," in the form of
support, acquiescence or opposition strengthen or moderate the murderous behavior of the Dergue and the Khmer Rouge?

Foreign alliances for the purpose of seeking military aid formed part
of the strategies and policies that the nationalistic and embattled
Dergue and the utopian and expansionist Angkar pursued to address
their frontier and security problems. Lip service to Marxism-Leninism
enabled the Dergue to claim ideological affinity with a superpower, the
Soviet Union, and also to forge a beneficial diplomatic relationship in

which the major interest of the Dergue was Soviet military equipment rather than the transformation of Ethiopia into a communist country. The Dergue's view of foreign relations as a means of obtaining weapons to sustain its martial honor only reinforced pre-1974 Ethiopian foreign relations which were "dominated by the search for sources of military supplies."[28]

In public, the Dergue promoted a view of the Ethiopian revolution as Africa's version of the Russian revolution. That was meant to deepen the Dergue's ideologically opportunistic relationship with Moscow for the sake of economic and military aid. Mengistu reminisced in March 1990:

> The fact that the Soviet Union, China and various other countries that made socialism their guiding ideology managed to overcome economic backwardness in a relatively short . . . time offered a vivid practical example. Moreover, the desire to redress the economic injustices imposed upon the people by the feudal system, particularly resolving the land question on a just basis, as well as the strong desire to cement the unity of Ethiopian nationalities on the basis of equality, . . . contribut[ed] to the choice of the path of development adopted by the forces of the revolution.[29]

There is a self-serving element in this statement. A former Vice-Foreign Minister of Ethiopia confirms that Mengistu's alliance with the Soviet Union, often cited by some scholars as evidence of the Dergue's "Afro-communist" nature, was a relationship of convenience provoked by the Somali invasion of Ethiopia in July 1977. The real priorities of the Dergue lay in national unity and stifling, in Ethiopia, the pursuit of the Leninist idea of ethnic self-determination up to and including secession.[30]

The Dergue and the Khmer Rouge could not have pursued their frontier objectives without a strong military posture. Prior to the revolution, the Ethiopian Army numbered fewer than 40,000 men. By 1984, it boasted of a 350,000 strong army.[31] The Khmer Rouge army grew from a small guerrilla force of less than 10,000 men, before the revolution, to a total of 72,248 regular troops, after April 17, 1975. It had nine divisions and four regiments.[32] Foreign allies of the Pol Pot and Mengistu regimes provided military equipment. China and North Korea provisioned both the Khmer Rouge and the Dergue army. The Dergue was initially dependent on U.S. military assistance because the Ethiopian army had been "entirely based on American technology." Between 1953 and 1969, the United States supplied $141.2 million worth of military aid to Ethiopia. That represented half of the total American military aid to the entire continent of Africa in those years. The United States also trained Ethiopian soldiers (such as Mengistu) in the 1960s, maintained a radio communication base in Eritrea and had American counter-insurgency teams assisting the Ethiopian government in opposing the Eritrean Liberation Movement.[33] The United States delivered M-60 tanks and new U.S.-made helicopters to Ethiopia in August 1975 to demonstrate its goodwill towards those who would soon assume power in Ethiopia. But when the Dergue executed 60 former officials of the Haile Selassie regime, including the Dergue's first Chairman, Aman Andom, in November 1974, U.S.-Ethiopian relations declined, but were not completely broken. With its desire to obtain aid without regard for ideology, the Dergue built the largest army in Africa with additional supplies from Israel, Czechoslovakia, Yugoslavia, China, North Korea and the Soviet Union.

For all the Marxist-Leninist bombast, Ethiopia's leaders accepted U.S. $37.6 million worth of American military aid in November 1975. The aid included 16 F-5 fighter aircraft. The United States also tripled its economic aid to the embattled regime in Addis Ababa. Henry Kissinger called it "taking a chance." But Assistant Secretary of State William Shaufele was convinced, in 1975, that the Dergue was "not systematically or instinctively anti-United States."[34] He was initially correct. From August 1976 onwards, however, Marxist and anti-American rhetoric dominated Ethiopia's political discourse. Radicals within and outside the Dergue prodded the regime to assume an anti-American position. Mengistu's vitriolic attacks on the United States represented, in part, a calculated strategy to delegitimize the Dergue's civilian political opponents by projecting the military regime as equally anti-American as they were. But as Merahehiwot Gabremariam notes, the "imperialist-armed anti-imperialist" Dergue was becoming more and more "embarrassed by its links with the U.S."[35] The United States was also becoming embarrassed by its support of the Dergue.

Senator Dick Clark (D-Iowa), Chairman of the U.S. Senate Subcommittee on Africa, summed up the American dilemma:

If [the Dergue] is such an anti-American government, if it is in such constant violation of human rights . . . , does it make sense for our Government to be its sole and greatest supporter? . . . if indeed . . . [the Dergue is] unstable and another government . . . [came] to power which, . . . for the sake of argument, might be more broadly representative, more popular at any rate, that new government . . . might view the U.S. association with . . . [the Dergue] in such a way that it would make [it] much more anti-American for future purposes.[36]

When Washington refused in 1977, during the Carter administration, to provide Ethiopia with the weapons it needed, the Addis Ababa regime switched suppliers.[37] Dawit Wolde Giorgis has revealed that:

[t]he Chinese shipped substantial amounts of small arms [to the Dergue], but were reluctant to give heavy weapons. North Korea shipped . . . small arms and promised to send more on the condition that [the Derge] expel the South Korean embassy from Ethiopia. That infuriated [the Mengistu regime] . . . Israel was approached secretly and supplied . . . vital spare parts and some light equipment.[38]

When Siad Barre unceremoniously kicked the Soviets out of Somalia, in August 1977, Ethiopia took advantage and switched its alliance from its traditional ally, the United States, to the former USSR. Mengistu signed the usual Twenty-Year Treaty of Friendship and Cooperation with the Soviet Union. By the end of 1977, Ethiopia had become a key destination of Russian advisors and weapons.

Paulos Milkias, political scientist and survivor of the Dergue's *Red Terror* campaign of political killings, has observed that in the late 1970s, and throughout the 1980s, Moscow had "over 5,000 advisers, diplomats and spies in Ethiopia." According to Paulos, 90 percent of the Soviet personnel in Ethiopia during the Brezhnev era had some connection with the KGB. The Soviet "advisers" turned Ethiopia's Ministry of Information into a "propaganda machine." As Paulos argues, "Mengistu bent over to please the Soviets because they supplied him billions of dollars worth of arms."[39] As the Ethiopian and Cambodian cases illustrate, in international affairs even if one state refuses to play the "accomplice" in the drama of arms supplies, as the United States did by cutting off military aid to the Dergue, there is always another state, or other states, eager, in their national interests, to provide the weapons and other instruments of violence that perpetrator states can use to commit murder.

The political necessity of pleasing Moscow for more arms now made the Dergue select for adoption key elements of Soviet communism. Soviet military aid came with pressure from Moscow to form that working class vanguard party which the Dergue lacked. The Dergue launched the Workers' Party of Ethiopia (WPE) in September 1984, the tenth anniversary of the revolution. But it was not devotion to communism which compelled the Dergue to work towards the formation of the WPE so late in the game, and which Mengistu later abandoned as we have already noted. It was pragmatism and opportunism. Hopes of securing Soviet diplomatic support in international affairs and military aid to defend the Dergue against its armed domestic political opponents converged with the Dergue's interest in organizing a political party to promote its pan-Ethiopian ideology and impose what it now called "communist morality." Here, a determination to crush domestic political opponents took precedence over any desire to become the first communist state in Africa. The contrast with the Khmer Rouge, which from the beginning owed its loyalty to a communist party, is clear.

Since the Dergue associated "communism" or what it called "communist morality" with "love of Ethiopian Unity," bolstered by Soviet arms, anti-Soviet attitudes, within and outside Ethiopia, acquired an anti-Ethiopian unity meaning for the Dergue. As the Dergue's ideological newsletter, *Meskerem*, stated:

> in the context of the . . . circumstances prevalent in Ethiopia, distorting the solidarity between the Ethiopian revolution and . . . the Soviet Union, and bellowing anti-Soviet propaganda is tantamount to adopting an anti-Communist stand and opposing the Ethiopian revolution.[40]

The Dergue applied this vision more in its domestic politics than in foreign relations. It found China's strained relations with the Soviet Union as inconsistent with Beijing's professed commitment to socialism. But criticism of China did not make Chinese military aid incompatible with the Dergue's struggle for *Ethiopian Socialism* (national unity).

The Dergue decorated Ethiopia with Socialist icons to make symbolic statements. The statues of Marx and Engels which guarded the entrance to Addis Ababa University (the former Haile Selassie I University) were meant mostly to reassure Ethiopian students who doubted the Dergue's Marxist credentials. The other visible displays of Marxist icons near the office of the United Nations Economic Commission for Africa proclaimed to international civil servants in Ethiopia the Dergue's faithfulness to the Soviet Union, even if it was only symbolic. But the Dergue's favorite Communist thinker was neither Marx nor Lenin. He was K.P. Artouski, a Soviet citizen and hero of World War II. In addressing the key question over which so much blood was shed during the Ethiopian revolution: "Who is a Communist?," the Dergue's ideological mouthpiece, *Meskerem*, heralded Artousky's view that:

> to be a communist is a great thing [but] it is not for anyone to have that honour. A Communist is a person of a special mould for whom duty constitutes the whole meaning of life. . . .

In revolutionary politics, Artouski, more than Marx, had the greatest appeal to the Dergue's leadership. Mengistu saw himself as a Communist in Artouski's definition. Duty to Ethiopia and towards Ethiopian unity were the meaning of life to Mengistu.[41]

Whereas the Dergue expanded its sources of military aid, and opportunistically labeled itself as Marxist, Communist and Socialist, the Khmer Rouge remained true to its foreign policy of engagement with its only one friend with the proper Marxist revolutionary characteristics: China. Kiernan notes that revolutionary Cambodia had received five convoys of military equipment from China by April 1977, and the last of these included "several ships carrying over thirty tanks and ten amphibious tanks." Cambodian port engineer Ung Pech actually witnessed the arrival in Kompong Som, in late 1976, of Chinese "tanks, armored personnel carriers, artillery, and guns." These eyewitness accounts of Chinese arms shipment to Cambodia have been corroborated by "a former staff member of the Chinese embassy" in Cambodia under the Khmer Rouge. He confirmed to Kiernan that "by the end of 1978, Beijing delivered to Cambodia two fast gunships of over eight hundred tons and four patrol boats, plus two hundred tanks, three hundred armored cars, three hundred artillery pieces, thirty thousand tons of ammunition, six jet fighters, and two bombers." The Khmer Rouge also hosted fifteen thousand Chinese technicians and advisors, as the Dergue did five thousand Soviet "advisors."[42]

ATTITUDES TOWARD WESTERN HUMANITARIAN AID

Anti-Americanism and references to the United States and Western countries as "imperialists" have formed part of the revolutionary politics of liberation movements in the developing world. But none went as far as seeing the United States as a perpetual enemy and totally closing itself to the West as the Khmer Rouge did in Cambodia. The Dergue's pragmatism, reflected in its relationship with Western countries such as the United States, contrasts sharply with Angkar's self-imposed isolation from the West.

Unlike the Pol Pot regime, the Mengistu regime was willing to downplay ideology and foreign policy principles for cooperation and even repudiate them if that served to enhance the Dergue's power and political survival. But pragmatism did not of course erase the Dergue's suspicion of the United States and other Western countries. The difference was in degree. The Khmer Rouge carried its suspicion of and antipathy towards the West farther than the Dergue's. Their different ideologies, revolutionary objectives and historical experiences with U.S. conduct shaped their views of the United States. Based on its 1969–73 experience of American bombardments, the Khmer Rouge raised its suspicion of the "American imperialists" to the level of a dogma.

The Khmer Rouge rejected offers of famine-aid and other humanitarian assistance given to Cambodia by Western humanitarian organizations such as the Save the Children Foundation and the International Committee of the Red Cross. The Cambodian regime had ideologically-rooted beliefs that food aid served as "means for foreign [read Western] powers to manipulate and subvert" the Cambodian revolution.[43] The Dergue's acceptance of military and food aid from every country willing to provide them, including the United States the Ethiopian regime called "imperialist," testifies to the Mengistu regime's pragmatism in comparison to the Khmer Rouge. By the end of 1984, the United States had offered, and Ethiopia had accepted, U.S. $112 million worth of American food, medicines and other assistance to relieve famine.[44]

The Ethiopian regime also sought U.S. arbitration in its war with its political opponents late in the 1980s, but failed to save itself in the process. It welcomed U.S. Assistant Secretary of State for African Affairs Herman Cohen to Addis Ababa in 1989 and showed great interest in U.S. attempts to negotiate peace between the Dergue and the EPLF. As Merahehiwot has accurately observed, at this time, the Dergue's armed opponents had "moved closer to the capital." The EPLF had captured "most of Eritrea." Military cooperation between the EPLF and TPLF had also brought the latter significant gains. All of Tigray province in the north was in the hands of the TPLF. The armed group also controlled parts of southern and western Ethiopia. The beleaguered Mengistu regime was "ready to talk."[45] More pragmatism was visible here; a sharp contrast with the Pol Pot regime.

The Dergue made some pragmatic compromises in the late 1980s. The often mistakenly labeled "Marxist" revolutionary military junta "completely dropped the use of Marxist vocabulary." Mengistu instructed the Ethiopian Mission to the United Nations to take a "helpful line . . . on the [first] Gulf War issue." The rhetorically anti-American Dergue robustly supported the U.S.-led campaign against Iraq in 1991. But as has often been the case in U.S.-Ethiopian relations, Washington did not reciprocate Ethiopia's diplomatic gestures. While the Mengistu regime, in its final days, frantically sought the attention of the United States to save itself from a looming defeat at the hands of a coalition of anti-Dergue armed groups, Washington was more interested in arranging the departure of the Ethiopian Jews for Israel. Under pressure from U.S. and Canadian government officials, and promises from them to guarantee Mengistu and his family a safe exit to Zimbabwe, Mengistu gave in. As Merahehiwot notes, the revolutionary Ethiopian government fell "72 hours after the last planeload of Ethiopian Jews left for Tel Aviv [on May 28, 1991]."[46] The Pol Pot regime had fallen twelve years before the demise of the Mengistu regime.

CONCLUSION

The Dergue and the Angkar followed different paths towards divergent though sometimes intersecting goals. And they struck different and contradictory foreign alliances to reach those goals. The Dergue found in the Soviet Union a reliable ally and had great affection for Vietnam, whereas the Khmer Rouge viewed the Soviet Union as an implacable ideological enemy, and Vietnam a hereditary foe. The Dergue was very critical of China, the country from which the Khmer Rouge derived its military, political and ideological support. But the Dergue's criticisms of Beijing did not bar the military regime from pursuing a beneficial relationship with China. The differing views of the Dergue and the Khmer Rouge on international affairs, and their divergent foreign relations, are further indications of the different nature and motivations of the Ethiopian and Cambodian revolutionary regimes.

The Dergue and the Angkar displayed the characteristics of twentieth century African and Asian nationalists. They were anti-American and anti-Western in their revolutionary politics. But the Khmer Rouge carried that politics farther. It refused to accept food aid from the United States and other Western countries while a million Cambodians died from famine during the revolution. That demonstrated the regime's fanaticism and its uncompromising outlook. By contrast, the Dergue was pragmatic. Its anti-Americanism was a propaganda tool and not a deep-seated ideology. It sought and accepted American and Western food aid and struck a good working relationship with various countries. That compromising outlook on foreign affairs helped the Dergue to save millions of lives that would otherwise have been lost as a result of the famine in Ethiopia during the revolution. In the process, the military regime also saved itself from early demise.

Both the Dergue and the Angkar hung the legitimacy of their revolutions on the fate of their national borders. But the Dergue emphasized preservation of those borders; the Khmer Rouge preferred expansion of them. Both regimes made militarism an element of their quest, but they met different fates from that choice. Khmer Rouge aggression provoked external invasion and its early demise at the hands of Vietnam. The Dergue, victim of unprovoked invasion by its eastern neighbor, Somalia, strengthened its nationalist credentials and power.

The Mengistu regime failed in its ultimate revolutionary objective of preserving Ethiopia's borders. Eritrea seceded from Ethiopia and became an independent state in April 1993. Pol Pot died on April 15, 1998. As at the time of the completion of this book, Mengistu Haile Mariam lives in exile in Zimbabwe. That gesture had been extended to him by Zimbabwe's Prime Minister Robert Mugabe in appreciation of for Mengistu's assistance in Zimbabwe's struggle for independence from

British colonial rule. Mengistu's flight to Zimbabwe was secretly facilitated by Canada and the United States.

NOTES

1. Kiernan, *The Pol Pot Regime*, 366. See also Democratic Kampuchea, Foreign Ministry Internal Document, "The Border History of Kampuchea-Vietnam," June 15, 1977, 24, 27.

2. Weitz, *Century of Genocide*, 158.

3. Author's interview with Col. Tadese Chernet, Army Ordnance Officer, Ground Forces, Addis Ababa, Ethiopia, May 12, 1999.

4. DK Foreign Ministry Internal Document, "The Border History," 4, 9, 10–13, 27. See also Kiernan, *The Pol Pot Regime*, 360.

5. Merahehiwot Gabremariam, "Ethio-U.S. Relations," *Ethioscope* (A quarterly magazine dealing with issues related to Ethiopia's foreign relationship), 1, no. 2 (January 1995): 11.

6. For the statement of the foreign policy objectives of the Dergue, see *The Ethiopian Herald*, September 12, 1974, 4.

7. Phat Kosal and Ben Kiernan, translators, *Ieng Sary's Regime: A Diary of the Khmer Rouge Foreign Ministry, 1976–79*, <http://www.yale.edu/cgp> (September 1998).

8. Kosal and Kiernan, "Ieng Sary's Regime," 8. See also DK Foreign Ministry, Internal Document No. 9, "Examining Vietnamese Reactions in the 5th Meeting on 14–5–76 morning," 15 <http://www.yale.edu/cgp>.

9. "Special National Congress Retains Sihanouk," *FBIS Daily Report*, 4, no. 82 (April 25, 1975): H1–2.

10. See Document 2, "Angkar's Political Line in Foreign Affairs," in "Ieng Sary's Regime" translated by Kosal and Kiernan.

11. DK Foreign Ministry, Internal Document, "Speech of Comrade Secretary [Pol Pot] in the First Ministerial Committee Meeting,"April 22, 1976, 14.

12. Kosal and Kiernan, "Ieng Sary Regime." See also DK Foreign Ministry, Internal Document No. 11, "Conversation Between Vice-President of the Cabinet, Ieng Sary, and Vice-President of Democratic Republic of Vietnam, Comrade Phan Phean, on 19–5–1976," <http://www.yale.edu/cgp>.

13. DK Foreign Ministry, "Speech of Comrade Secretary [Pol Pot] in the First Ministerial Committee Meeting," 18.

14. Diary of the Khmer Rouge Foreign Ministry, Internal Document 34, "Objectives to Direct the Work of the Ministry of Foreign Affairs from July 1976 to

July 1977," July 14, 1976; "Objectives to Direct the Work of the Ministry of Foreign Affairs from July 1976 to July 1977," <http://www.yale.edu/cgp>.

15. DK Foreign Ministry, Internal Document, "The Minutes of the Standing Committee Meeting," <http://www.yale.edu/cgp> (May 3, 1976), 2.

16. DK Foreign Ministry, "Speech of Comrade Secretary," April 22, 1976, 13.

17. See "Who Is a Communist," *Meskerem* (the Ideological newsletter of the Dergue), 1, no. 2 (January 1981): 19.

18. DK Foreign Ministry, "The Border History," 1.

19. DK Foreign Ministry, Internal Document, "Examining Vietnamese Reactions in the 5th Meeting on 14–5–76 morning."

20. Kiernan, *The Pol Pot Regime*, 357.

21. Kiernan, *The Pol Pot Regime*, 360.

22. Merahehiwot, "Ethio-U.S. Relations," 17.

23. DK Foreign Ministry, "Examining Vietnamese Reactions."

24. Kiernan, *The Pol Pot Regime*, 362, 366.

25. Becker, *When the War Was Over: Cambodia and the Khmer Rouge Revolution*, 293.

26. Dawit, *Red Tears*, 40.

27. Merahehiwot, "Ethio-U.S. Relations," 15.

28. Amare Tekle, "Continuity and Change in Ethiopian Politics," in *The Political Economy of Ethiopia*, ed. Marina Ottaway (New York: Praeger, 1990), p. 36. See also Dawit, *Red Tears*, 40.

29. Dawit, *Red Tears*, 20.

30. Interview with Tesfaye Mekasha Amare.

31. Dawit, *Red Tears*, 70.

32. See "Khmer Rouge National Army: Order of Battle," <http://www.yale.edu/cgp/translate/army.htm> (January 1976).

33. Dawit, *Red Tears*, 36; Merahehiwot, "Ethio-U.S. Relations," 13.

34. Merahehiwot, "Ethio-U.S. Relations," 12.

35. Merahehiwot, "Ethio-U.S. Relations," 12.

36. United States Congress, Senate, Committee on Foreign Relations, *Ethiopia and the Horn of Africa: Hearings Before the Subcommittee on African Affairs*, 2nd Session, 94th Congress, August 4–6, 1976, 90, 96, 128.

37. Merahehiwot, "Ethio-U.S. Relations," 13.

38. Dawit, *Red Tears*, 70.

39. Paulos, "Mengistu Haile Mariam," 52.

40. See *Meskerem*, "The Content of Ideology and the Means of Its Dissemination," 2, no. 6 (September 1981): 25, 40.

41. See "Who Is a Communist?," *Meskerem*, 1, no. 2 (January 1981): 19.

42. Kiernan, *The Pol Pot Regime*, 378–79.

43. Becker, *When the War Was Over: Cambodia and the Khmer Rouge Revolution*, 170.

44. U.S.-Ethiopian relations in the area of famine relief was not without acrimonious political disagreements. See Kissi, "Famine and the Politics of Relief," chapter 8.

45. Merahehiwot, "Ethio-U.S. Relations," 17.

46. Merahehiwot, "Ethio-U.S. Relations," 17.

CONCLUSION

.

The Ethiopian and Cambodian revolutionary experiences compared in
this book offer many lessons for the comparative study of genocide. Not
only does the comparison represent one important example of a fault-
line in the connection between revolution and genocide, but also it
helps us to reflect on the implications that false comparisons and analo-
gies could have for the study of genocide and its underlying ethics. As
Robert Cribb has reminded us, genocide scholarship could encounter a
major ethical dilemma if scholars equate political mass murder with
genocide or conflate the two. That would mean that for the study of
genocide to have any analytical and predictive value, it would need to
examine the entire political circumstances that led to the killing of one
group of political activists in a two-way political conflict. The complaints
of accused officials of the Dergue in Ethiopia's ongoing "genocide" trial
of perpetrators of political murder illuminate Cribb's point.

If political killing (politicide) is included in the rubric of genocide as
Ethiopian law does, then the study and prosecution of politicides of the
kind that occurred in Ethiopia, in which other non-state groups (guerrilla
movements and liberation fronts) also participated in the killing of people, would require examination of both sides of the situation that produced mass murder. It would be unthinkable to apply the same method
of analysis to investigation of the other form of genocide (ethnic-based

killing) because the implication that the victims may also have partici-pated in murder or could bear some responsibility for what happened to them would be conceptually, analytically and ethically outrageous. Ethi-cally, no victim group in a political killing (politicide) or ethnic-based massacres (genocide) should be blamed or can be deemed to deserve their fate. Hence, it is not only the bewildering implications of equating political killing with racial and ethnic massacres that should trouble us. We should also be concerned about the implications for the study of genocide of not defining the amorphous category called "political groups" and drawing distinctions between the many types and guises in which "political groups" come.

The Ethiopian case reinforces the argument against inclusion of the killing of particular political groups in the concept of genocide. The Dergue did not kill political opponents because they held a dissenting political view. The political opponents the revolutionary regime targeted were mainly organized armed groups bent on eliminating the leadership of the Ethiopian military regime and those who supported it. Scholars who argue that separating "ethnic groups" and "political groups" is im-possible because political groups, like ethnic and religious groups, can-not cease to be who they are in their corporate or collective identity as holders of particular beliefs are conceptually correct. An analytical ar-gument can also be made that it is not impossible for political groups who hold and pass on particular beliefs to members of their group to cease pursuing those political beliefs with violence. If the ultimate goal of studying how and why genocides happen is to provide the ideas needed to prevent genocide and thereby create stable and functioning societies able to preserve the sanctity of human life, then a clear dis-tinction ought to be drawn between "[armed] political groups" and other "political activists" who pursue their objectives through violence and "[defenseless] political groups" and other "political organizations" whose members are not armed, but just hold opinions that may differ from conventional views and pursue their aims without violence. Such a distinction should also emphasize that unless the killing of political groups (both armed and defenseless) includes or leads to the destruc-tion of the families and the ethnic groups from which such groups orig-inate (which did not happen in Ethiopia), then such killing should be called politicide and not genocide.

There is no convincing evidence that perpetrators in Ethiopia (the Dergue and its armed opponents) who committed politicide went beyond their principal political targets to obliterate the families of their victims or many or all of the members of the ethnic groups from which their opponents came. This is a significant difference between what happened in Ethiopia and what took place in Cambodia. Redefining political groups and distinguishing between politicide and genocide can benefit from the insights provided in this book into why genocide did not take place in Ethiopia, but did in Cambodia though both societies experienced a violent and bloody revolution.

Differences in social structure and the political contexts of the two revolutions offer one of many explanations. Ethiopia was much more plural. And the Dergue, which itself was multi-ethnic in its composition, could not target one particular ethnic group for destruction without encountering dissension within its own ranks and opposition from the larger society. The mono-ethnic Khmer Rouge, however, did not have the restraints of a pluralist social structure that the Dergue had and, therefore, had no scruples in targeting particular ethnic groups for destruction. Furthermore, in Ethiopia armed non-state groups and other politicized ethnic groups pursuing competing political objectives with violence could defend themselves. Second, differences in ideology also explain why genocide occurred in the context of revolution in Cambodia, but not in Ethiopia. Khmer Rouge Maoist revolutionary ideology was totalitarian, millenarian and racist. Ethiopian revolutionary marxism, if such existed at all, was pragmatic, opportunist and egalitarian. Thus, the Dergue in Ethiopia was driven to use opportunistic ideological formulas and alliances for political survival. The Khmer Rouge, on the other hand, was driven by Marxist, racist and utopian dogma as an end in itself. Unlike the Khmer Rouge which abolished religion and upheld the supremacy of Khmer identity against ethnic and religious minority rights, the Dergue saw racial and religious equality as the essence of a pan-Ethiopian identity.

A comparative study of the Ethiopian and Cambodian revolutions demonstrates that the potential for genocide and politicide of the magnitude committed in the two revolutionary societies becomes greater under circumstances that go beyond social structure, ideology or even war and revolution. How revolutionary regimes acquire power, the control they exercise in the revolutionary society, the domestic opposition they face, the international support they receive and the cultural contexts in which they operate are equally important. In Ethiopia, a reform-minded group of soldiers had power thrust upon them by a convergence of circumstances at a historical juncture when they least expected it, and in a political culture where they feared losing it. Fear of losing power, and sustained domestic opposition from armed civilian competitors, turned the Dergue into a repressive regime. By contrast, well-known Khmer Communists seized power after a five-year civil war and pursued a repressive and exclusionary policy of racial purification without any organized and determined domestic opposition. Hence, whatever the similarities between the Khmer Rouge and the Dergue in their use of terror and violence in the course of their revolutions, there was no Ethiopian equivalent of the dogmatic adherence to ideology and the genocidal racism of the Khmer Rouge.

Pol Pot and Mengistu may seem to be revolutionary bedfellows to scholars who mistake political rhetoric for ideological convictions. But, it is in closer scrutiny of what lay behind their rhetoric that Mengistu and Pol Pot appear to be the revolutionary oddfellows that they were. The outlook of the Pol Pot regime and the Mengistu regime on world politics, the foreign policy principles they enunciated, the compromises they made or refused to make in their foreign relations and the international alliances they forged reveal the different nature and motives of the Cambodian and the Ethiopian revolutions and their leaders. The Dergue was opportunistically pro-Soviet and anti-China. The Khmer Rouge was ideologically pro-China and anti-Soviet. From their attitude towards foreigners and foreign aid and their varying approaches to their border problems, the differences between the Dergue and the Khmer Rouge become even more manifest.

The Khmer Rouge rejected offers of aid from Western countries to relieve the famine which occurred during the revolution. That accorded with its doctrinaire outlook on world politics and ideological antipathy towards the West. The Dergue asked for and accepted aid from Western countries, and indeed from everyone who offered it, to relieve famine which occurred during its revolution. Ethiopia became the symbol of international famine-relief operations in the late twentieth century. That was consistent with the Dergue's pragmatic outlook on world politics and its opportunist approach to revolution. Here, the primacy of power and political survival in the Dergue's revolutionary practice is highlighted in the compromises it made and the cooperative relations it struck with its "foreign enemies." By contrast, the Khmer Rouge's fanaticism is clearly distinguished by its uncompromising pursuit of a self-destructive ideology of self-reliance.

Both revolutionary regimes were instigated by fear of enemies: the Dergue of enemies within and the Angkar of enemies without. The Khmer Rouge had visions of an imperial reign over greater territory. The Dergue sought to defend a territorial status quo. But the difference between the Dergue and the Khmer Rouge was how each responded to insecurity. The Khmer Rouge responded to insecurity by surging ahead with racial purges and rapid Communist transformation of Cambodia. The Dergue moved cautiously about its social reforms and sacrificed a communist transformation of Ethiopia to enforced national unity. The Khmer Rouge provoked a Vietnamese invasion of Cambodia through bellicose attacks on its eastern neighbor in furtherance of its racial hatred of Vietnam and apparent determination to retake Vietnamese territories inhabited in part by ethnic-Khmer. The Dergue was the victim of unprovoked external aggression from its eastern neighbor, Somalia. It repulsed the invasion by defending the Ogaden, Ethiopian territory inhabited by ethnic-Somalis, in its determination to preserve Ethiopia's traditional borders. What happened in revolutionary Ethiopia was, therefore, not a mirror image of what occurred in revolutionary Cambodia as Dawit Wolde Giorgis, Robert Kaplan and John Dunn have inaccurately argued.

While the Khmer Rouge committed crimes against humanity and genocide as defined in the UN Genocide Convention, the pattern of violence against political opponents in revolutionary Ethiopia makes the Dergue's crimes acts of politicide and crimes against humanity, not genocide under international law. There is, however, a common lesson that can be drawn from Ethiopia's and Cambodia's uncommon experience of social revolution. The Dergue and the Angkar became so ruthless, and unpopular, that very few regretted their demise. Vietnamese troops entered Phnom Penh on January 7, 1979 to overthrow the Khmer Rouge without popular resistance. And Ethiopians hailed the entry of a coalition of anti-Dergue groups to Addis Ababa on May 28, 1991 to oust one of the most repressive military regimes in the history of the twentieth century.

SELECT BIBLIOGRAPHY

PRIMARY SOURCES: INTERVIEWS WITH INDIVIDUALS

Andreas Eshete. Former member of EPRP. Current President of Addis Ababa University.

David Korn. Former U.S. Charge d'Affaires in Ethiopia.

Gebru Mersha. Former member of the EPRP, and Professor of Political Science, Addis Ababa University.

Kifle Wodajo. Former *Dergue* Minister of Foreign Affairs.

Kong Peng. Cambodian student at the University of Oregon.

Melaku Tegegne. Former member of the EPRP.

Merera Gudina. Former member of *Me'ison*.

Merid Wolde Aregay. History Department, Addis Ababa University.

Mesfin Wolde Mariam. Chairman, Ethiopian Human Rights Council.

Tadese Chernet. Former Member of Ethiopian Army, Ground Forces.

Tekalign Wolde Mariam. History Department, Addis Ababa University.

Tesfaye Mekasha Amare, ex Vice-Foreign Minister, Imperial Ethiopian Government.

Yeraswork Admassu. Former member of the EPRP.

Zegeye Asfaw. Former *Dergue* Minister of Settlement, Dergue regime.

INTERVIEWS WITH GROUPS

Interview with Amhara and Oromo resettlees at Pawe Resettlement villages 14 and 23. Pawe, East Gojjam Administrative Zone. Ethiopia. October 1, 1995.

Interview with Kembatta resettlees. Pawe, East Gojjam Administrative Zone. Ethiopia. October 1, 1995.

Interview with 8 farmers including ex-peasant association leaders at Kutaber, North Wollo Administrative Zone. Ethiopia. October 20, 1995.

Interview with a group of peasants at Mersa, North Wollo Administrative Zone. Ethiopia. October 20, 1995.

Interview with 8 peasants at Wegel Tena, North Wollo Administrative Zone. Ethiopia. October 12, 1995.

GOVERNMENT DOCUMENTS AND ARCHIVAL SOURCES

Agreement between the United Nations and the Royal Government of Cambodia Concerning the Prosecution Under Cambodian Law of Crimes Committed during the Period of Democratic Kampuchea. http://migs.concordia.ca/links/Cambodia.html (June 6, 2003).

Christian Relief and Development Association (CRDA) Archives. RRC Reports and Minutes Files. January–December 1985, and January–December 1986.

Convention on the Prevention and Punishment of the Crime of Genocide, Approved and Proposed for Signature and Ratification or Accession by UN General Assembly Resolution 260 A (III) of December 9, 1948.

Democratic Kampuchea. Foreign Ministry Internal Document. "The Border History of Kampuchea-Vietnam."

———. Foreign Ministry Internal Document No. 9. "Examining Vietnamese Reactions in the 5th Meeting on 14–5–76 morning." <http://www.yale.edu/cgp>

———. Foreign Ministry Internal Document. "Speech of Comrade Secretary in the First Ministerial Committee." April 22, 1976.

———. Foreign Ministry Internal Document No. 11. "Conversation Between Vice President of the Cabinet, Ieng Sary, and Vice President of Democratic Republic of Vietnam, Comrade Phan Phean, on 19–5–1976." <http://www.yale.edu/cgp>

———. Foreign Ministry Internal Document No. 43. "Objectives to Direct the Work of the Ministry of Foreign Affairs from July 1976 to July 1977. <http://www.yale.edu/cgp> (May 3, 1976).

——. Foreign Ministry Internal Document. "The Minutes of the Standing Committee Meeting." <http://www.yale.edu/cgp> (May 3, 1976).

——. "Khmer Rouge National Army: Order of Battle." <http://www.yale.edu/cgp/translate/army.htm> (January 1976).

Empire of Ethiopia. *Penal Code of the Empire of Ethiopia of 1957.*

Food and Agricultural Organization (FAO) Archives. Addis Ababa, Ethiopia. RRC Files No. IL 2/2. February 1986–August 1987, and Jananuary–December 1988.

Ministry of Agriculture Archives. Addis Ababa Ethiopia. Provisional Military Government of Socialist Ethiopia. Planning and Programming Department. "Food Crop Development Information, July 1978."

Ministry of Natural Resources Development and Environmental Protection . Archives. Addis Ababa. World Bank Office Memorandum. "Ethiopia: Recent Political Developments and Bank Operations." December 13, 1974.

Ministry of Agriculture. Documentation Center. Addis Ababa. "General Agricultural Survey: Preliminary Report, 1983–1984." vol. 1.

Relief and Rehabilitation (RRC) Documentation Center. Addis Ababa. File No. A6.91.

Rome Statute of the International Criminal Court. http://www.iccnow.org/romearchive/romestatue/rome-e.doc (1998).

Transitional Government of Ethiopia. Central High Court. *Genocide and Crimes Against Humanity.* Part 1. Unofficial Draft Translation. Addis Ababa, October 1994.

United Nations War Crimes Commission. Law Reports of Trials of War Criminals. Vol. 15 (1948).

United States National Archives. Washington, D.C. Record Group (RG) 59: British Africa: 1955–1959. Box 4881. Joseph Simonson, U.S. Ambassador to Ethiopia, to Secretary of State. "Comments on a New Generation of Ethiopians." April 21, 1955.

——. RG 59. Lot File No. 57, D616, Box 13. "Summary of Remarks Made by His Imperial Majesty at Audience Granted on March 12, 1957 to the Vice President of the United States.

U.S. Congress. Senate. Committee on Foreign Relations. Ethiopia and the Horn: *Hearings Before the Subcommittee on African Affairs.* 94th Congress. 2nd Session. August 4–6, 1976.

World Food Program Archives. Addis Ababa. Incoming Cables. "Canadian Broadcasting Corporation Interview with Ethiopia's Head of State." February 27, 1985.

Workers Party of Ethiopia. *Report by Mengistu Haile Mariam: Resolutions Adopted by the Plenum.* Addis Ababa. March 6, 1990.

SECONDARY SOURCES: BOOKS AND ARTICLES

Addis Hiwet. Ethiopia: *From Autocracy to Revolution*. London: Review of African Political Economy, 1975.

Amnesty International (Canadian Section). "File on Torture: Ethiopia." vol. 14, no. 3 (April 1987).

Andargachew Tiruneh. *The Ethiopian Revolution 1974–1987: A Transformation from an Aristocratic to a Totalitarian Autocracy*. Cambridge: Cambridge University Press, 1993.

Bahru Zewde. *A History of Modern Ethiopia, 1855–1974*. Addis Ababa: Addis Ababa University Press, 1991.

Balsvik, Randi R. *Haile Sellassie's Students: The Intellectual and Social Background to Revolution, 1952–1977*. East Lansing, MI: Michigan University Press, 1985.

——— et al. "Bureaucracy of Death: Documents from Inside Pol Pot's Torture Machine." *New Statesman* 99 no. 2563 (May 1980): 669–76.

Becker, Elizabeth. *When the War Was Over: The Voices of Cambodia's Revolution and Its People*. New York: Simon and Schuster, 1986.

———. *When the War Was Over: Cambodia and the Khmer Rouge Revolution*. New York: Public Affairs, 1998.

Boua, Chanthou. "Genocide of a Religious Group: Pol Pot and Cambodia's Buddhist Monks." Pp. 669–676 in *State-Organized Terror: The Case of Violent Internal Repression*, edited by Timothy Bushnell et. al. Boulder: Westview, 1991.

Chalk, Frank and Kurt Jonassohn. *The History and Sociology of Genocide: Analyses and Case Studies*. New Haven: Yale University Press, 1990.

Chandler, David P. *The Tragedy of Cambodian History: War, Politics and Revolution Since 1945*. New Haven: Yale University Press, 1991.

———. *The Land and People of Cambodia*. New York: Harper Collins Publishers, 1991.

———. *Brother Number One: A Political Biography Pol Pot*. Boulder, CO: Westview, 1992.

———. *Voices from S-21: Terror and History in Pol Pot's Secret Prison*. Berkeley: University of California Press, 1999.

——— and Ben Kiernan. *Revolution and Its Aftermath in Kampuchea: Eight Essays*. Yale Southeast Asia Studies Monograph Series No. 25, 1983.

———, et al., ed. *Pol Pot Plans the Future: Confidential Leadership Documents from Democratic Kampuchea, 1976–1977*. Yale Southeast Asia Studies Monograph Series 33, 1988.

Charny, Israel W. "Towards a Generic Definition of Genocide." Pp. 64–94 in *Genocide: Conceptual and Historical Dimensions*, edited by George Andeopoulos. Philadelphia: University of Pennsylvania Press, 1997.

————, ed. *Encyclopedia of Genocide*. Vols 1 & 2. Santa Barbara, CA: ABC-CLIO, 1999.

Chigas, George. "The Politics of defining justice after the Cambodian genocide." *Journal of Genocide Research* 2, no. 2 (June 2000): 245–65.

Chorbajian, Levon and George Shirinian. *Studies in Comparative Genocide* (New York: St. Martin's Press, 1999).

Clapham, Christopher. *Transformation and Continuity in Revolutionary Ethiopia*. Cambridge, MA: Cambridge University Press, 1988.

Clymer, Kenton J. "The Perils of Neutrality: The Break in U.S.-Cambodian Relations, 1965." *Diplomatic History* 23, no. 4 (Fall 1999): 609–31.

Cook, Sisan. "Prosecuting Genocide in Cambodia: The Winding Path Towards Justice." <http://www.yale.edu/cgp>.

Courtois, Stephane et al. *The Black Book of Communism: Crimes, Terror, Repression* (Cambridge, MA.: Harvard University Press, 1999).

Cribb, Robert. "Genocide in the Non-Western World." *International Institute for Asian Studies Newsletter* 25 (July 2001): 6.

————. "Genocide in the non-Western World: Implications for Holocaust Studies." Pp. 123–140 in *Genocide: Cases, Comparisons and Contemporary Debates*, edited by Steven L.B. Jensen. Copenhagen: The Danish Center for Holocaust and Genocide Studies, 2003.

Criddle, Joann and Teeda Butt Mam. *To Destroy You is No Loss: The Odyssey of a Cambodian Family*. New York: The Atlantic Monthly Press, 1987.

Davidson, Basil, Lionel Cliffe and Bereket Habte Sellassie. *Behind the War in Eritrea* (Nottingham: Spokesman, 1980).

Deac, Wilfred P. *Road to the Killing Fields*. College Station: Texas A&M University Press, 1997

De Nike, Howard J. et. al. *Genocide in Cambodia: Documents from the Trial of Pol Pot and Ieng Sary*. Philadelphia: University of Pennsylvania Press, 2000.

Dessalegn Rahmato. *Famine and Survival Strategies: A Case Study from Northeast Ethiopia*. ppsala: Nordiska Afrikainstitutet, 1991.

Donham, Donald L. *Marxist Modern: An Ethnographic History of the Ethiopian Revolution*. Los Angeles: University of California Press, 1999.

Dunn, John. *Modern Revolutions: An Introduction to the Analysis of a Political Phenomenon*. Cambridge, MA: Cambridge University Press, 1989.

Etcheson, Craig. "The Politics of Justice in Cambodia." Paper presented at the Montreal Institute of Genocide and Human Rights Studies, Montreal, Canada, September 12, 2003.

Ethiopian News Agency. Ethiopia: *State Terrorism on Trial: Genocide and Crime Against Humanity*. Addis Ababa: Ethiopian News Agency, 1998.

Ethiopian Students Union in North America. *Repression in Africa*. Cambridge, MA.: Africa Research Group, 1971.

Fein, Helen. "Revolutionary and Antirevolutionary Genocides: A Comparison of State Murders in Democratic Kampuchea, 1975 to 1979, and in Indonesia, 1965 to 1966," *Comparative Studies in Society and History* 35, no. 3 (July 1993): 796–823.

———. "Genocide, Terror, Life Integrity, and War Crimes: The Case for Discrimination." Pp. 95–107 in *Genocide: Conceptual and Historical Dimensions*, edited by George Andeopoulos. Philadelphia: University of Pennsylvania Press, 1997.

———. *Genocide: A Sociological Perspective*. London: Sage, 1993.

Firebrace, James (with Stuart Holland). *Never Kneel Down: Drought, Development and Liberation*. Trenton, NJ: The Red Sea Press, 1986.

Gebru Tareke. *Ethiopia: Power and Protest, Peasant Revolts in the Twentieth Century*. Cambridge, MA: Cambridge University Press, 1991.

Gellately, Robert and Ben Kiernan. ed. *The Specter of Genocide: Mass Murder in Historical Perspective*. Cambridge, MA: Cambridge University Press, 2003.

Gilkes, Patrick. *The Dying Lion: Feudalism and Modernization in Ethiopia*. New York: St Martin's Press, 1975.

Goldstone, Jack A., Ted Robert Gurr and Farrokh Moshiri. *Revolutions of the Late Twentieth Century*. Boulder: Westview, 1991.

Greenfield, Richard. Ethiopia: *A New Political History*. London: Pall Mall, 1965.

Guillebaud, Jean-Claude. "Dergue's red terror." *The Guardian Weekly* 118, no. 9 (February 1978): 11.

Gurr, Ted Robert and Barbara Harff. "Systematic Early Warning of Humanitarian Emergencies." *Journal of Peace Research* 35, no. 5 (1998): 551–79.

Halliday, Fred and Maxine Mollyneux. *The Ethiopian Revolution*. London: Unwin Brothers, 1981.

Harff, Barbara. "No lessons Learned from the Holocaust?: Assessing Risks of Genocide and Political Mass Murder since 1965." *American Political Science Review* 97, no. 1 (February 2003): 57–73.

——— and Ted Robert Gurr. "Victims of the State: Genocides, Politicides and Group Repression Since 1945." *International Review of Victimology* 1 (1989): 23–41.

Hegel, Friedrich G.W. *The Philosophy of History*, translated by J. Sibree. New York: Dover Publications, 1956.

Heuveline, Patrick. "Between One and Three Million: Towards the Demographic Reconstruction of a Decade of Cambodian History (1970–79)." *Population Studies* 52 (1998): 49–65.

Hinton, Alexander. ed. *Annihilating Difference: The Anthropology of Genocide* (Berkeley: University of California Press, 2002).

———. "A Head for an Eye: Revenge, Culture, and the Cambodia Genocide." Paper presented at the meeting of the Association of Genocide Scholars, Montreal, Canada, November, 1997.

Jackson, Karl D. *Cambodia: Rendezvous with Death.* Princeton, NJ: Princeton University Press, 1989.

Kaplan, Robert D. *Surrender or Starve: The Wars Behind the Famine.* Boulder, CO: Westview Press, 1988.

———. Kaplan, Robert D. "The African Killing Fields." *The Washington Monthly,* Vol 28, No.8 (September 1988): 27–36.

Kaufeler, Heinz. *Modernization, Legitimacy and Social Movement: A Study of Socio-Cultural Dynamics and Revolution in Iran and Ethiopia.* Zurich: Ethnologische Schriften, 1988

Keller, Edmond J. *Revolutionary Ethiopia: From Empire to People's Republic.* Bloomington: Indiana University Press, 1988.

Kiernan, Ben. *The Pol Pot Regime: Race, Power and Genocide in Cambodia Under the Khmer Rouge, 1975–79.* New Haven: Yale University Press, 1996.

———. *How Pol Pot Came to Power: A History of Communism in Kampuchea, 1930–1975.* London: Verso, 1985.

———. *How Pol Pot Came to Power: Colonialism, nationalism, and Communism in Cambodia, 1930–1975.* 2nd edition. New Haven: Yale University Press, 2004.

———. "The Cambodian genocide—1975–1979." Pp. 334–71 in *Century of Genocide: Eyewitness Accounts and Critical Essays,* edited by Samuel Totten, W.S. Parsons and Israel W. Charny. New York: Garland, 1997.

———. "Conflict in the Kampuchean Communist Movement." *Journal of Contemporary Asia* 10, nos. 1–2 (1980): 7–65.

———. "Genocidal Targeting: Two Groups of Victims in Pol Pot's Cambodia." Pp. 207–225 in *State-Organized Terror: The Case of Violent Internal Repression,* edited by Timothy Bushnell et al. Boulder: Westview, 1991.

——— and Chanthou Boua. *Peasants and Politics in Kampuchea, 1942–1981.* London: Zed Press, 1982.

——— and Phat Kosal. translators. *Ieng Sary's Regime: A Diary of the Khmer Rouge Foreign Ministry, 1976–79.* <http://www.yale.edu/cgp>.

Kiflu Tadesse. *The Generation, Part I: The History of the Ethiopian People's Revolutionary Party.* Trenton, NJ: Red Sea Press, 1993

———. *The Generation, Part II: Ethiopia, Transformation and Conflict: The History of the Ethiopian People's Revolutionary Party.* Trenton, NJ: Red Sea Press, 1998

Kissi, Edward. "Famine and the Politics of Food Relief in United States Relations with Ethiopia: 1950–1991." Ph.D. diss., Department of History, Concordia University, Montreal, Canada, 1997.

Kuper, Leo. Genocide: *Its Political Use in the Twentieth Century.* New Haven: Yale University Press, 1981.

Lefort, Rene. *Ethiopia: An Heretical Revolution?* (London: Zed Books, 1983).

"Letter Written by jailed Derg officials to Prime Minister Meles Zenawi." <http://www.ethiopianreporter.com/displayenglish.php?id=614> (February 9, 2004).

Lijphart, Arend. "Comparative Politics and the Comparative Method." *American Political Science Review*, 65, no. 3 (1971).

Maier, Charles. *The Unmasterable Past: History, Holocaust and German National Identity.* Cambridge, MA: Harvard University Press, 1997.

Markakis, John, and Nega Ayele. *Class and Revolution in Ethiopia.* Nottingham: Spokesman, 1978.

Medhane Tadesse. "EPRP vs TPLF: The Struggle for Supremacy over Tigray, 1975–1978." Paper presented at a Department of History seminar, Addis Ababa University, Ethiopia, June 1995.

Meister, Ulrich. "Ethiopia's Unfinished Revolution." *Swiss Review of World Affairs* 33, no. 2 (May 1983): 10–17.

Melson, Robert. *Revolution and Genocide: On the Origins of the Armenian Genocide and the Holocaust.* Chicago: The University of Chicago Press, 1992.

———. "My Journey in the Study of Genocide." Paper presented at the Sawyer seminar of the Genocide Studies Program, Yale University, September 2000.

Merahehiwot Gebremariam. "Ethio-U.S. Relations." *Ethioscope* 1, no. 2 (January 1995): 6–21.

Mesfin Wolde Mariam. *Rural Vulnerability to Famine, 1958–1977.* London: Intermediate Technology Publications, 1986.

Miller, John K. "An Analysis of the Ethiopian, Iranian and Nicaraguan Revolutions from the Perspective of United States Involvement." Ph.D. diss., the University of Texas at Austin, 1985.

Mosyakov, Dmitry. "The Khmer Rouge and the Vietnamese Communists: A history of their relations as told in the Soviet archives." Yale Center for International and Area Studies, *Genocide Studies Program Working Paper no. 15.*

Ngor, Haing (with Roger Warner), ed. *A Cambodian Odyssey.* New York: Warner Books, 1987.

Niggli, Peter. *Ethiopia: Deportations and Forced Labour Camps: A Study by Peter Niggli on Behalf of the Berliner Missionswerk, 1986.* Berlin: Berliner Missionswerk, 1986.

Ottaway, Marina, ed. *The Political Economy of Ethiopia.* New York: Praeger, 1990.

—— and David Ottaway. *Ethiopia: Empire in Revolution*. New York: Holmer and Meier Publishers, Inc., 1978.

Paulos Milkias. "Mengistu Haile Mariam: Profile of a Dictator." *Ethiopian Review* (February 1994): 45–56.

Relief and Rehabilitation Commission. *Ethiopia: An Overview*. Addis Ababa: RRC Public Relations and Information Service, 1995.

Ryle, John. "An African Nuremberg." *The New Yorker*. October 2, 1995: 50–61.

Schabas, William. *Genocide in International Law*. Cambridge: Cambridge University Press, 2000.

——. "Cambodia: Was it Really Genocide?" *Human Rights Quarterly* 23, no. 2 (May 2001): 470–77.

Scocpol, Theda. *States and Social Revolutions: A Comparative Analysis of France, Russia and China*. Cambridge: Cambridge University Press, 1979.

Stahl, Michael. *Political Contradictions in Agricultural Development*. New York: Africana Publishing Company, 1974.

Stanton, Gregory H. "Seeking Justice in Cambodia: Realism, Idealism, and Pragmatism." <http://www.genocidewatch.org>.

Teferra Haile Selassie. *The Ethiopian Revolution, 1974–1991: From a Monarchical Autocracy to a Military Oligarchy*. London: Kegan Paul International, 1997.

Tekalign Wolde-Mariam, "A City and Its Hinterlands: The Political Economy of Land Tenure, Agriculture and Food Supply for Addis Ababa, Ethiopia, 1887–1974." Ph.D. diss., Department of History, Boston University, 1995.

Teshale Tibebu. *The Making of Modern Ethiopia: 1896–1974*. Lawrenceville, NJ: The Red Sea Press Inc, 1995.

The Wall Street Journal. Editorial. "Today's Holocaust." January 27, 1986.

Totten S., et al., eds. *Century of Genocide: Critical Essays and Eye Witness Accounts*. New York: Garland Press, 1995.

Tubiana, Joseph, ed. *Modern Ethiopia: From the Accession of Menelik II to the Present*. Rotterdam: A.A. Balkena, 1980.

Varnis, Stephen L. *Reluctant Aid or Aiding the Reluctant?: U.S. Aid Policy and Ethiopian Relief*. New Brunswick, NJ: Transaction, 1990.

Vickery, Michael. *Cambodia: 1975–1982*. Boston: South End Press, 1985.

Weaver, Mary Anne. "Annals of Political Terror: Burying the Martyrs." *The New Yorker*, December 28, 1992–January 4, 1993: 106–29.

Weitz, Eric D. *A Century of Genocide: Utopias of Race and Nation*. Princeton, NJ: Princeton University Press, 2003.

Wolde Giorgis, Dawit. *Red Tears: War, Famine and Revolution in Ethiopia*. Trenton, NJ: The Red Sea Press, 1989.

Young, John. *Peasant Revolution in Ethiopia: The Tigray People's Liberation Front*. Cambridge: Cambridge University Press, 1997.

Zenner, Walter P. "Middleman Minorities Theories: a Critical Review." Pp. 255–76 in *The Persisting Question: Sociological Perspectives and Social Contexts of Modern Antisemitism*, edited by Helen Fein. Berlin: de Gruyter, 1987.

INDEX

ABOUT THE AUTHOR

Edward Kissi is Assistant Professor of African History in the Department of Africana Studies at the University of South Florida, Tampa. His doctoral dissertation examining the role of famine in the origins of the Ethiopian revolutionary government and the charges of genocide lodged against its leaders was written under the direction of the distinguished genocide scholar Frank Chalk at Concordia University in Montreal, Canada. Between January 1998 and December 1999, Kissi began the two-year archival and field research that ultimately produced this book as a Mellon postdoctoral fellow in the Genocide Studies Program at Yale University directed by Ben Kiernan, the leading scholar on the Pol Pot regime. Prior to joining the faculty at South Florida, Kissi taught African history, U.S. foreign relations and comparative genocide in the Department of History, and at the Strassler Family Center for Holocaust and Genocide Studies, at Clark University, in Worcester, Massachusetts, from January 2000 to May 2003. In recognition of his work on the comparative study of genocide, Kissi was one of the scholars interviewed for the BBC and KCET television documentary, *Auschwitz: Inside the Nazi State*, aired nationally on PBS on January 19, 2005.

DATE DUE

#47-0108 Peel Off Pressure Sensitive